Home Screens

Home Screens

Public Housing in Global Film and Television

Edited by Lorrie Palmer

BLOOMSBURY ACADEMIC
LONDON • NEW YORK • OXFORD • NEW DELHI • SYDNEY

BLOOMSBURY ACADEMIC
Bloomsbury Publishing Plc, 50 Bedford Square, London, WC1B 3DP, UK
Bloomsbury Publishing Inc, 1385 Broadway, New York, NY 10018, USA
Bloomsbury Publishing Ireland, 29 Earlsfort Terrace, Dublin 2, D02 AY28, Ireland

BLOOMSBURY, BLOOMSBURY ACADEMIC and the Diana logo are
trademarks of Bloomsbury Publishing Plc

First published in Great Britain 2024
This edition published in 2025

Cover design: Ben Anslow
Cover images: Apartment Buildings In Hong Kong (© Chunyip Wing/iStock/Getty
Images Plus); *Candyman* (1992), dir. Bernard Rose (© TriStar Pictures/Photofest)

Bloomsbury Publishing Plc does not have any control over, or responsibility for,
any third-party websites referred to or in this book. All internet addresses given
in this book were correct at the time of going to press. The author and publisher
regret any inconvenience caused if addresses have changed or sites have ceased
to exist, but can accept no responsibility for any such changes.

A catalogue record for this book is available from the British Library.

ISBN: HB: 978-1-3502-5395-7
         PB: 978-1-3502-5394-0
       ePDF: 978-1-3502-5397-1
      eBook: 978-1-3502-5396-4

Typeset by Integra Software Services Pvt. Ltd.

For product safety related questions contact productsafety@bloomsbury.com.

To find out more about our authors and books visit www.bloomsbury.com
and sign up for our newsletters.

I dedicate this book to Peggy, a single mom, seashell archivist, farmer, artist and educator, who raised me with books and a love for lifelong learning.

Contents

List of figures

Contributors

Liat Savin Ben Shoshan, BArch, Ph.D., teaches in Bezalel Academy of Arts and Design and studied architecture in Bezalel Academy of Arts and Design and Bar Ilan University. Her postdoctoral research at the Technion Institute of Technology, Haifa, focused on the architect and town planner Yitzhaq Perlstein and his cinematic documentation of his own works. She writes and lectures on film, culture and space, and on writing and filming as research methodologies in architectural planning. Her publications appear in a variety of academic journals.

Chua Beng Huat is Professor of Urban Studies, Yale-NUS College and Professor, Department of Sociology, National University of Singapore. Public housing policies and East Asian Pop Culture are two areas of his research interests. He has published *Housing and Political Legitimacy: Stakeholding in Singapore* (1997) and *Structure, Audience and Soft Power in East Asian Pop Culture* (2012). He is co-executive editor of *Inter-Asia Cultural Studies*.

Michael D. Dwyer is Associate Professor of Media and Communication at Arcadia University, with a research focus in Hollywood film and popular music of the late twentieth century. He is the author of *Back to the Fifties: Nostalgia, Hollywood Film, and Popular Music of the 1970s and 1980s*. His next book, *Tinsel and Rust: How Hollywood Manufactured the Rust Belt*, is under contract. He lives in Philadelphia.

Heike Kumpf has a B.A. in German (Luther College) and a Master of Architecture degree (Illinois Institute of Technology), with her architectural license (Illinois 2014) taking her career to multiple locations within the United States and Canada. Primarily engaged in healthcare and institutional architecture, she maintains research interests in spatial interpretation and appreciation. Recently, she co-wrote a paper on character and home in Max Frisch's *Biedermann und die Brandstifter*, and has guest lectured on the spatial context of the Secret Annex in Anne Frank's diary in university course settings as well as to the local community.

Kirsten Kumpf Baele (Ph.D. in German) is director of the Anne Frank Initiative and faculty in the Department of German at the University of Iowa. Recent publications examine the aesthetics and politics of hair in prewar era film and forced adoption practices in Belgian film. Youth voices and agency (placemaking, opposition and peacemaking), trees in literature and the arts, and diaristic modes of writing through the lens of ecobiography drive her scholarship and teaching. She is currently serving as co-editor/contributing author to the volume *Teaching Anne Frank & Other Difficult Life Stories*.

Daphna Levine, Ph.D. Architect, is a postdoctoral associate at Jacobs Technion-Cornell Institute at Cornell Tech. Levine's doctoral research at the Technion-Israel Institute of Technology created models for representing abstract social phenomena through cutting-edge technology and qualitative method and was awarded the Azrieli Fellowship for outstanding academic merit. Levine graduated from the Bezalel Academy of Arts and Design in architecture and the Hebrew University of Jerusalem in philosophy and comparative literature. Levine has published articles in leading journals and a few books: *The Third Space – Center and Periphery in Israeli Literature* (2016) and *No House Is Bereft of a City* (2022); *Architecture in Flip-Flops: Bat Yam 1920–1990* (2023); and *Delphine* (2023).

Alberto Lo Pinto, Ph.D., University of Notre Dame, is an independent scholar based in Rome and a former Fellow at the Bibliotheca Hertziana Max Planck Institute. He is interested in the various interactions between cinema and architecture, such as the architecture of film sets, the architecture of movie theatres and films directed by architects. His current research is on film exhibition in Rome in the 1970s and 1980s.

Steve Macek is Professor of Communication at North Central College and author of *Urban Nightmares: The Media, the Right and the Moral Panic over the City* (2006). In recent years, he has published chapters and scholarly articles on David Simon's *The Wire*, media coverage of police misconduct in Chicago and representations of the dual city and the urban precariat in global media.

Isabelle McNeill is the Philomathia Fellow in French and Film at Trinity Hall, University of Cambridge, where she has taught film studies and French literature since 2005 and is chair (and co-founder) of the Cambridge Film Trust. She is the author of *Memory and the Moving Image: French Film in the Digital Era* (2010) as well as articles and essays on film in relation to memory, the city, home, tourism, Internet culture and girlhood. She is currently making video essays and writing a book on the cinematic rooftops of Paris.

Helen Morgan Parmett is the Edwin W. Lawrence Forensic Professor of Speech and Associate Professor in the Department of English and Film and Television

Studies at the University of Vermont. Her research centres on critical media studies, where she focuses especially on relationships among media, identity and space/place.

Lorrie Palmer, Ph.D. Indiana University, is an Associate Professor of Film and Media Studies at Towson University. Her scholarship on film history, film and television genres (noir, horror, sci fi, action), gender/race/technology and city space appears in *Cinema Journal, The Velvet Light Trap, Jump Cut, Science Fiction Film and Television, Camera Obscura, Mediapolis: A Journal of Cities and Culture, Senses of Cinema, Slayage* and several anthologies.

Dr. Anna Viola Sborgi is a Marie Skłodowska-Curie Research Fellow at the Department of Film and Screen Media, University College Cork, Ireland. Her current Horizon 2020-funded project, *MEDIAHOMES: Housing Precarity on Screen in Ireland, Portugal and the UK from the 2008 Crisis to COVID-19*, investigates transnational mediations of housing inequality in Europe, their production and circulation. She has recently published on housing and documentary, and film and architecture and is currently co-editing a Special Issue of *Alphaville* on *The Home as a Space of Resistance*. She co-chairs the Society of Cinema and Media Studies (SCMS) Urbanism/Geography/Architecture Scholarly Interest Group.

Meisen Wong is a doctoral candidate at the Technische Universität (Darmstadt) in Germany and a teaching assistant at the National University of Singapore (Sociology). Her doctoral dissertation critically examines the phenomenon of ghost cities in China and the impact on its residents' future orientations.

Kalima Young is an Assistant Professor in the Department of Electronic Media and Film at Towson University. She received her Ph.D. in American Studies from the University of Maryland College Park. Her research explores the impact of race and gender-based trauma on Black identity, media and cultural production. A Baltimore native, videographer and activist, Dr. Young is also a member of Rooted, a Black LGBTQ healing collective. Her book, *Mediated Misogynoir: The Erasure of Black Women's and Girls' Innocence in the Public Imagination*, was released in 2022.

Acknowledgements

The editor wishes to thank the contributors herein for their graceful collegiality during some challenging years for the world, as well as for their professionalism and rigorous scholarship. It has been a pleasure to share in this journey and to learn so much from all of them.

At Bloomsbury, thanks to Camilla Erskine for her enthusiasm and guidance on the proposal process and to Veidehi Hans for great assistance thereafter. I (and we) also wish to thank our two readers for their productive and well-informed feedback during peer review.

Thank you to the College of Fine Arts and Communication at Towson University for their funding support and to Nicholas Regine for preparing the images.

On a personal note, I would like to thank Mark Shiel, King's College, London, for responding to my description of current research interests at the Society for Cinema and Media Studies conference (Montreal 2015) with the jolting statement: 'That's a book.' Also, a tip of the hat to Elissa Favero for her 2012 blog post, 'Attack the Block. Allow it.'[1] This was the first scholarship I ever read on cinema and public housing – my fascination for the histories, architecture, people and screen spaces of this topic happened right there.

Lorrie Palmer
Towson University
April 2023

---

[1] Favero, Elissa. (2012), 'Attack the Block. Allow it.' *Yellow Umbrella Adventures*, 24 January. Available online: http://yellowumbrellaadventures.blogspot.com/2012/01/attack-block-allow-it.html (accessed 12 January 2014).

Introduction: Public housing in global film and television

Lorrie Palmer

Between the ages of six and nine, I lived in St. Louis, Missouri, not far from the 57-acre Pruitt-Igoe housing project on the city's North Side, which opened in 1955. On 21 April 1972, the demolition of Building C-15 was undertaken by the St. Louis Housing Authority. As the sparse, symmetrical structure that came to define the iconography of public housing fell, it prompted cultural critic and architectural historian Charles Jencks to declare that this was the moment modern architecture died (see Figure 0.1). Archival footage of that explosion of terrible beauty was included in Godfrey Reggio's 1982 experimental film, *Koyaanisqatsi*, after the director first unspooled almost three minutes of aerial footage shot from a helicopter above the stark abandoned blocks, comprised of thirty-three eleven-storey brick buildings. Pruitt-Igoe's lead architect Minoru Yamasaki, who would later go on to design the St. Louis Lambert International Airport terminal (1956) and the World Trade Center towers (1976), was commissioned by Mayor Joseph M. Darst, who was eager to put St. Louis on the modernist map after visiting public housing sites in New York City. The Housing Act of 1949[1] provided the $36 million in federal funding to build Pruitt-Igoe, which was heralded as a shining postwar solution to the city's previous overcrowded and disease-ridden slums. Less than twenty years after the buildings opened, demolition crews placed their explosive charges, and a spectacular ruin was born – nationally televised and broadcast worldwide.

That image, of a dystopian urban zone of decay and trauma and failure – social, political, ideological, architectural – has persisted. Although this has become the dominant perception of public housing in news media and policy discourse, the present volume traces its more nuanced depictions across a set of representative fiction and non-fiction narratives in global film and television. Public perceptions that link buildings with people, particularly through the

Figure 0.1 The demolition of Building C-15 in the Pruitt-Igoe housing project, April 1972, by the St. Louis Housing Authority. Photo courtesy of the U.S. Department of Housing and Urban Development Office of Policy Development and Research, public domain.

oft-deployed metaphors of disease ('blight', for example), have been deployed in real-world contexts to justify demolition of these sites. When public housing structures come down in controlled blasts of billowing concrete dust, such as the last six (of eight) towers in the Red Road council estate in Glasgow, Scotland (2015), or the Barre Debussy in the Cité des 4000, La Courneuve *banlieue* on the periphery of Paris (1986), or the Las Gladiolas complex in Hato Rey, Puerto Rico (2011), the spectacle is often met by the cheers of onlookers and/or by prideful speeches about urban renewal by local authorities. However, former tenants may perceive it differently. Outsiders – reformers, city planners, business and real-estate interests, the news media – see uninhabitable waste(d)lands of poverty and crime while often and ironically, it is frequently the case that 'public housing residents – the insiders – liked their homes' (Leavitt 1993: 114), having developed kinship networks to improve their collective living conditions. Disjunction between public perception and private experience ripples across time and place – and screens. Season three of the HBO series, *The Wire* (2002–08), opens with a scene that frames this dichotomy as the fictional Franklin Terrace Towers are demolished by the Baltimore Housing Authority, amid cheers and speeches, and echoes of Pruitt-Igoe, 'whose famous demolition *The Wire*'s own demolition scene undoubtedly channels' (Clemoes 2018), even as two young men who once lived there share their nostalgia about it as it falls (see Young, this volume).

Just as modernist architecture – the design – of public housing was once blamed for its failure (at those sites where it did fail)[2] rather than the underlying culprits of shifting politics, culture, economics and complex urban histories, we will argue that the deliberate aesthetic and narrative design of public housing in film and television likewise frames a bigger story. Our primary way into this story is *home* (and how it is designed for living in), something often forgotten in the surveillance and spectacle branded onto public housing. While existing academic discourse includes rich scholarship in fields from social science to architectural history to urban studies, we build upon these by looking through a diverse set of lenses that media makers have aimed at the onscreen buildings and homes of public housing. This introduction will trace the ripples between the city as an institutional-architectural-social form with public housing as its shadow and will lay the foundation for a collection of interdisciplinary essays through which we will show how screens across decades, genres and formats have depicted these sites, whether perpetuating or challenging popular perceptions of public housing and those who live there.

To guide us into those onscreen spaces explored by the twelve chapters comprising this collection, I will first consider the built environment and how it has become an uneven foundation for homes devised as uniquely *public*. Although my focus here is predominantly US- and UK-based, the essays that follow expand outwards from there through the expert gaze of global scholars, which I hope will serve as a model for future scholarship that goes even further.

Constructions and demolitions

'To approach a city, or even a city neighborhood, as if it were a larger architectural problem, capable of being given order by converting it into a disciplined work of art, is to make the mistake of attempting to substitute art for life' – Jane Jacobs, in *The Death and Life of Great American Cities*.

(1961: 373)

Beginning with Baron Georges-Eugène Haussmann's massive renovation (1853–70) of the medieval jumble of streets, alleys and haphazard structures of Paris from a chaotic labyrinth to a modern metropolis, the drive to rationalize urban space was set in motion. Haussmann tore down approximately 19,730 buildings and erected structures on a monumental scale along his new wide straight boulevards. The goal of Haussmann and his employer, Emperor Napoléon III, was to modernize the city; this included parks, public squares, schools, hospitals, railway hubs, a new sewage system and an aqueduct for clean water. The reconstruction was a material articulation of rational capitalism and an opportunity for the 'technological mastery of urban space and the search for progressively greater degrees of social and spatial order' (Gandy 1999: 28–9). As is always the case with cities and ambitious urban planning projects, poor people (approximately 350,000) and the communities they carved out of the built environment were displaced and razed, to clear the way for commerce and affluent city dwellers first. This strategy created an architectural and spatial aesthetic that increased the visibility of economic inequality between rich and poor. The French-Swiss architect, Le Corbusier, imagined taking this urban reorganization a step further with his Plan Voisin (1925) which proposed to strip away the existing topography of the 3rd and 4th arrondissements on the Seine's right bank and to lay in an extensive parkland dominated by eighteen identical modernist high-rise towers. His plan never materialized; its monumental scale was widely reviled as dehumanizing and alienating, a costly knife to the heart and soul of the city, especially the popular Marais Quarter which would have been gutted. However, his goal to replace urban disorder with an architectural solution steeped in rationality and efficiency (and its corresponding paternalistic assumptions about such an environment's pedagogical impact on the habits and behaviours of residents) reflects an authoritarian elitism drilled in social engineering and exclusion. Although his Plan Voisin was unrealized in the private market, its echo reverberated forwards in time to public housing, where the 'sprawling outer city housing estates that went up in *banlieues* such as Clichy-sous-Bois consisted of clusters of tower blocks that didn't look so different from Le Corbusier's ideas 40 years prior' (Beanland 2015). His design aesthetic *of* the future was reborn as a segregated social reality *in* the future. In his 1920s response to criticisms that his plan would demolish historic neighbourhoods where people lived and worked, 'the architect said these "troglodytes" could be relocated to garden cities in outer Paris' (Lubin 2013). Regeneration meant relocation and, as has continued to be the global case into present times, renewal means removal. This also informed his theory that 'the abolition of the street, and with it the type of crowd and the range of activities associated with it' was the optimum way forward in city planning (Donald 1999: 59). Here the design principles of the 'concept city' (Donald 1999: 59) espoused by men like Le Corbusier (*The Radiant City*, 1935), Lewis Mumford (who famously hated cars), and architectural historian, Siegfried Giedion and his New Monumentality (1944), bristled with an ethos of urban control only thinly disguised as benign functionalism. At the core of their philosophy was the notion that '*planned* changes in that environment would be sufficient to produce *predictable* changes in people's perception, mental life, habits, and conduct' (Donald 1995: 89). A way to decrease unpredictability was the erasure of the street, of the chance encounter with strangers (often marked as Other), of the chaotic city. 'The desire to tame the street became a staple of modernist architectural thought' (McQuire 2008: 137). This form-as-function approach was likewise clear in the work of two Le Corbusier disciples, Lucio Costa and Oscar Niemeyer, when they designed Brazil's capital city, Brasilia (1956–61). They followed his concepts that 'a modern city needed to be deliberate, orderly, rational, and systematic – the opposite of messy, over-crowded cities that grew and developed organically over time' (Budds 2019) as the *favelas* on the margins of Rio de Janeiro had done. The same desire for rational control is evident in Neighborhood Gardens, a St. Louis housing project developed in 1935. Joseph Heathcott notes that the city 'offered a planned, orderly landscape that was clear in its design, purpose, and aspirations for urban order' through a 'reorganization of urban space [that] was not just a physical exercise but a social one as well, as reformers sought to discipline both the land and the racial, social, and family composition of the people who dwelt there' (2011: 88).[3] In a precursor to the planned segregation of Pruitt-Igoe in the late 1950s, the 1930s and 1940s saw St. Louis propose the Carr Square Village (for Black residents) and the Clinton-Peabody homes (for white residents) which stripped out the shops, warehouses, junkyards and other small businesses to inspire a more orderly city, opting for single-use zoning (Heathcott 2011: 96). This is the same impulse that drove Le Corbusier and Giedion to advocate for a single-use approach to city space – to keep commerce, cars, pedestrians and homes in separate zones. As cities go, so goes housing. This ideologically driven quest for control and its offshoot, the spatial isolation of public housing, has accumulated globally wherever we see '"urban outcasts", living in the ghettos, *favelas*, inner cities, *villa miserias* or *banlieues*' (Levasseur 2008: 97) in cities large and small. These undervalued tracts are frequently where displaced (and equally undervalued) urban dwellers are relocated – either as the result of a grand architectural vision or as a naked land grab – and this paradox of progressivism and neglect is a pattern repeated in the microcosmic history of public housing.

In the UK, that history began with the 1890 Housing of the Working Classes Act, which led to the Boundary Estate opening in Bethnal Green, East London, in 1900. Socialized housing legislation in Britain at this time 'was heavily influenced by public health policy' (Myles 2019), focused on the need to avoid disease outbreaks endemic to the overcrowding of people and structures. The first move towards public housing in the United States began in 1933 with President Roosevelt's New Deal. In 1935, 'the Housing Division of the Public Works Administration (PWA), United States Housing Authority, and Atlanta Housing Authority constructed nearly five thousand units' (Rodriguez 2021: 7) of row houses and garden apartments called Techwood Homes. Like Techwood, other low-rise developments of the era were also 'solidly built and well designed', such as those in the New Orleans projects of Iberville and Lafitte and in the art deco 'Outhwaite Homes in Cleveland, built in 1935' (Goetz 2013: 26). The institutional objectives that drove American public housing of the 1930s and 1940s indicate a philosophical arc. Initially conceived as a 'resource for the working poor' (Goetz 2013: 13) it later split, with the Progressive movement's desire to improve the lives of poor families as a publicly funded alternative to the private market through a 'more enlightened urban design' and the Modern Housing movement based on the European model of public housing 'more as a public utility than as a social service initiative' (Goetz 2013: 25); after the Second World War came 'urban clearance and renewal' (Goetz 2013: 29), launching the contemporary rhetoric of exclusion and demarcation (see also Zipp 2012).

How else have urban spaces and public housing cohabitated around the world? In most US cities, for instance, 'the construction of public housing followed established patterns of racial segregation' as a means of 'marginalizing races and spaces in the modern city' (Rodriguez 2021: 7). Although, in Britain, because 'there were no preexisting racial ghettos, public housing was sited without racial considerations in mind'; rather it 'was built in working class districts, which were not racially defined' (Weir 1993: 25). In countries like Brazil, Colombia and Mexico, a different approach: 'While US policies revolve around questions of segregation, ghettoization, and concentration of poverty, Latin American housing programmes' (Libertun de Duren 2018: 178) instead work 'with a dynamic mostly based on land markets rather than on segregation by race' (Libertun de Duren 2018: 179). The relationship may also be geopolitical. For example, the 1961 Alliance for Progress, initiated by

President John F. Kennedy to foster cooperation and avert communist influence in the region, partially funded a 'mammoth project' in Bogotá – called Cuidad Kennedy completed in 1965 – as 'one of the largest public housing projects in the hemisphere' (Handelman 1979, 8), where still today 14 per cent of the city's low-income population lives. Elsewhere, in Hong Kong, public housing stock has been developed as undifferentiated in terms of design, location, 'technical specification' and unlike many sites in the United States, the UK and Europe, 'has not been constructed solely in remote areas and has avoided a segregated pattern' of tenancy (Lau and Murie 2017: 282). Sweden and Denmark built livable postwar socialized housing in which nature was prioritized, with provision for children's outdoor play spaces and careful landscaping, at sites already integrated with existing urban transport systems (Carolin 2008). Housing policies, these and others, do not remain static over time and certainly the current collection will explore several national contexts in great detail by authors with expertise in their fields. But my snapshot here suggests that policies are influenced by prevailing attitudes towards race, class, money, space and control. And much of any conversation about policy or media representation begins with how public housing *looks*. In simplistic terms: Is it a blighted ruin? Tear it down. Is it a dramatic dystopian backdrop? Film it.

How public housing looks depends on what kind of investment a municipality or local council or housing authority or national government wants to make, how much autonomy architects have been given, what social group it is intended to be occupied by, and myriad other aspects unique to each time and place. Because it is publicly funded, the design aesthetic tends to be driven by economical function, not luxury. How it looks on camera or onscreen is similarly complex – its mode and format (fiction, documentary, home movies, photography,[4] videogame, music video, film and television), its national context, its conditions of production, its historical period, its genre, how and why it matters that its characters/residents are framed in or near public housing. What meaning does this location create for the viewer? Is it designed to be literal or symbolic, as realism or fantasy? How will that meaning translate across the global circulation of media imagery? For both policymakers and media makers, one of the most powerful images in their toolkit is the high-rise tower. On the planning desk, its architecture is monumental but cost-effective. Onscreen, it conveys everything from gendered power to social alienation to utopian rebranding. The tower satisfies. In the onscreen narratives under discussion in this volume and in the real-world contexts they reflect or resist, public housing lives somewhere between appearance and experience.

Building up

Samuel Zipp has traced the aspirational origins of urban renewal through livable spaces, with its roots in the ideals of 'ethical city rebuilding' (2012: 367). He describes the ideological image (and disconnect) evoked by the words 'housing' and 'home'. Urban reformers in 1940s New York realized that *home* had a universal public meaning: a 'single-family house with a patch of yard' while *housing* instead primarily suggested 'government aid for the underprivileged' (Zipp 2012: 272). It is how media makers use these spaces (in film, television and other formats) to create relatable narratives for viewers that builds the story of public housing we present in this volume. The setting may be used for social critique, to make the unfamiliar familiar through character and action, to humanize. And onscreen characters may use the spaces to dance, to create community or even seek escape. In reality, it is clear that many of the aspirational aims of urban reformers and architects did not succeed. The same may be true for some of the onscreen characters we encounter here. The point is to contextualize the image (housing) by aiming our lens inwards to the lived space (home) – where the bigger stories always are.

In 1974, the American TV sitcom, *Good Times* (co-created by Eric Monte, who grew up in Chicago public housing; see Dwyer, this volume) was the first US television series to depict a Black two-parent family – already a challenge to the prevailing perceptions of the 1970s (when the first large-scale demolitions of public housing high-rises began) – as intact, loving and supportive. Challenging conventional stigmas, the show is rightly celebrated for 'providing proper and positive representation for those living in America's public housing' (Marten 2019). The Evans family talked about lean paychecks, they helped neighbours experiencing food insecurity and they cared about art and education in the lives of their children, while residing in a family unit made cosy with floral curtains, natural light and an active dinner table. While the show was criticized for omitting the harsher realities endured by real-life residents of Cabrini-Green (a name which was never mentioned on the show), its opening title sequence nevertheless cuts away from the aloof gaze of aerial perspectives to frame the camaraderie and play of boys on bicycles at street level alongside the brick towers where they live. This shot is B-roll of real residents on location and looks more like the lived-in fictional world of *Good Times*. Moving from the tower to the street is about this: 'Rescaling the projects from the overwhelmingly large size and forceful control to a more human scale' (Faisst 2016: 275) and it reflects the aim of this volume as we move into the home.

Likewise, in another genre and another medium, the 2011 British horror/sci fi/comedy *Attack the Block* situates its imposing tower like a spaceship landed in the wilds of Brixton, South London. Director Joe Cornish never adopts the typical media or surveillance perspective of the tower from an aerial view, opting instead to repeatedly aim up at it from a low angle, from street level. The film was shot on location at the Heygate estate, whose high-rise towers were built in 1974 in the style of 1950s–60s Brutalism. This style included exposed pre-cast concrete slab exteriors 'widely seen as the architectural style of the Welfare State – a cheap way of building quickly, on a large scale' (Boughton 2018: 119–20) for council housing, stamping its inhabitants' class position straight onto its unmissable architecture. In this film's resistance to that image, its teen characters identify positively with 'the block' and, to illustrate, Cornish includes scenes from their individual flats – warm lamp glow, meals being prepared in their kitchens, pets, generational families – all in personalized, lived-in domestic spaces.[5] When aliens attack, the teens' assured navigation of the tower's stairwells, corridors and exterior elevated walkways allows the multi-racial group – and the film – to counter the dystopian media narrative and public perception of council housing youth that dominated Britain in the riot-strife summer of 2011 (see Palmer 2014; see Wong/Chua, this volume). The Heygate was demolished (between 2011 and 2014) for a regeneration project to reclaim this valuable site convenient to central London. Its 1,260 council homes were replaced by 3,300 units, mostly for private sale, with only 25 per cent designated for affordable housing – dispersing (or 'decanting' in the vernacular of developers) the community that made their home there.

Regeneration

To see what it looks like when public housing is regenerated without demolition, in reality and onscreen, I would point to the ways in which British film and television screens have depicted London's Thamesmead estate, an ambitious modernist new town built in the mid-1960s on the former site of the Royal Arsenal munitions dump on the southeast bank of the Thames. 'Thamesmead was London County Council's bold attempt to build a new town to address the city's housing shortage after the Second World War' and noted for 'its daring, experimental design – concrete modern terraces, blocks of flats and elevated walkways built around a system of lakes and canals – the town received attention from architects, sociologists and politicians throughout the world but also gained notoriety as the backdrop to Stanley Kubrick's film, "A Clockwork Orange"' in 1971 (Baker 2019). In choosing Thamesmead for his film, Kubrick selected the location not to convey the dystopian image that his film ultimately spawned as the enduring public perception of the place but because of its architectural modernism for a story set in the future (the LCC originally billed the site as 'The Town of Tomorrow'). In *A Clockwork Orange*, Alex (Malcolm McDowell) and his ultraviolent Droogs roam the 'unspeakable concrete disaster' with its 'vast, dismal, windswept collection of tower blocks connected by intimidating walkways' ('A Clockwork Orange | 1971'), where Alex kicks Dim (Warren Clarke) into the man-made lake at Flat Block Marina, Binsey Walk, alongside the 'labyrinth of angular, asymmetric balconies' (White 2019) of Thamesmead South.

Kubrick's film has perpetuated a lingering and poisonous image. To resist this negative public association of Thamesmead 'with the "physical brutality" of the fictional Droogs' nihilistic crime and vandalism' (de Coo 2017), the Greater London Council (GLC) released a 25-minute promotional film, *Living at Thamesmead* (directed by Charmian and Jack Saward, Tara Films), in 1974, in which a young couple (played by Julie Dawn Cole and Spencer Banks) stroll at leisure through the exteriors and interiors of the estate on a bright sunny day. Their passage provides a mobile perspective as children play on the concrete terraces, families and fun fairs brighten the lakeside in the exact location where Alex attacked Dim, residents gather in the evening for dart games and pints, the Thamesmead community association meets, teens watch television in a cosy maisonette, teachers take young students on nature walks in the surrounding marshlands and 'people of various colours and creeds go about their day' (de Coo 2017). Christopher Beanland describes this film's 'proto-*Gregory's Girl* social realism' in his praise of postwar British new towns as being far more successful and livable than the media and politicians have given them credit for, as 'whole functioning places with jobs, shops and services' (2017).

Peabody, London's oldest housing association and current owner of Thamesmead, has a compilation on its website of the estate's screen presence from dystopian images of youth crime and urban violence in Aphex Twin's music video *Come to Daddy* (1997) and the Channel 4 series *Misfits* (2009–13) (de Coo 2017). Yet, it also references a short film, *The Bard of the Street* (Mary McCartney 2016), commissioned by Selfridges department store, that envisions at the site a new *West Side Story* of sweeping aerial views approaching Thamesmead over the water, tracking shots up the angular concrete walkways, young people in designer fashion taking slow-motion strolls against a backdrop of high-rise towers, accompanied by ethereal piano and a spoken word recitation by James Massiah on 'the ballers from the blocks on mopeds and ninja bikes' ('Selfridges HOT AIR Presents' 2016: 00:48-00:50). The youth here are far from the brutal Droogs in their defensively masculine cricket codpieces, instead wearing white Elizabethan neck ruffs and kissing each other against soft blue shutters, posed above green parkland and pastoral lake views.

This romanticizing of Thamesmead at the contemporary intersection of music video and advertising is joined by the 1996 coming-of-age queer romantic comedy *Beautiful Thing* (adapted from Jonathan Harvey's stage play), which was produced for television but successful enough to warrant a cinematic release. Two teens, Jamie and Ste (Glen Berry and Scott Neal), explore their relationship and their identities within the iconic spaces of Thamesmead. The marketing poster for the film shows the two young men in the foreground, with tower blocks dominating vertical space behind them. The Thamesmead shooting location becomes a character in the film, most visually present in the final scene, in which the teens slow dance in front of a community of neighbours, friends and family to the 1968 Cass Elliot tune, 'Dream a Little Dream of Me'. The concrete courtyard is warmly lit by sun flares as the camera rotates around them, with high rises, elevated walkways and geometric rooflines acting as the urban stage for their romance. The new romanticism of the site has been further re-imagined more recently in a 'dance-theatre piece – as part of Pride in a co-production between Greenwich+Docklands International Festival (GDIF) and Peabody' of Harvey's *Beautiful Thing* in a 2018 return to Thamesmead (co-directed by Bradley Hemmings and Robby Graham). An *Evening Standard* review acknowledges the mediated visual experience and the chameleon possibilities of the architecture, alongside the estate's more dystopian screen history:

> Perched on a grassy hill opposite, the audience can gaze in through the windows, Rear Window-style. We see teenagers Jamie and Ste fall in lust, while Jamie's mum teases her toyboy and rows with her neighbour. The action is conceived as series of split narratives – dancers perform in around the buildings, while dazzling digital projections by NOVAK animate the block. One minute the concrete is drenched in technicolour flowers; the next it resembles a prison. … But watching working-class boys slow dance in a housing estate where Clockwork Orange was filmed creates a real frisson.
>
> (Hoggard 2018)

This spectrum of mainstream cinema, government and commercially sponsored narratives, produced-for-TV and theatrical works across documentary and fiction modes as well as urban arts performance, shows the protean representation of Thamesmead over time. The interplay between dominant imagery and more positive portrayals, some based on the voices and experiences of real-life residents, is all part of how we will examine public housing and media in this volume. And 'home' being public: therein lies the paradox of it *and* the often-uncomfortable reason we can look inside.

At home

There is no other form of domestic space so opened up to a public gaze, or archived onscreen, in the way that public housing is. Inhabitants are frequently denied the same presumption of privacy and autonomy enjoyed by those served by the private housing market (and its attendant, almost invisible economic support by an alliance of government and business). In postwar America, housing and media synched up in the form of government-backed low-interest home loans, the banking and real-estate industries' collusion in redlining and blockbusting[6], and the cultural ubiquity of white, nuclear family domesticity powering the proliferation of broadcast network TV programming. Viewers can be invited in to see how people live, to relate to the domestic scene and its characters onscreen, or they can be kept at a distance, to view the inhabitants of the space (and the space itself) as Other.

The private urban home, examined by Pamela Robertson Wojcik as the 'apartment plot', concerns the mapping of the 'protagonist's identity into his or her spatial location' while it simultaneously 'delimits a character's identity in terms of gender, race, ethnicity, and class' (2018: 4–5). Yet, the gaze relationship between public and private in film and television apartment narratives does not implicate the state as having a vested financial interest in what goes on there. When public monies even partially fund housing, the privacy of domestic life is laid bare to the institutional and bureaucratic – and media – gaze in a way that private homes are not. This occurs at the level of policy, and it translates into film and television characters, settings and perspectives. Contested terrain is where public housing lives.

The worlds encompassed in *Home Screens: Public Housing in Global Film and Television* view this terrain in architectural, political and social settings where residents may not have an assumption of privacy about family income, leisure spending, entertainment and communication technologies, female and male labour, identity, family demographics, marital status, health, addiction, contraception, personal freedoms or choices. To illustrate, I will consider Frederick Wiseman's

1996 observational documentary, *Public Housing*. The filmmaker (immersed into the community as part of a three-person crew) includes a scene of teen mothers in the Ida B. Wells housing project, holding their infants during a demonstration by two nurses on the proper usage of condoms. The gaze of Wiseman's camera at this moment lays bare the institutional disconnect of the Chicago Housing Authority while simultaneously rendering public its inhabitants' private lives. However, Wiseman's unobtrusive camera on the dailiness of real people, such as his quiet unmediated long take of an elderly woman meticulously picking over a head of cabbage at her kitchen table, gently brings privacy home, resisting the more widely circulated spectacularized and stereotyped image of violent men in violent places (see the prevalence of these, for example, in 'Further Viewing' this volume). In 1996, a local bi-monthly Chicago newspaper, the *Residents' Journal*, was entirely produced by local public housing residents with the aim to resist negative public perception, conflating buildings and people, held by outsiders.

> In contrast to the dystopian interpretations and imagined reputations traditionally shackled to representations of the 'ghetto' or 'slum,' *Resident's Journal* appreciates the actual daily practices of those who inhabit this environment: The neighbor*hood* (home) of public housing becomes a specific space of place-based attachments and spatial mobilization.
>
> (Mann 2012: 276)

Acknowledging the multivalent meanings people ascribe to their homes should be part of how we interpret these sites and their onscreen representations (including relevant production and reception contexts). This is, after all, why our exploration of public housing in global film and television is being undertaken.

Our challenge is to find this value in constructions of home or domestic space made unique by their very nature as 'public' (and publicly funded). The political/institutional *largesse* implicit in this arrangement gives tacit permission to media makers and media consumers, to urban planners and architects and to authorities to observe, study and surveil these sites and their inhabitants in a way they would not do with privately owned homes, homeowners or even private renters, who not-coincidentally tend to possess more social and political capital. Since so many of these residents in multiple global contexts tend to be on the lower end of the socio-economic spectrum – and in many locations are viewed as Other in terms of race, class, gender, immigration and citizenship – this dominant public mediated gaze has the power to narrativize and stigmatize these urban sites and those who live in them. There is no other type of domestic space framed by the media through a lens rooted in such a power imbalance.

Intersecting markers of identity – gender, race and class – in architects, planners, media makers and tenants are always embedded in public housing policies and representations. For example, male-centric visions drove the construction of socialized housing in Britain just after the Second World War, which 'was about top-down, total design; men smoking pipes in committee rooms and deciding what was best for women and children' (Beanland 2017). From that same time period came the film adaptation of Ayn Rand's *The Fountainhead* (screenplay by Rand, 1949). Although male urban planners and male filmmakers alike typically dismiss or fail to acknowledge that public housing is a 'largely woman's world' (Leavitt 1993: 109), this film does acknowledge it and attacks it on that basis. Merrill Schleier notes the film's architectural metaphor of monumental masculinity embodied by Howard Roark (Gary Cooper) whose superior physicality is conflated with his buildings. What Roark (and Rand) despises is the feminization of the architect's vision in the construction of public housing, which reeks of un-American socialism: government skimming the hard-earned dollars of real Americans to subsidize the weak in sub-par housing projects. In fairness and in real-world terms, many architects have experienced ambivalence towards public housing due to governmental imposition of strict 'standardization and economies of scale' (Heathcott 88–9) leaving little creativity or challenge for their talents. Rand equated tall buildings 'with masculine heterosexual virility' (Schleier 2002: 314) while also disdaining any architectural ornamentation as being akin to feminine fashion and frippery. Ironically, tall utilitarian American buildings (in the postwar period) were part of a moralizing public housing discourse in which 'plain architecture suited the puritan view of many Americans – and certainly of the housing reformers – who felt that social housing should not be fancy' ('Greenbridge' 2008). And 'fancy' often meant closet doors and toilet seats. For all his attention to architectural designs that would give urbanites air and light in his high-rise utopias, even Le Corbusier trafficked in this classist rhetoric and went just a bit further, writing in 1923: 'Decoration … is suited to simple races, peasants and savages' (McQuire 2008: 179). Along these lines, *The Fountainhead* celebrates a raced, classed, gendered urban avatar for the ideology of rugged individualism and Manifest Destiny from the myth of the American frontier – a skyscraper cowboy – and culminates in Roark's privileged, self-righteous demolition of Cortland Homes, a public housing project he was asked to design (Schleier 2002: 316). Seemingly unconcerned with the working-class and poor tenants who might have found a home there, Roark is only incensed that superfluous bas-relief ornamentation was added to his work.

This collection explores how film and television screens imagine people in public housing – how they live, work, play, struggle and define *home*. What we believe matters about how public housing is framed here – and across the national contexts not discussed, and in digital media such as game design and interactive multi-media formats using Virtual Reality (VR) and online interfaces[7] – are these very aspects of living. Media makers choose characters, plots, locations, mise-en-scène and they choose how public housing looks to the viewer. Genres, production techniques, cultural frameworks, social commentary and echoes of real-world public housing experiences are some of the mysteries to be explored by the twelve authors whose work animates this collection.

I didn't witness the implosion of Pruitt-Igoe as a child, but I have since imagined that moment and found the photographs and film footage both powerful and melancholy. Now, when I cross the Mississippi River over the Stan Musial Veterans Memorial Bridge and look towards the north and west, I wonder why that big patch of the St. Louis landscape still sits empty. Perhaps this project can begin to fill in this blank site – and others – where people once came home and where they still do, on our screens. I am honoured to share these perspectives with the thoughtful and talented scholars herein. I hope that our voices are only the start of this conversation.

Summary of chapters

These essays travel the globe to locations in Chicago, Singapore, St. Louis, Paris, London, Berlin, Baltimore, New York, New Orleans, Rome, Hong Kong and Tel Aviv. They shine a light on frequently marginalized urban spaces and integrate the historical with the cultural, the fictional with the real and the domestic with the institutional. The mise-en-scène in these media visualizes the mysterious geographies of public housing while this volume includes case studies of real-world housing projects in unique global cities and how they are depicted in their respective onscreen worlds.

Part I – *Design, Architecture and Space* begins with five essays that enter a diverse array of public housing sites in which the materiality of aesthetics and spatial urban geographies are foregrounded in the narrative and/or visual depiction of real-world locations. These design elements drive perceptions of housing inhabitants as well as how livable these spaces are (or are not) based on their built structures. The relationship between larger entities (society, government, city planners, media makers) and individuals is revealed through architecture in this set of essays covering both fiction and non-fiction works.

Chapter One, 'Uncanny Architecture: Haunted Structures in *Candyman* and *The Pruitt-Igoe Myth*' (Lorrie Palmer), examines how unseen forces driving the design of Chicago's Cabrini-Green and St. Louis' Pruitt-Igoe render uncanny the exteriors and interiors of their isolated high-rise structures and – too powerful to be repressed – return to haunt residents in notably harmful forms. Chapter Two, '*Die Architekten* (1990): East/West Ideology, Concrete Topography and the Shadow of *Plattenbau*' (Heike Kumpf and Kirsten Kumpf Baele), contrasts state-controlled city planners and Communist-era architecture (made visible in Plattenbau's prefabricated concrete slabs) with creative non-traditionalist architects trying to make an aesthetic, expressive divergence from industrial mass production. Chapter Three, 'Architect and Amateur Documentarian, Yitzhaq Perlstein: Planning Israeli Public Housing (1960–70)' (Daphna Levine and Liat Savin Ben Shoshan), views Tel Aviv public housing through the home movies shot onsite by architect Yitzhaq Perlstein, viewing mass industrialized construction methods alongside his aspirational neighbourhood unit planning. Chapter Four, 'Pier Paolo Pasolini's *Mamma Roma* (1962): INA-Casa Public Housing and Remaking Rome's Postwar Social Landscape' (Alberto Lo Pinto), finds the director's critique of postwar INA-Casa's architectural traits as mere replicas of prewar fascist housing aimed at stimulating petite bourgeois aspirations against which he frames the anti-urban ruins in green spaces nearby. Chapter Five, 'Aerial Transitions: Drone Airspace and Domestic Space in the *Banlieue*' (Isabelle McNeill), explores fluid interior/exterior drone footage in the 2016 documentary, *Swagger*, where a collaborative and fantastical urban space of housing block rooftops and architecture suggests possibilities of freedom and community for schoolchildren living in Aulnay-sous-Bois.

Part II – *Spatialization of Race, Class and Gender* probes the interior and exterior spaces of public housing to reveal the impact of the built environment on its inhabitant. The collection begins to move more deeply into the relationship between powerful housing entities and the confinement or stigmatizing effect felt by those at the other end of the social and economic spectrum. At this intersection between space and human characters, themes of entrapment, alienation, escape and the possibility (or not) for mobility and freedom become entwined with issues of identity: race, class and gender. The architectural becomes personal – at home.

Chapter Six, 'Precarious Homes in Britain and France: Girlhood, Escape and Dance in *Fish Tank* and *Divines*' (Anna Viola Sborgi), follows two troubled teenage girls whose appropriation of the institutional spaces of their council estate and *banlieue*, through dance and restless movement, reflects the fleeting, temporary nature of escape and mobility within their socio-economic realities. Chapter Seven, '*Cooley High*, Cabrini-Green and Early-Onset Rusting in Chicago' (Michael D. Dwyer), frames this 1975 coming-of-age film through industry, infrastructure and geography to argue that the negative effects of deindustrialization are confined to lower-class Black neighbourhoods while the benefits of postindustrialization are devoted to white, upper-class areas of Chicago. Chapter Eight, 'Franklin Wong's *Below the Lion Rock* Television Series: Community Dialogue in 1970s Hong Kong Public Housing' (Chung-kin Tsang), frames this television drama through the blurred public/private spaces of the Resettlement Estates where family and community interrogate the role of the colonial government as Hong Kong was transitioning from a traditional to a modern city. Chapter Nine, 'Within the Public Housing Flats: Interiorization of Class Drama in Singapore Cinema' (Meisen Wong and Chua Beng Huat), exposes the myth of communal class harmony interpreted by the public (and encouraged by the state) to show that class-based alienation and isolation are made visible through home interiors in a range of fiction films.

Part III – *Home Screens: Public Housing in Serialized Television Drama of The Wire, Treme and Show Me a Hero.* These interior/exterior distinctions explore the concept of 'home', which prompts a personal and complex connection to public housing, no matter its architectural aesthetic or the prevailing discourses of identity and representation around it. The aim of these three essays is not so much an industrial-commercial analysis of HBO as a prescription streaming service or of producer/writer David Simon as an *auteur*. Rather, this section will explore the complex world-building in these series to better understand real-world activism and housing policies. The narratives here simultaneously entertain, critique or fail the public housing (and its real-world inhabitants) that make these stories and characters indelible, articulated alongside a domestic urban space designed to provoke complex emotions, fictions and realities.

Chapter Ten, 'Ignoring Women and Communities of Care: Public Housing in *The Wire*' (Kalima Young), challenges the dominant critical discourses of this landmark Baltimore series – and media surveillance constructing the 'hypervisibility' of crime and poverty – to demonstrate the show's erasure of kinship networks spearheaded by female-led households to help manage social ills. Chapter Eleven, '"People Need to Come Home": *Treme*, Abandoned Housing and Post-Katrina New Orleans' (Helen Morgan Parmett), interrogates the HOPE VI programme as a cover for gentrification by the city government and real-estate developers after the storm, while the series refuses to stereotype or pathologize Black life in favour of optimistic community building. Chapter Twelve, 'Public Housing, Social Problems and Defensible Space in David Simon's *Show Me a Hero*' (Steve Macek), notes how the series endorses architect and city planner, Oscar Newman's, largely discredited theory of high-rise modernism for failures in Black and Latino/a working-class housing yet demonstrates that embedded NIMBY ('not in my back yard') racism in local 1980s Yonkers, New York, politics as the real cause.

Conclusion

The world's first public housing museum is inside the only remaining building of Chicago's Jane Addams Homes, built in the New Deal 1930s, where housing insecurity can become part of a larger conversation about social justice. The mission of the National Public Housing Museum 'is to preserve, promote, and propel the right of all people to a place where they can live and prosper – a place to call home' (Mortice 2019). Opening its doors in 2023, the interiors include intimately scaled replicas of residents' apartments representing some of the different groups who once lived in the complex, 'including Jewish, Puerto Rican, Polish, and African-American families' (Mortice 2019). A 2009 open house previewed one of the museum's multi-media installations in which video, audio and music were projected inside the building's original domestic space (see Fennell 2012). The value of experiential immersion into homes and lives is what we aim to share in this volume and, as we argue here, aim matters. Aim can be cities, urban planners, governments; it can be viewers, writers, the camera. How these entities see and show 'home' in the real world as well as in those screenspaces of drama, horror, social critique, rebellion, violence, bodies in motion, race relations, political intrigue, architectural design and the narrative power of outsiders who become the centre of their own story – this is the core of everything that follows.

Notes

1   Aiming to balance public and private provisions through the construction
of a 'decent home and suitable living environment', the Housing Act of 1949
'overwhelmingly directed public resources toward private home building' and did
not require a one-to-one replacement of units demolished through slum clearance,

eminent domain and urban redevelopment, with $1 billion in loans and $500 million in capital grants directed primarily towards 'private, single-family homes' in the suburbs, as well as civic and commercial construction by private developers; only one provision in the Act related to public housing, promising to build 810,000 new low-income homes over the ensuing six years, a goal not reached until 1975 (Heathcott 2012: 366). Julia Faisst notes that the white flight to the suburbs, driven by this government programme, meant that 'no other law contributed as much to racial segregation as the housing laws that went into effect in the United States in 1949' (2016: 282).

2   Not all public housing failed (including that by modernist architects). See Jenny McComas, 'Modernist Housing Between the World Wars: Aesthetics, Politics, and Economics' for examples from 1919 to 1933 (Indiana University, Bloomington 2022), available online: https://artmuseum.indiana.edu/collections-online/features/european-american/swing-landscape-modernist-housing.php. For examples of successful recent constructions, from 2003 to 2013, see Rebecca Hani Romeli, 'The 19 World's Best Public and Social Housing Projects You Need to Know' (iProperty.com.my 2021), available online: https://www.iproperty.com.my/guides/best-public-and-social-housing-around-the-world-70972. Perhaps media makers will set their films, TV shows, videogames, music videos, etc. at these sites for future scholars to build upon our discussion here.

3   As another measure of control by city planners: Neighborhood Gardens was designed from the start to be exclusively for white working-class families (see Heathcott 2011: 87).

4   See, for example, *Photography and Modern Public Housing in Los Angeles* (Nicole Krup Oest, arthistoricum.net, Heidelberg University Library, 2021), from *Art & Photography* series, editor Bettina Gockel (https://d-nb.info/1248239105/34). Similarly, an unpublished manuscript, *Aliso Village USA* (by Leonard Nadel, *c.* 1948–9), uses photography to show the optimism (and racial integration) of this postwar modernist Los Angeles housing project (see Ventura 2021).

5   *Attack the Block* set designer, Marcus Roland, gave cameras to the young cast members to photograph their own council estate homes – and based his design of the onscreen teens' flats on these (see Palmer 2014).

6   Redlining is a series of discriminatory practices first instituted with the 1933 New Deal which built up US housing stock and segregated it along racial lines; the Federal Housing Administration (FHA) refused to insure home mortgages for African Americans, while subsidizing whites-only suburbs. The government created color-coded maps of every major US city, with the African American areas lined in red, indicating (fabricated) financial risk to banks, insurance companies, mortgage lenders and appraisers, thereby prohibiting African Americans from moving into suburban housing in the 1940s–60s. Blockbusting occurred when

realtors convinced homeowners to sell at a reduced price by manipulating them to believe non-whites were about to move into the neighbourhood and depress property values. The owners would sell in a panic and the realtors then profiteered by re-selling those homes at inflated prices.

7   Examples: Videogames include *Dot's Home* (Rise-Home Stories Project 2021) a 2-D single player narrative-driven game which puts the player in Dot's shoes as she finds a time-traveling key and goes back into previous decades of her family to choose different housing options in hopes of a better outcome. 'But because it is a game and because of the limitations of technologies, the choices are rigged for the player, and they get an ending that has already been pre-constructed for them. So in essence, it's sort of this mirror of reality. I don't think a story or comic book or video could quite convey that feeling of false agency and false choices', says Christina Rosales, co-producer of the game (see Poon 2022). Other digital media: an interactive, mixed-media five-feature documentary project, *Highrise* (Katerina Cizek 2010–15); the multi-media project, *Between Two Homes: Story of Dakota Crescent* (Singapore), combining social media, educational workshops and public exhibition; and the interactive, immersive VR documentary, *Common Ground* (Darren Emerson 2019) (Aylesbury Estate, London).

References

Baker, Tora (2019), 'Photography of 50 Years of Thamesmead, the Backdrop of Stanley Kubrick's "A Clockwork Orange"', *Creative Boom*, 18 February. Available online: https://www.creativeboom.com/inspiration/photography-that-reveals-50-years-of-thameshead-the-backdrop-of-stanley-kubricks-a-clockwork-orange/ (accessed 18 July 2021).

Beanland, Christopher (2015), 'Canned Designs: Rip It Up and Start Again in Paris', *The Long + Short*, 15 December. Available online: https://thelongandshort.org/cities/le-corbusier-rebuild-paris-plan-voisin (accessed 14 July 2021).

Beanland, Christopher (2017), 'Just Like Starting Over: When Britain (briefly) Fell in Love with New Towns', *The Long + Short*, 7 March. Available online: https://thelongandshort.org/cities/new-towns (accessed 14 July 2021).

Beautiful Thing (1996), [Film] Dir. Hettie MacDonald, UK: Channel Four Films.

Boughton, John (2018), *Municipal Dreams: The Rise and Fall of Council Housing*, London: Verso.

Budds, Diana (2019), 'Inside Brazil's "cautionary tale" for utopian urbanists', *Curbed*, 7 June. Available online: https://archive.curbed.com/2019/6/7/18657121/brasilia-brazil-urban-planning-architecture-design (accessed 14 July 2021).

Carolin, Peter (2008), 'Sense, Sensibility and Tower Blocks: The Swedish Influence on Post-War Housing in Britain', *Twentieth Century Architecture*, 9: 98–112.

Clemoes, Charlie (2018), 'Memories, Steel and Concrete: *The Wire*'s Season 3
     Opener', *Failed Architecture*, 15 March. Available online: https://failedarchitecture.
     com/2018/03/memories-steel-and-concrete-the-wires-season-3-opener/ (accessed
     6 July 2021).

'A Clockwork Orange | 1971'. *Movie-Locations*. Available online: https://www.movie-
     locations.com/movies/c/Clockwork-Orange.php (accessed 8 July 2021).

Cunha Linke, Clarisse (2018), 'Shortcomings of Brazil's Minha Casa, Minha Vida
     Programme', *Urbanet*, 27 September. Available online: https://www.urbanet.info/
     brazil-social-housing-shortcomings/ (accessed 14 July 2021).

de Coo, Inez (2017), 'Ultraviolence in Representation: The Enduring Myth of the
     Thamesmead Estate', *Failed Architecture*, 15 December. Available online: https://
     failedarchitecture.com/ultraviolence-in-representation-the-enduring-myth-of-the-
     thamesmead-estate/ (accessed 18 July 2021).

Donald, James (1995), 'The City, the Cinema: Modern Spaces', in Chris Jenks (ed),
     Visual Culture, 77–95, London: Routledge.

Donald, James (1999), *Imagining the Modern City*, Minneapolis: The University of
     Minnesota Press.

Faisst, Julia (2016), 'Ghetto Aesthetics: Performing Spatial Inequality in The Pruitt-Igoe
     Myth', in Birgit M. Bauridl and Pia Wiegmink (eds), *Approaching Transnational
     America in Performance*, 265–88, New York: Peter Lang.

Fennell, Catherine (2012), 'The Museum of Resilience: Raising a Sympathetic Public in
     Postwelfare Chicago', *Cultural Anthropology*, 27 (4): 641–66.

The Fountainhead (1949), [FILM] Dir. King Vidor, USA: Warner Bros.

Gandy, Matthew (1999), 'The Paris Sewers and the Rationalization of Urban Space',
     Transactions of the Institute of British Geographers, 24 (1): 23–44.

Goetz, Edward G. (2013), *New Deal Ruins: Race, Economic Justice, and Public Housing
     Policy*, Ithaca: Cornell University Press.

Good Times (1974–1979), [TV programme] US: CBS.

'Greenbridge: The Failure of the Cabrini-Green Model of Public Housing and the Rise
     of the New Urbanism'. *White Center Now*, 28 November 2008. Available online:
     http://whitecenternow.com/2008/11/28/greenbridge-the-failure-of-the-cabrini-
     green-model-of-public-housing-and-the-rise-of-the-new-urbanism/ (accessed
     18 September 2021).

Handelman, Howard (1979), 'High-Rises and Shantytowns: Housing the Poor in Bogotá
     and Caracas', *American Universities Field Staff Report*, No. 9.

Heathcott, Joseph (2011), '"In the Nature of a Clinic": The Design of Early Public
     Housing in St. Louis', *Journal of the Society of Architectural Historians*, 70 (1):
     82–103.

Heathcott, Joseph (2012), 'The Strange Career of Public Housing', *Journal of the
     American Planning Association*, 78 (4): 360–75.

Hoggard, Liz (2018), 'Beautiful Thing Review: Backdrop of Thamesmead Estate Gives
     Dance Re-imagining Real Frisson', *Evening Standard*, 5 July. Available online: https://

www.standard.co.uk/culture/theatre/beautiful-thing-review-backdrop-of-thamesmead-estate-gives-dance-re-imagining-real-frisson-a3879756.html (accessed 8 September 2021).

Jacobs, Jane (1961), *The Death and Life of Great American Cities*, New York: Vintage Books.

Lau, Kwok Yu, and Alan Murie (2017), 'Residualisation and Resilience: Public Housing in Hong Kong', *Housing Studies*, 32 (3): 271–95.

Leavitt, Jacqueline (1993), 'Women under Fire: Public Housing Activism in Los Angeles', *Frontiers: A Journal of Women's Studies*, 13 (2): 109–30.

Levasseur, Bruno (2008), 'De-essentializing the Banlieues, Reframing the Nation: Documentary Cinema in France in the Late 1990s', *New Cinemas: Journal of Contemporary Film*, 6 (2): 97–109.

Libertun de Duren, Nora Ruth (2018), 'The Social Housing Burden: Comparing Households at the Periphery and the Centre of Cities in Brazil, Colombia, and Mexico', *International Journal of Housing Policy*, 18 (2): 177–203.

Living at Thamesmead, 1974 (1974), [VIDEO] Available online: https://www.youtube.com/watch?v=NtqX9PJv-Nk&t=340s (accessed 9 June 2021).

Lubin, Gus (2013), 'Why Architect Le Corbusier Wanted to Demolish Downtown Paris', 20 August, *Business Insider*, 20 August. Available online: https://www.businessinsider.com/le-corbusiers-plan-voisin-for-paris-2013-7 (accessed 12 July 2021).

Mann, Nicola (2012), 'Do Not Believe the Hype: The Death and Resurrection of Public Housing in the American Imagination', in Chris Richardson and Hans A. Skott-Myhre (eds), *Habitus of the Hood*, 271–98, Chicago: The University of Chicago Press.

Marten, Dan (2019), '"Good Times" and Representation: Media in Cabrini-Green', *TechNews*, 11 March. Available online: https://technewsiit.com/good-times-and-representation-cabrini-green (accessed 1 March 2022).

McQuire, Scott (2008), *The Media City: Media, Architecture and Urban Space*, London: Sage.

Mortice, Zach (2019), 'The National Public Housing Museum Eyes a 2021 Opening', 3 December, *Bloomberg CityLab*. Available online: https://www.bloomberg.com/news/articles/2019-12-03/plans-evolve-for-a-national-public-housing-museum (accessed 1 March 2022).

Myles, Sarah (2019), 'The Expansion of the British Social Class Divide', *Medium*, 3 October. Available online: https://medium.com/@sjmyles79/the-expansion-of-the-british-social-class-divide-861a05c499b (accessed 30 June 2021).

Palmer, Lorrie (2014), '*Attack the Block: Monsters, Race, and Rewriting South London's Outer Spaces*', *Jump Cut*, 56. Available online: https://www.ejumpcut.org/archive/jc56.2014-2015/PalmerAttackBlock/index.html (accessed 23 January 2022).

Poon, Linda (2022), 'Can You Game Your Way Out of American Housing Injustice? A new video game uses a choose-your-own adventure format to interrogate the

illusion of choice in the U.S. housing system', 12 January, *Bloomberg CityLab +*
Equality. Available online: https://www.bloomberg.com/news/articles/2022-01-12/
video-game-spotlights-racism-in-u-s-housing-system (accessed 9 March 2022).

Rodriguez, Akira Drake (2021), *Diverging Space for Deviants: The Politics of Atlanta's*
Public Housing, Athens: The University of Georgia Press.

Schleier, Merrill (2002), 'Ayn Rand and King Vidor's Film "The Fountainhead":
Architectural Modernism, the Gendered Body, and Political Ideology', *Journal of the*
Society of Architectural Historians, 61 (3): 310–31.

Selfridges HOT AIR Presents: The Bard of the Street, A Film by Mary McCartney (2016),
[VIDEO] Available online: https://www.youtube.com/watch?v=xaNbyYeJRZI
(accessed 4 September 2021).

Ventura, Anya (2021), 'The Rise and Fall of an American Dream', 15 July, *Getty*.
Available online: https://www.getty.edu/news/the-rise-and-fall-of-las-aliso-village/
(accessed 21 March 2023).

Weir, Margaret (1993), 'Race and Urban Poverty: Comparing Europe and America',
The Brookings Review, 11 (3): 22–7.

White, Ryan (2019), 'Photographing Thamesmead: The Town of Tomorrow',
I-D Vice, 4 March. Available online: https://i-d.vice.com/en_uk/article/mbzx78/
photographing-thamesmead-the-town-of-tomorrow (accessed 18 July 2021).

Wojcik, Pamela Robertson (2018), 'Introduction: What Makes the Apartment
Complex?', in Pamela Robertson Wojcik (ed), *The Apartment Complex: Urban Living*
and Global Screen Cultures, Durham: Duke University Press.

Zipp, Samuel (2012), 'The Roots and Routes of Urban Renewal', *Journal of Urban*
History, 39 (3): 366–91.

Part One

Design, architecture and space

1

Uncanny architecture: Haunted structures in *Candyman* and *The Pruitt-Igoe Myth*

Lorrie Palmer

In the urban imaginary, public housing is the uncanny of the city. When it fails, it becomes the architectural expression of alienation, estrangement, exile and unhomeliness (the *unheimlich* of Freud's early twentieth-century notions of the uncanny). Public housing is experiential, architectural and, by the nature of the forces behind it, institutional. The 'uncanny specific to the modern metropolis arises in the disquieting distinction between the city as object of government and the city as frame of mind' (Donald 1999: 73), a simultaneity of the rational, bureaucratic city with the phantasmagoric 'uncanny architecture of experience, symbol, myth, and fantasy' (Donald 1999: 84). In other words, the urban uncanny is that zone between the external and the internal, the built and the lived. When *home* is built in this zone, it becomes an architectural uncanny likewise characterized by doubleness – the home as a space of familiarity as well as concealment. The dominant image of public housing in the failed tower blocks central to the two films I will discuss here is one of architectural darkness but because the filmmakers go inside – to the homes of the fictional characters and the real-world residents – we can also see the uncanny in the distinction between architectural design and the unique uses made of those spaces. Uncanny architecture occurs 'first in the house, haunted or not, that pretends to afford the utmost security while opening itself to the secret intrusion of terror, and then in the city, where what was once walled and intimate, the confirmation of community … has been rendered strange', merging the real with the unreal (Vidler 1992: 11). Therefore, I will find in the homes of these public housing-based films – in their modes of documentary and horror, the rational and the irrational – what haunts the high-rise architecture of the structures in 2011's *The Pruitt-Igoe Myth* (set in St. Louis) and the 1992 film, *Candyman* (located in Chicago's Cabrini-Green).

While James Donald finds in *Candyman* the opportunity to divine the uncanny space between the city as a planned external environment and its irrational, labyrinthine interior, his perspective of the film's setting relies primarily on the former, in the 'dehumanised geometry' (1999: 69) he notes in the aerial shots of Chicago at the start of the film. Donald's incursion into the streets below is brief, where he rightly identifies the presence of a racialized 'underclass' of the city focused on fear and myth, in contrast to the anthropological detective work done by the female protagonist wishing to understand those legends by opening herself up to their horror (1999: 69–70). In pairing *Candyman* with *The Pruitt-Igoe Myth* through the uncanny doubleness of their architecture and their uses of it – through onscreen structures and mediating lenses – I would suggest a point at which to build upon Donald's approach. He never goes inside *Candyman*'s domestic space and does not associate the uncanny urban labyrinth with home. Therefore, I will go inside (as these two films do) to view how destructive external forces, whose presence is repressed through rationalized design policies, inevitably unleash monsters where home should be. Real-world contexts of public housing in Chicago and St. Louis will also help me frame the alienating exteriors of the two films' tower block structures, their residents' (and filmmakers') resistance to these through their (initially) livable homes, the holes that eventually blur exterior/interior spaces and, finally, the haunting urban history of water and waste that connects them all – as it intrudes from outside to inside and upwards from below. These liquid eruptions are simultaneously the logical as well as the phantasmagoric consequences of Le Corbusier's modernist desire to repress the city's messy 'history, memory and desire' through 'architecture and city planning' (Donald 1999: 84). This and other forms of repression play out in the material construction and narrative symbolism that drive the architectural design of Cabrini-Green and Pruitt-Igoe, onscreen and off.

Both films use the design of elevators, bathrooms, stairwells, open spaces at ground level, communal galleries and the geography of structures to reveal the institutional repression intruding from without. The buildings we see onscreen include the *heimlich* (homely) cosy spaces where people are doing the best they can in desperate circumstances. We also see a gentrified palimpsest of segregation defined by race and class, as well as the decay and neglect visible in the holes broken through brick and concrete and glass. All uncanny.

Bernard Rose, the British director of *Candyman* (which he transposed from the port city of Liverpool in the original 1985 short story *The Forbidden* by Clive Barker to the housing projects of Chicago), describes his framework: 'Definitely the film is about architecture and the way that people can exist in the same space, but it's how the space is designated that affects the nature of the building, in a way'; thus, Rose reveals 'architecture as a malevolent force' (Landekic 2016). The horror of Candyman's (Tony Todd) haunting of Cabrini-Green emerges from the trauma of his nineteenth-century human self as Daniel Robitaille, a portrait artist and son of a freed slave, who now returns with a bloody hook hand to slash anyone who dares to say his name five times into a mirror. For his sin of loving a white woman, Robitaille was brutalized by her father's mob; his painting hand was roughly amputated, and he was covered in honey and stung to death by hungry bees. In a new century, the Cabrini-Green complex is eventually built on the site of this racist murder and in present-day Chicago white anthropology graduate student Helen Lyle (Virginia Madsen) arrives there to research urban myths, along with Bernadette Walsh (Kasi Lemmons), her African American thesis-writing partner from the University of Illinois. The women make the mistake, however, of dismissing the myth of Candyman and standing together in Helen's bathroom and saying his name into her mirrored cabinet, a design feature that I will show sutures real-world public housing into the invasions we see onscreen. This film's use of its architectural spaces echoes philosopher Friedrich Schelling's take on the uncanny as that which 'ought to have remained secret and hidden but has come to light' (Freud 1955: 225). This uneasy urban overlap of home and horror is revealed as Helen and the Candyman meet at Cabrini-Green.[1]

Rose's aerial views trace highways crisscrossing the city, bridges over the Chicago River and streets passing beneath commercial buildings, all facilitating the unfettered flow of traffic, an effect of government urban planning. The movement of mass transit through the city frequently had the opposite effect on the North Side projects of Cabrini-Green, however (as well as the Robert Taylor Homes and Stateway Gardens in the Bronzeville neighbourhood on the South Side), limiting their access to the rest of the city, with some highways, for example, having no exit ramps. One fourteen-lane road in particular made it personal: 'the mammoth Dan Ryan Expressway certainly formed a psychological boundary for public housing residents' (Hunt 2009: 343n59). Chicago's urban topography materializes bureaucracy in the form of these concrete barriers, forcing immobility upon designated residents of the city (see Dwyer, this volume). In parallel, the film narrates the institutional construction of Cabrini-Green itself as an act of repression – where haunted structures sit on the bloody ground of Robitaille's murder. The consequence is Candyman's monstrous intrusion into the city's public housing as well as its gentrified Gold Coast.

In Chad Freidrichs' documentary, *The Pruitt-Igoe Myth*, the director shares a journalistic, film and photographic archive of lives lived in the projects of St. Louis, articulated on camera by five former residents. Friedrichs outlines the 'myth' that the site's high-rise modernist architecture, along with the poor and Black residents, was to blame for (take your pick) crime, unemployment, fractured families, the drug trade, violence, broken infrastructure (water pipes, elevators, lights) and, ultimately, the heavily publicized demolition that brought down the buildings less than twenty years after they went up. Instead, the film argues that the failure of this public housing development stemmed from a complex nexus of white flight to the (subsidized) suburbs, urban divestment, lack of funding for onsite management and maintenance (which depended on rental income from full occupancy), deindustrialization, wildly overestimated urban population growth projections, race-based inequalities and the ways in which Pruitt-Igoe and its residents were cut off from the larger city of St. Louis. The director also challenges the perception of public housing residents as problems to be solved – the conflation of people with the built environment – as he gives voice to the men and women who lived in Pruitt-Igoe and who made it a home, with memories of community behind the increasingly stigmatized modernist image of public housing. That perception was fostered by design as Pruitt-Igoe was spatially isolated from the city. In 'The Story of Segregation in St. Louis' (2014), Jeannette Cooperman explains that the city's eminent domain policies 'harnessed architecture as a barrier' to maintain spatial and racial segregation through evictions, redevelopment and highway construction (*St. Louis Magazine*). With this power of urban planning, the uncanny of the haunted house extends to the 'carceral architectures of detention' (Wasson 2019: 37), a monster lurking inside the homes of Pruitt-Igoe, concealed by rationalized design.

In both films, such homes are experienced by residents forced to navigate buildings with a political and ideological provenance. Much like civic monuments, these structures are imbued with the omnipresence of the state, its surveillance, its prohibitions, its will to subservience; the buildings are 'haunted with power' and the 'ghost of authority' (Hook 2005: 699) rooted in the bureaucratic control of their architectural and spatial environment. These films enable me to examine the ways in which the powers that planned the public housing sites and directed the designs of architects impact them and their residents. Freud explicitly linked that which is repressed (and later returns) to the uncanny. These powers cannot be repressed, they will always return in harmful forms to haunt the structures – outside and in.

Exteriors

The archival aerial photography used by director Chad Freidrichs in *The Pruitt-Igoe Myth* illustrates the architectural uncanny 'as an aesthetic category … reconceived as the very sign of modernism's propensity for shock and disturbance' (Vidler 1992: 8). The site's thirty-three buildings in 1700-foot-long rows, 'oriented East-West in parallel' (Montgomery 1966: 33) reared up out of the flat Midwestern plain even more inorganically than did Le Corbusier's eighteen cruciform steel-grid towers lord over Paris in his unrealized 1925 Plan Voisin. The rational control visible in their 'rigid sightlines, and insistent verticality' (Heathcott 2011: 100) already evoked the uncanny by this material misfit. High-angle images, with the 638-foot (190-meter) stainless steel Gateway Arch on the city's riverfront, emphasize the distance from downtown to the modernist towers to the north and west. Pruitt-Igoe never fit the city; the unadorned blocks instead seemed designed for spatial disorientation, 'looking utterly alien to the miles of low-rise 19th and early twentieth-century brick structures surrounding it' (Marshall 2015) (see Figure 1.1). Archival film footage makes visible their design feature of an open grid of structural concrete columns (*pilotis*) 'at the base of each tower' with these allowing 'at least two circulation routes' to the tower interiors through the stairwells and elevators (Major 2021: 62). The Corbusian architectural philosophy behind this design was that it would create a space for air and light to circulate as well as for neighbours to gather. The reality was that this cut-through feature instead

Figure 1.1 Aerial view of Pruitt-Igoe, St. Louis, Missouri (date unknown). Photo courtesy of United States Geological Survey, public domain.

facilitated the penetration by outsiders and strangers into the community along with uncontrolled access to the elevators, which became zones of darkness (constantly broken light fixtures) and assault. 'Bodies enter, becomes displaced, leave, becomes replaced, and so on. Residents have remarked that it came to a point where it became impossible to distinguish resident from intruder because of the fluidity, and perhaps the transitory nature of these said bodies' (Koh 2014).There was, in this way, a distinction between the design of the structures' architectural features and the reality lived by people on site – and there lies the uncanny.

Filmmaker Freidrichs takes on the originating myth that rose up in academic, political and architectural discourses about Pruitt-Igoe, that 'the rational and orderly architecture' of the site 'was supposed, in accordance with modernist urban design principles … to change poor people for the better, supposedly improving their characters by changing their living conditions' (Faisst 2016: 266–7). However, Katharine Bristol, whose 1991 *Journal of Architectural Education* article, 'The Pruitt-Igoe Myth', is a significant influence on Freidrichs' documentary, notes that architects at Minoru Yamasaki's Detroit firm,[2] in designing the 'glazed galleries, the skip-stop elevators … and the minimalist surface treatment reflected the prevailing interest in Modernism' at the time, but do not 'demonstrate that the architects had particular intentions for social reform' (169). Indeed, Yamasaki's initial plans called for a mixed-rise development of two-storey townhouses and eleven-storey modular structures, but the city insisted on building only the cost-saving, land-efficient towers instead. Between the city's intentional design and the lived experience of residents is the architectural uncanny, where repression has an immediate effect. Former tenant, Brian King, felt this at a visceral level, saying that Pruitt-Igoe seemed 'strategically planned' to make people feel isolated, restricted, inhuman – 'You're bad, we have to restrain you, we have to curtail what you're doing. It was void of humanity. It was void of caring. It seemed more like a prison environment that you have to escape from' (*TP-IM* 2011: 00:35:00:42-36:12). What disoriented residents even more acutely was how fast it all happened.

The transformation from the comfort and cleanliness of residents' apartments and the surrounding grounds when they first moved in, to the later deterioration of the buildings and city services stifled the early sense of kinship they felt in the community. We see a grainy television interview with Mrs. Ruby Russell: 'Well, one day we woke up and it was all gone' (*TP-IM* 2011: 00:04:28). Freidrichs previews the coming transformation: he opens in the mid-1950s with both colour and black-and-white footage of well-maintained green spaces and children of different races (in the early days)[3] enjoying playground equipment. Subsequent shots then reveal the change – the buildings' facades, dotted with the eerie openness of hundreds of broken windows, derelict cars, sagging chain-link fences and rusted children's swing sets. Audio of contemporaneous newscasts narrates these shots and sustains the media and popular understanding of public housing within a 'scenario of failure and dysfunction' (Goetz 2013: 41), intoning that 'Pruitt-Igoe looks like a battleground' (*TP-IM* 2011: 00:05:00). The archival footage here shows only exterior or common areas, indicating that media reportage at the time (roughly the late 1960s up to when the demolitions began in 1972) avoided going into residents' homes once things started going downhill in the projects.

This exterior focus also initially holds true in *Candyman*, as Rose helicopters his camera over and into Cabrini-Green to establish the visual and architectural terrain of the projects from which the urban uncanny will erupt. However, 'Rose's camera departs its spectral vantage point, swooping down to street level' (Mann 2012: 284) as he follows Helen and Bernadette in a small red car traversing expressways and bridges into Cabrini-Green. The combination of aerial and ground views conveys the site's isolation and its desolate landscape of red brick towers jutting up from deserted lots. In contrast, the quiet security of Helen's neighbourhood, and her high-rise condominium, is clear in an exterior pan across its old-growth trees and sculpted streetlights, with a leisurely tilt up to the building's glowing windows and trim balconies. We later see from Helen's apartment window that there are physical barriers between her neighbourhood and the nearby public housing complex. The city and the Chicago Housing Authority (CHA) envisioned the expressway and mass transit lines as boundaries around the superblocks of Cabrini-Green, spatially isolating the projects and drawing a stark contrast between wealth and poverty, along with disparities of race and class. On this night, Bernadette has come to Helen's home to work on their graduate thesis. Helen lays out microfiche printouts of two architectural drawings published in a city newspaper, side by side, and prompts Bernadette, 'Do you spot it?' (*Candyman* 1992: 00:12:52). One high-rise is from Cabrini-Green and the other is Helen's own building, Lincoln Village. She informs her partner, 'My apartment was built as a housing project' (00:13:04). However, a closer look at these two drawings reveals that their designs are quite different: the Cabrini-Green 'Reds' building is a nineteen-storey slab design (a straight-line structure rather than the cross- or H-shaped type) with 'exposed concrete frames and red brick infill with two perpendicular wings at the rear of each building' (Clark 1996). Lincoln Village, on the other hand, is taller (twenty-eight storeys), square in configuration and more resembles an urban skyscraper, with smooth glass sides, expansive balconies at all four corners of the building and, visible in the previous exterior pan, although not in the drawing, a zig-zag overhang (in a folded plate design) embellishing the first floor. Why does writer/director Rose juxtapose these two drawings in the shot then have Helen say they are virtually indistinguishable (and Bernadette is unable to spot the difference)? Perhaps image alone is enough. The dystopian public perception of high-rise public housing haunts any sparse urban tower, averted here by extra glass, balconies and the drama of the folded plate aesthetic. The social and spatial distinction between Lincoln Village and Cabrini-Green, formed by the city's transportation infrastructure, recurs at the level of design – keeping one tower the architectural uncanny of the other.

In another on-location scene, Rose reveals much of Cabrini-Green's blasted landscape, its exterior walls and its walk-through passages when a young boy, Jake (DeJuan Guy), leads Helen from Anne-Marie's (Vanessa Williams) building to an adjacent public outhouse to show her where one of Candyman's attacks took place. The structure does not include the *pilotis* design, but there is a similar ground-level cut-through with columns; the graffitied red brick surfaces where the two characters exit reveal a clear line of sight through to the back of the building. The camera tracks alongside them as they cross an empty parking lot behind a Cabrini tower block and past children's swing sets with no swings on them, to the small out-building (see Figure 1.2) where ransacked stalls are smeared with excrement and, in the last one, a toilet swarming with Candyman's hungry bees.

Inside this space, Helen visibly struggles with the overwhelming stench, as the boundary between the orderly mechanics of modern toilets and the city's hidden sewage system has broken down. 'The sewer has consistently been associated with what we might term the "urban uncanny": a spatially defined sense of dread in modern urban societies' (Gandy 1999: 34). The dread is embodied, across people and places, with shifting philosophies and practices around waste and human hygiene. In this *Candyman* outhouse, we see that 'human excrement [takes] on an intensely abject quality as part of a multiplicity of flows that [have] integrated the body and urban society into an uneasy whole' (Gandy 1999: 35). The uncanny emanating from such a place has always been the underlying reality of urban housing design. From the early days of slums and tenement housing for the poor, one consistent feature has been 'that urban working-class neighborhoods remained without water and other modern sanitary services'

Figure 1.2 Jake leads Helen to the outhouse of Cabrini-Green, with the skyscrapers of Chicago in the distance, from *Candyman* directed by Bernard Rose © Polygram Filmed Entertainment, 1992. All rights reserved.

(Bauman 2000: 9). The flows of water and waste are where both *Candyman* and *The Pruitt-Igoe Myth* signal the uncanny nature of public housing, which will be my final point in this chapter. How we arrive there first requires a continuation of our journey through the architectural spaces they depict.

In between

Moving from the exterior spaces of these housing projects to the interior, we encounter in both films the structure of flows, of passage and process, designed into the buildings onscreen and into their real-world counterparts in stairwells, galleries and elevators. Helen and Bernadette venture into 'Candyman country' (00:29:16) on their first visit to Cabrini-Green to see the apartment where the hooked monster is believed by the locals – and reported in the newspaper – to have murdered a fourth-floor tenant named Ruthie Jean. The two grad students are confronted by gang members on the ground floor and then, realizing the elevator is broken, they ascend a brick stairwell. In this passage, we see the absence of building maintenance, the omnipresent graffiti in the common areas, the wide-open access to outsiders and, as they arrive on the fourth floor, the open-air gallery bounded on one side by wire mesh. The CHA fenced in the galleries at most of the city's high-rises in 1968 so that the streets-in-the-sky envisioned by the architects instead 'looked like cages, a devastating aesthetic that defined perceptions of Chicago's projects thereafter' (Hunt 2009: 167; Vale 2013: 226–7). The visual and thematic bridge between outside and inside is the graffiti on the outer wall of the apartment opposite the wire mesh, spelled out in bright spray-paint, 'Sweets for the Sweet', a menacing enticement the residents attribute to Candyman; the same phrase is smeared in excrement in the public toilet that Helen investigates. The symbolic and literal juxtaposition is jarring in these uncanny repetitions, these unwelcoming entryways. Director Rose, in describing his film as being about how architecture is designated, how the spaces are named and used and experienced, likewise helps frame the memories of Pruitt-Igoe's former tenants in Freidrichs's documentary.

The Pruitt-Igoe Myth introduces us to two such tenants – Sylvester Brown, Jr. and Brian King – who appear onscreen and describe what it was like to live there as children. Their experiences with in-between spaces diverged significantly. Sylvester remembers that his building was a place of wonderful cooking smells and had spaces where kids could 'play hard' in the 85-feet long galleries (what he calls 'breezeways') and run up and down in the stairwells (*TP-IM* 2011: 00:16:15), although he also makes clear that things did change. Eventually, the elevators stopped working due to an absence of onsite management and maintenance; kids would use the elevators as toilets (further blurring the public/ private boundary) and the elevators would frequently get stuck between floors (00:15:56-00:16:24). But his early positive experiences helped temper what came later. In contrast, Brian King hated Pruitt-Igoe on sight; he arrived there once the decline had begun and did not have the backlog of warm memories that Mr. Brown had. He remembered the smell of the garbage piled up in front of the corridor incinerators on the ground floor and adds that he 'never really recovered from that first day' (*TP-IM* 2011: 00:20:24-00:20:48). Valerie Sills, another former resident, describes how people would set this accumulated trash on fire themselves, sending the smoke along the corridor and seeping into the elevator shaft, leaving anyone stuck on the elevator in the dark with 'no place to go' (00:52:52). A similar intrusion of the elements is visible in a black-and-white photograph of a young boy pushing a mop against a large puddle of water in one of the galleries (00:54:24), as there is no glass, only wire mesh to keep the outside out.

The haunting of these in-between spaces may be summed up in the design of the elevators. To save money, planners required the architects to install elevators that did not stop on every floor – this cost-saving measure was a popular modernist feature (Le Corbusier designed it into his Marseilles *Unité d'Habitation*[4] in 1952) but, in the Pruitt-Igoe context, it only reflected failed building maintenance, the isolation of tenants trapped on dark elevators, the forced resort to dangerous stairwells and the mechanical and spatial severing of safe passage home.

> Internally, each building has a single 'skip-stop' elevator which stops only on the fourth, seventh, and tenth floors. All other floors are served by stairways from the galleries at the elevator floors or from the ground. The buildings average about seventy dwelling in each vertical stack, and all the units open from the dark landings of the unlit stair shafts.
>
> (Montgomery 1966: 33)

Freud's uncanny (his *unheimlich*) is bound to a particular experience of uncertainty in which a 'lack of orientation' – of not 'knowing one's way about' – transforms the familiar world of home into an uneasy hostile terrain (Vidler 1992: 23). Rather than being a high-rise double of the urban sidewalk where people might pass their neighbours' front doors on the way home, might engage in community connection as the architects intended, the forced economy of the elevator design instead deposited tenants into the very *unheimlich* core of an unknowable space.

Interiors

It is in the domestic interiors in *Candyman* and *The Pruitt-Igoe Myth* that the architectural uncanny penetrates the visible and mediated outer walls to the hidden homes inside – and where the real haunting begins. In *Candyman*, we get a tour of Helen's converted condominium in Lincoln Village as she walks Bernadette from the kitchen to the living room, then down the hall to the bathroom and its fatal mirror so she can demonstrate its identical floor plan with the units at Cabrini-Green. She knocks on the living room wall and tells her friend that the original cinder blocks were plastered over and painted as it morphed from affordable public housing to high-priced private property. In all the interior scenes of Helen's home, the film's production designer, Jane Ann Stewart, personalizes it with full bookshelves (fitting the academic profession she shares with her husband, Trevor), a fireplace, textured couch pillows and throws in orange, brown, gold and black, houseplants, woven baskets, painted walls, carved wooden totems and a floor-to-ceiling living room window. This *heimlich* environment is not made uncanny until the Cabrini-Green spectre of Candyman invades it, first, by thrusting his bloody hook through her bathroom mirror and then by eviscerating Bernadette while Helen is unconscious on the kitchen floor. The home interiors on both sides of the city's constructed boundaries are paired nevertheless, fused by Candyman's violent undoing of each. He invades the Cabrini-Green home of Anne-Marie McCoy as well, to frame Helen for his kidnapping of the single mother's infant son, Anthony. Production designer Stewart has likewise carefully crafted the McCoy apartment a cozy, albeit thrifty, version of Helen's condo, as she is determined to raise her child in a positive home environment, regardless of the 'assholes downstairs' (*Candyman* 1992: 00:26:06) who station themselves near the cut-through areas at ground level. The cinder block walls of her kitchen and living room are painted in soft hues; there are textile wall hangings, a crocheted couch pillow, a console television, framed family photos, floral curtains in the kitchen and a color palette of gold, orange, red and brown in the living room (in a similar range to the colours in Helen's unit). All of these details serve to disarm any 'preconceptions about what the home of a single mother from public housing *should* look like' (Mann 2012: 290). In both homes, the kitchens, bedrooms and bathrooms are painted, decorated and lived-in, with common and relatable personal touches – the very essence of homeliness. As each is eventually torn by violence (Candyman beheads Anne-Marie's guard dog and murders Helen's best friend), what was outside has come in, haunting the homes and making them unrecognizable. In the filmmaker's use of these interiors, we see architectural copies as each is rendered *unheimlich*. They are doubles drawn in blood.

Facilitated by the cut-through feature of Le Corbusier's *pilotis*, the outside can freely enter into the St. Louis projects as well. But first, director Freidrichs displays the bare template of Pruitt-Igoe's interiors through black-and-white as well as colour photographs from the 1950s and early 1960s. We see a living room, a child's bedroom, and an adult's bedroom, where residents' use of these spaces made it a home. Former tenant, Ruby Russell, who had never lived higher than two storeys, loved her eleventh-floor apartment; she said, 'It was like an oasis in the desert – all this newness' (00:13:45). That shiny polished interior, like a dream, is another way that outside institutional forces haunt the lived experiences inside the structures of St. Louis public housing, as seen in *The Pruitt-Igoe Myth*. Resident Jacquelyn Williams describes where the line was drawn by official policy: 'We couldn't have a telephone. We couldn't have a television' (00:35:26). This effectively cut people off from the civic life of the city and from the flow of information these technologies would bring into the home. However, she describes her mother later getting a letter[5] from the St. Louis Housing Authority eventually giving permission for them to get a TV. Even this seemingly positive change communicates spatial inequality. As a girl, Jacquelyn was fascinated by TV families with fathers; this stems from the lack in her own home, as the SLHA barred all husbands and fathers from living with their families (the punitive prerequisite for women and children on welfare assistance). Over his subject's narration here, Freidrichs cuts in archival shots of a slow pan over the sparkling mid-century interior of a Barbie Dream House (complete with a miniature console television and telephone on a teenage girl's desk), as well as scenes from the sitcom, *My Little Margie* (Roland Reed Productions, 1952–5). Ms. Williams remembers enjoying this series because it depicted a father deeply involved in his daughter's life. It is interesting that the establishing shot of this television series is of a residential high-rise where Margie lives (and where she has a radio on her nightstand, visible in the scene Freidrichs includes here). As Jacquelyn watched this show on the television that the authorities finally allowed her family to have, she noticed the racialized housing it revealed, but never questioned it: 'This was just the way white people lived' (00:38:02). Both girls, Jacquelyn and Margie, lived in modernist high-rises but only one had an exiled father.

Holes

The wholeness of *My Little Margie's* sitcom world contrasts with lives inside Pruitt-Igoe. As the documentary progresses forward in time, holes begin to appear. Repeated shots of walls broken through, showing rooms on the other side through the gaping, violated boundaries between units. There were so many holes through windows in the structures that it was possible to see through them to the other side. As tenant occupancy continued to shrink in the 1960s and early 1970s, vandals and local drug dealers began to strip the buildings for parts and to move in and set up shop, knowing the community was under-policed. As a result, remaining residents were even more cut off from city services and increasingly isolated by fear inside their homes. Despite the in-between zones of galleries, stairwells and elevators designated for convenience and access, the way they were used now fostered only alienation. As in his use of exterior shots of broken windows, missing doors along the galleries and repeated framings through jagged holes in glass, Freidrichs now sequences interior photographs of empty rooms displaying rough holes knocked through the walls, including a black-and-white image of an abandoned bathroom in which exposed copper pipes have been cut out and there is no longer a sink, just a large hole where it used to be.

Similarly, *Candyman* utilizes the cut-through (and see-through) function of holes, of broken architectural boundaries – in walls and ceilings – to convey the growing uncanny of the lost homes of Cabrini-Green. Helen's discovery of her condo's shared design with the projects – in those architectural drawings and the hole behind her mirrored bathroom cabinet – continues after hearing the story of Ruthie Jean's murder in Cabrini-Green. She and Bernadette find the same feature in the dead woman's apartment (which is next door to Anne-Marie). Helen opens the mirrored cabinet and climbs through the hole behind it. After passing through larger holes in several walls, she crosses one more and, in the reverse shot, we see that the face of Candyman has been painted on the other side, with his gaping mouth the portal through which Helen enters into the building's deep interior labyrinth. Rose holds this shot (and Helen photographs it), emphasizing the easy violation of a building opened up to bodies and cameras through literal and symbolic holes. Anne-Marie tells Helen and Bernadette later, after allowing them into her apartment, that she hears noises and feels unsafe; her bathroom cabinet has the same design, after all. Here is another hole through which visible architecture lays bare the hidden structures beneath – made uncanny by how these spaces are used. Through this most intimate of domestic spaces, vulnerability and exposure lead to even deeper architectural recesses of public housing where waste and sewage form the shadow of the city, repressed by design.

Under the structures: water and sewage

As urban life progressed, from the 1920s and that decade's 'spread of private bathrooms' to the 'sanitized, piped, wired, plumbed house – the classic icon of the 1950s and 1960s', the modernized networks of water and waste were banished to the underbelly of the city (Kaika and Swyngedouw 2002: 134). The domestication of these flows and processes rendered them invisible in what should be the pure spaces of the metropolitan home. However, 'sewers form an enduring element of the "urban uncanny", through their integral interrelationship with changing conceptions of bodily abjection and urban order' (Gandy 1999: 25). In the uncanny spaces of public housing depicted in *Candyman* and *The Pruitt-Igoe Myth*, any control over the boundaries between 'the body, technology and urban architecture' (Gandy 1999: 32) is illusory at best. Why? Because 'the sewer [is] also haunted' (Donald 1999: 24). The remainder of my discussion here will locate architectural haunting through the networks of water and sewage and the related site-specific depictions of toilets/bathrooms which both films use to distinguish the rational from the irrational.

The Pruitt-Igoe Myth replays excerpts of a 1970 TV news story about the brutal winter at the projects that year, describing 'buildings on the verge of physical collapse' (01:03:00). Colour footage from this broadcast shows water leaking through a concrete support in the ceiling of a stairwell. The camera starts at a low angle aiming upwards at this dripping stain, then a quick vertical tilt follows the water straight down to where it freezes into thick layers on the metal railings below. We also see shots of a building's exterior with heavy icicles hanging from gaping window frames. The reporter narrates this view saying, 'the dam finally broke' (1:03:13) in the sub-zero (Fahrenheit) temperatures when 'water lines in several of the Pruitt-Igoe apartment buildings broke and the subsequent flow of water turned into ice' (1:03:21-1:03:24). We see four women working together to mop the flood of water out to a stairwell where it cascades down the concrete steps and continues to freeze every part of the structure all the way down. The uncontrolled return of the hidden networks below ground only gets worse: 'At 2311 Dixon, a sewer line is broken, so now raw sewage bubbles out of the ground like a malevolent spring' (1:03:26-1:03:31), which the TV reporter illustrates with an exterior shot of saturated earth. 'This sense of a once-buried spring bursting forth unexpectedly, of the *unheimlich* compared to a disquieting return' (Vidler 1992: 25), is in this transition from the homely to the unhomely and, further, we see 'the role of architecture in staging the sensation and in acting as an instrument for its narrative and spatial manifestation' (Vidler 1992: 27) – the disruption of design into disaster. The work of architects is not only what is visible on the structures' exteriors, but what lies beneath – and the St. Louis Housing Authority demanded strict design budgets: 'Heaters, toilets, garbage incinerators and electricity all malfunctioned, and at one point the faulty plumbing let loose floods of raw sewage through the hallways' (Marshall 2015). The structure and infrastructure of Pruitt-Igoe could no longer contain what was repressed and monstrous at its core.

That same uncanny return – of what must burst out – also drives the centrality of toilets/bathrooms in *Candyman*. Much of the antagonist's mayhem occurs in these spaces: his killing of a babysitter in a suburban home, the ritual evocation of his name in Helen's bathroom mirror, the public outhouse where a young boy was murdered, the now-derelict bathroom where Ruthie Jean died; Helen wakes up in a pool of blood in Anne-Marie's bathroom, Helen's unfaithful husband Trevor utters her name into the bathroom mirror after Helen dies destroying Candyman to save Anthony and, finally, Helen is resurrected as the new Candyman to slash Trevor and leave him dead and bloody in their bathtub. There are additional images of toilets throughout the narrative. The intended designation of bathrooms and 'urban water networks' with the rise of modernity – cleanliness, purity, sanitary efficiency – 'were gradually translated into the cultural and the domestic sphere, into design and architecture' (Kaika and Swyngedouw 2002: 132), but that all breaks down in *Candyman*.

Helen first encountered a violation of intended designation in the maw of the outhouse toilet – with its teeming cauldron of bees – echoed later when Helen escapes the mental hospital and crosses even more deeply into the architectural darkness of Cabrini-Green. Once again climbing through Ruthie Jean's bathroom mirror, she traverses several gaping holes in interior walls (all dripping with uncontrolled water leakage), then up a stack of debris through a hole in the ceiling to emerge into a wide-open loft space in the abandoned top floor of the structure. From a high angle, the camera tracks over bare I-beams and a derelict toilet. What used to be a private bathroom has been stripped of the walls and ceiling that once enclosed it and is now open to our gaze. Helen has found Candyman's lair – a deeply unhomely space without rooms, electricity or furniture. This is the core of Cabrini-Green and an uncanny mirror of public housing's misused and haunted architecture. Here, she bargains with him – to trade her life for that of Anne-Marie's baby – and there follows a shot of actor Tony Todd's open mouth, spilling over with bees as he bends down to her for a 'kiss' to seal the deal. In this space and with his emphatic association with toilets and bathrooms, Candyman represents an embodied and architectural orifice (as we saw with his open mouth painted around a hole in a wall), collectively connoting waste, sewage and the invaded home.

Conclusion

In 2021, a new *Candyman* film (directed by Nia DaCosta) builds public housing and collective Black trauma into an architectural palimpsest of gentrification where Cabrini-Green once stood – and the haunting returns. Whatever is repressed always does. It only needs a way out. *The Pruitt-Igoe Myth* reveals that way out through real-world holes in its broken walls and widows and *Candyman* (1992) paints a monster around them. In their respective cities of 'haunted housing policies' (Mock 2021), *unheimlich* homes are likewise framed by monstrous structures. As the camera eye and the human (and non-human) figures we encounter move together through the exterior, in-between and interior spaces of these films, we see that 'the "Uncanny" reveals sinister and hidden qualities behind the superficial curtain called architecture' (Deckers 2010: 126). The planning and design of public housing at Pruitt-Igoe and Cabrini-Green invaded the homes inside – merging documentary and horror in the process – where unseen institutional power rendered uncanny the rational city alongside its phantasmagoric domestic shadow. James Donald sees urban space in this way as 'doubly textured', containing both the concrete and the fantastic (1999: 69), where the uncanny, disquieting space between them is most readily visible from a distance (aerial, omnipresent, 'the *dieu voyeur*') (1999: 55). From this vantage point, he even wonders: 'How can such a bewildering and alien environment – the city as unsolvable enigma – provide a home?' (Donald 1999: 71). The impossibility of home, in this perspective, is based on that distance. Between the rational city/housing of urban planners (the aerial views of photography and blueprints) and the fear and myth inside the metropolis (slashers born of repressed memory and history) is the same monster the documentary and the horror film here share. Their haunted structures – where repressed institutional power bursts out as harmful architectural violations – are nevertheless used (by characters, tenants, filmmakers) to suggest the possibility of home in the uncanny city. That resistant use of domestic space is unique to public housing; private homes do not have the same monsters.

Notes

1   The Cabrini-Green complex consisted of the Frances Cabrini Homes (built in 1942, by architects Holsman, Burmeister, et al.), with fifty-five two- and three-storey rowhomes in the Near North Side area of Chicago; next to these were built in 1958 the Cabrini Extension (called 'the Reds' for their red-brick exterior, by architects A. Epstein & Sons), fifteen buildings of seven, ten or nineteen storeys; then north and west of these were built in 1962 the William Green Homes (called 'the Whites', with 'concrete panels, middle and precast concrete panels below the windows on the front and rear walls', see Clark 1996) by architects Pace Associates; in all, the complex included over seventy buildings, twenty-one of these were high-rises, with over 3,600 units.

2   That firm was Hellmuth, Yamasaki and Leinweber.

3   In the planning stage of Pruitt-Igoe, Jim Crow segregation was still in place, so the Wendall O. Pruitt Homes were designated for Black residents and the William Igoe Apartments for white residents. However, with the 1954 *Brown v. Board of Education* ruling by the Supreme Court (ending school segregation), Pruitt-Igoe

was racially integrated. This meant that, shortly after the first units were open in 1954, white residents who had the means to do so moved out.

4   There were eight *Unité* buildings, this one is called *La Cité Radieuse*.

5   No year is given for this letter.

References

Austen, Ben (2018), *High-Risers: Cabrini-Green and the Fate of American Public Housing*, New York: HarperCollins.

Bauman, John F. (2000), 'Introduction: The Eternal War on the Slums', in John F. Bauman, Roger Biles and Kristin M. Szylvian (eds), *From Tenements to the Taylor Homes: In Search of an Urban Housing Policy in Twentieth-Century America*, University Park: The Pennsylvania State University Press.

Bristol, Katharine G. (1991), 'The Pruitt-Igoe Myth', *Journal of Architectural Education*, 44 (3): 163–71.

Candyman (1992), [Film] Dir. Bernard Rose, USA: TriStar Pictures.

Candyman (2021), [Film] Dir. Nia DaCosta, USA: MGM.

Clark, Cecelia A. (1996), 'A History of Cabrini-Green', *We the People Media: Residents' Journal*, 3 October. Available online: https://wethepeoplemedia.org/a-history-of-cabrini-green/ (accessed 11 March 2022).

Cooperman, Jeannette (2014), 'The Story of Segregation in St. Louis', *St. Louis Magazine*, 17 October. Available online: https://www.stlmag.com/news/the-color-line-race-in-st.-louis/ (accessed 7 July 2020).

Deckers, Karel (2010), 'The Disquieting Workings of the "Uncanny": A Creative Device for Architectural Representation', *Interiors*, 1 (1–2): 119–32.

Donald, James (1999), *Imagining the Modern City*, Minneapolis: University of Minnesota Press.

Faisst, Julia (2016), 'Ghetto Aesthetics: Performing Spatial Inequality in the Pruitt-Igoe Myth', in Birgit M. Bauridl and Pia Wiegmink (eds), *Approaching Transnational America in Performance*, 265–88, Frankfurt and New York: Peter Lang.

Freud, Sigmund ([1919], 1955), 'The "Uncanny"', in James Strachey (ed), *The Standard Edition of the Complete Psychological Works of Sigmund Freud, Vol. XVII*, 217–56, London: Hogarth Press.

Gandy, Matthew (1999), 'The Paris Sewers and the Rationalization of Urban Space', *Transactions of the Institute of British Geographers*, 24 (1): 23–44.

Goetz, Edward G. (2013), *New Deal Ruins: Race, Economic Justice, and Public Housing Policy*, Ithaca: Cornell University Press.

Heathcott, Joseph (2011), '"In the Nature of a Clinic": The Design of Early Public Housing in St. Louis', *Journal of the Society of Architectural Historians*, 70 (1): 82–103.

Hook, Derek (2005), 'Monumental Space and the Uncanny', *Geoforum*, 36: 688–704.

Hunt, D. Bradford (2009), *Blueprint for Disaster: The Unraveling of Chicago Public Housing*, Chicago: The University of Chicago Press.

Kaika, Maria and Erik Swyngedouw (2002), 'Fetishizing the Modern City: The Phantasmagoria of Urban Technological Networks', *International Journal of Urban and Regional Research*, 24 (1): 120–38.

Koh, Michael (2014), 'The St. Louis Problem: Pruitt-Igoe and the Social Factors That Led to Its Eventual Destruction', *Thought Catalog*, 9 May. Available online: https://thoughtcatalog.com/michael-koh/2014/05/the-st-louis-problem-pruitt-igoe-and-the-social-factors-that-led-to-its-eventual-destruction/ (accessed 7 July 2020).

Landekic, Lola (2016), 'Candyman (1992)', *Art of the Title*, 26 October. Available online: https://www.artofthetitle.com/title/candyman/ (accessed 15 August 2020).

Major, Mark David (2021), '"Excavating" Pruitt-Igoe Using Space Syntax', *Architectural Research Quarterly*, 25 (1): 55–68.

Mann, Nicola (2012), 'Do Not Believe the Hype: The Death and Resurrection of Public Housing in the American Visual Imagination', in Chris Richardson and Hans A. Skott-Myhre (eds), *Habitus of the Hood*, 271–98, Chicago: The University of Chicago Press.

Marshall, Colin (2015), 'Pruitt-Igoe: The Troubled High-Rise That Came to Define Urban America', *The Guardian*, 22 April. Available online: https://www.theguardian.com/cities/2015/apr/22/pruitt-igoe-high-rise-urban-america-history-cities (accessed 9 July 2021).

Mock, Brentin (2021), 'In Slasher Film 'Candyman,' the Horror Is U.S. Housing Policy', *Bloomberg CityLab*, 9 September. Available online: https://www.bloomberg.com/news/articles/2021-09-09/in-candyman-the-horror-is-u-s-housing-policy (accessed 12 February 2022).

Montgomery, Robert (1966), 'Comment On: "Fear and House-as-Haven in the Lower Class"', *Journal of the American Institute of Planners*, 32 (1): 31–7.

The Pruitt-Igoe Myth (2011), [Film] Dir. Chad Freidrichs, USA: First Run Features.

Vale, Lawrence J. (2013), *Purging the Poorest: Public Housing and the Design Politics of Twice-Cleared Communities*, Chicago: University of Chicago Press.

Vidler, Anthony (1992), *The Architectural Uncanny: Essays in the Modern Unhomely*, Cambridge: The MIT Press.

Wasson, Sara (2019), 'Gothic and the Built Environment: The Architectural Uncanny and the Urban Sublime', in David Punter (ed), *The Edinburgh Companion to Gothic and the Arts*, 36–51, Edinburgh: Edinburgh University Press.

2

Die Architekten: East/west ideology, concrete topography and the shadow of *Plattenbau*

Heike Kumpf and Kirsten Kumpf Baele

Though not exactly synonymous with 'public housing', the terms *Plattenbau*[1], *Plattenbauten* or simply the *Platte* (respectively translated as panel construction; those buildings comprised of said construction; 'the panel' as short-form, or nickname for this sort of building itself) evoke a strong correlation, in part due to their substantial prevalence in such state-subsidized or state-sanctioned endeavors. Amidst a capitalist perspective, public housing is often associated with those at society's margins, who cannot afford other means of habitation, especially on an open market. In this application, the first half of the term subsumes the nature of financial resources and the manner of the decision-making process. Often considered onerous in a capitalist society, public housing renders itself obsolete and simultaneously pervasive when seen through a communist lens. Housing of the masses becomes a fundamental responsibility of the State when its citizens are the engine that drives society forward. Communism,[2] in its simplest and most utopian interpretation, seeks to utilize individual talents in support of the State, which in turn provides a living wage and standardized accommodations, thereby striving to eliminate class hierarchies often based on birthright, inheritance, intelligence or even coincidence. This may improve base conditions, but undoubtedly also limits opportunities. In addition to being defined by governmental funding and municipal input, communism puts an ironic spin on the term: public housing which is indeed *for* the public.

All quotes whose original source is German were translated by the authors, unless otherwise noted. Film dialogue is based on the English subtitles and translated by the authors to accurately reflect the message or tone intended.

In *Die Architekten* (*The Architects*, 1990), director Peter Kahane attempts to unravel the concept of public housing and all of its relentless tentacles which have grabbed hold of its main protagonist, architect Daniel Brenner (Kurt Naumann). Produced by the prolific *Deutsche Film Aktiengesellschaft* (German Film Joint Stock Company[3]), commonly referred to simply as DEFA, *Die Architekten* embodies bureaucratic control over filmic expression within the DEFA-system just as it illustrates authority governing the design and construction industry. Kahane's constant reference to and depictions of *Plattenbauten* are no mere accident. Public housing provides the backdrop to the story, arguably because of the familiar territory it evokes in the eyes of the movie's intended audience, whereas the new cultural centre, the proposed building at the centre of the film's plot, arrives on scene like a sliver of light cutting through a cloudy sky. By not being one of the countless residential towers but rather a singular support space nestled amongst them, it should, by its very nature, allow for some freedoms of expression. However, as the architects in the film discover to their disappointment, it is not immune to the same strict oversight. The film outlines the extent of the government's grasp, the iron fist which clutches the reality of daily life and chokes the efforts of those who dare to dream.

Enter Daniel Brenner, mid-career architect living and working in East Germany[4], who is unexpectedly granted the opportunity to design this cultural centre to be located within the massive public housing blocks which he himself calls home, a *Trabantenstadt* (satellite city)[5] far removed from East Berlin's city centre. Having spent his career thus far relegated to designs of bus shelters and other sidelined structures, Daniel welcomes this opportunity with open arms and resounding energy. Not only can he finally exercise his architectural knowledge and skill on a building that will actually affect people's lives, he has also been given leniency in assembling a collective of fellow architects. Although the architectural project at the heart of the story is called a cultural centre, in essence its true function is to be a place for amenities central to the many *Plattenbauten* nearby, which sorely lack any such comforts or conveniences. People everywhere fantasize about improvements to their lives and surroundings, but the nature of dreams expressed by this group speaks volumes about life in the East.

> We're designing pleasant spaces rather than elaborate façades. Malls, squares, and streets custom-made to human proportions. Full of variety. Where people meet instead of getting lost, which is currently so often the case. Only if we adhere to this will we be able to make the people of our city feel at ease and accept it as home.

>   (*Die Architekten* 00:17:22)

Of note is Kahane's decision for this conversation (as well as other creative brainstorming sessions) to take place in Renate Reese's (Uta Eisold) old-build apartment, rather than Daniel's (or another's) *Plattenbau* unit. Not only is her place more spacious allowing the group to gather comfortably but it seems generally a more creative space, one that is actively being personalized, evidenced by paintbrushes, drop cloths and paint splatter. The group's list of programmatic enrichments for what is all to be housed in the cultural centre changes over time as they respond to the powers that be, but among them are a cinema, a Vietnamese restaurant, an ice cream parlour, a shopping centre and a swimming pool – places that offer activities outside of the home, at various times of day, encouraging interaction and connection. As evidenced by their conversations and subsequent design, the physical manifestations of comfort also cover a wide range of commodities such as green roofs, skylights, building-integrated sculpture and natural ventilation, among others.

The story arc is one of rapid ascent – pure elation at the chance to improve not only their own lives, but also the lives of others – and soul-crushing defeat at their eventual inability to override the governmental dictates and truly change the status quo. To add insult to injury, Daniel Brenner's personal life rises and falls according to the same tide. His professional success and the joy it brings him early in the film leaves his wife, Wanda (Rita Feldmeier), feeling alone in the despair they previously shared, to seek a divorce. Similar to her husband's grief, hers is also rooted in the *Platte*; its inability to offer any variation in life has stifled her outlook. The film makes numerous references to the Brenners' previous life in the city as a happier time. A multitude of cultural outlets (cinema, theatre, restaurants) and friends nearby offered variety and distraction, but the urban conditions, air quality specifically, drove them to the *Plattenbauten* located on the outskirts where their daughter's asthma was less pronounced.

The constant thread throughout the film is the architectural project which Daniel and his team design, iteration after iteration, concept after concept. Apprehension and disbelief loom large amongst the group initially as none can imagine that the Ministry of Construction,[6] which has to sign off on the project, will agree to do so. Beyond the doubts they express at having their ideas realized, lurks uncertainty that they even possess the ability to come up with a design that will actually address their general grievances. In an early brainstorming session, Daniel attempts to combat the negativity: 'Now, let's think a bit about everything without limitations' to which one of the group callously responds, 'If that's even still possible' (*Die Architekten* 00:16:08). Eventually Daniel is able to counteract the team's scepticism with his enthusiasm and logic. Repeatedly he reminds them that, with this project, they finally have the chance to address many of the problems they see and experience every day. Likewise, he claims, there are ways to circumnavigate the system if they just rely on their creativity; knowing that budget is paramount, the collective finds ways to utilize 95 per cent prefabricated construction components to minimize cost thereby reserving funds for moments of 'extravagance'. His appeal to logic even convinces the staunch party economist, Endler (Christoph Engel), to acknowledge that the ministry cannot object to their design on the basis of cost. Over time, and as a result of Daniel's passionate overtures, their creativity grows, as does their attachment to the project – one which seeks to solve many of the issues of daily life in the GDR in a single stroke. This largely boils down to versatility and options, in short: humanity. As the architects present their final design, complete with green roof, skylights and natural ventilation, among other features, the government board's harsh review is solidly rooted in communist ideology and effectively delivers a reprimand rather than a constructive critique. In the end the team disperses, each for their own reasons but all reflective of their respective frustration, distrust and disenfranchisement. Only Daniel Brenner is left standing, forced to toe the party line, appearing lost on the podium as they break ground on a cultural centre which speculatively bears little if any resemblance to the work of the collective, but instead touts the traditional and expected hallmarks of party politics. Although the scene is devoid of dialogue, Kahane does not mince words in the final shot showing a broken Brenner drunkenly lying in his own vomit at the very location of the project site.

Constructive fields

Director Peter Kahane admits that the arena of architecture and city building is not a far cry from that of the East German film industry, citing similar heavy-handed governmental censure and limits on creative expression. Sebastian Heiduschke even claims that the character of Daniel Brenner is essentially Kahane's alter ego, as both men experienced comparable stunted professional growth (2013: 124). The architects in *Die Architekten* could be representative of a multitude of professions, particularly ones with creative aspects, since seemingly no vocation was spared oversight from the East German ruling regime. Rosemary Stott notes that, '[T]hrough the control of film industry personnel, the ruling Socialist Unity Party (SED) tried to ensure that the films exhibited in East German cinemas promoted party interest and did not fuel audience discontent or disillusionment with the government' (2016: 20). Not only did the government control content and limit critique, it also expected all filmic endeavours to reinforce communist ideology. And yet, the criticism that Kahane puts forth in *Die Architekten* is neither veiled nor subtle.

Most films which seek to cast an acrimonious eye towards East Germany, East Berlin, etc., do so via strong imagery of the physical embodiment of the GDR's communist ideology, notably, the Berlin Wall. In effect erected in a single night, 13 August 1961, and later built out to its full extent to include guard towers, trenches and mines, the Wall was the East's response to increasing numbers of defectors capitalizing on West Berlin's proximity and ease of access. Built to physically separate Easterners from the temptation of freedom presented by the West, the Wall was euphemistically referred to as an *antifaschistischer Schutzwall* (anti-fascist protection rampart) by GDR authorities. Regardless of name or purpose, it quickly became the visual incarnation of a divided country, and thus carries justifiable symbolic weight when depicted in film. However, the Berlin Wall makes only a scant cameo appearance in *Die Architekten*. Instead, Kahane chooses to highlight the endless rows of *Plattenbauten*, those stacks of prefabricated concrete boxes which the SED saw as the clear, quick and initially only solution to the housing problem. The *Platte* features heavily in the film: viewers get a good sense of the Brenner family's small flat through various scenes set at home; their widespread proliferation is chronicled through B-roll montages during story-line transitions; the remoteness of these housing complexes is stressed by footage of extensive roadways and underscored with dialogue proclaiming the very same.

The argument could be made that all creative professions were, in some form or other, controlled by the GDR government. However, that of the architect is particularly on the nose in a film showcasing the qualitative effects such control bears on the human condition for two main reasons. First, although not everyone is an architect, trained to formally assess the current existing conditions, pinpoint problems and offer creative solutions, everyone does experience architecture. And by the late 1980s, *Plattenbauten* were widespread – the film's anticipated audience would undoubtedly already be quite familiar with, or at least aware of, the often-dreary reality of life in the *Platte*. Second, criticism of any aspect of the *Wohnungsprogramm* (State housing programme) carries singular effect since it was such a source of pride for the GDR and ever so intricately intertwined with socialist ideals – not just that the State was providing housing for the masses, but that workers were coming together to achieve a common goal. Kahane acknowledges, 'the whole appreciation of the construction workers was more than just an appreciation of their practical work. It was a piece of the ideology. It referred to the founding myth of the GDR. Out of the rubble, the country emerged'[7] (*A Regular DEFA Film?* 2004: 03:30). Beyond the visual overtures of endless *Platten*scapes, the film is riddled with commentary which constantly reinforces the depressive state, and any mention of *Heimat*[8] results in fierce consternation and disbelief. Mere criticism of communist ideology permeating through various professions and livelihoods could have taken on many forms. However, Kahane recognizes that the architectural expressions of socialism serve more than their reported utilitarian functions and fall in line with a legion of propagandist ploys – a harsh reality he attempts to shine some light on in *Die Architekten*.

The prevalence of *Plattenbauten* – a topography develops

Not unique to East Germany, or the greater Communist Bloc, *Plattenbauten* grew out of the modernist movement. In the era[9] that rebuked ornamentation, explored new material usages and found meaning in machinery, the flat unarticulated prefabricated housing that assembled quickly and efficiently from a kit fit with the times. Le Corbusier, one of the most influential modernist architects, proclaimed that '[t]he house is a machine for living in' (1931: 4). With an eye directed at automobile, ocean liner and airplane design, Le Corbusier made the argument that a home has its various functions and should be designed around those needs, as opposed to fitting those needs into an overall design. Moreover, it does not have to ascribe to any notions of permanence; houses or living quarters are as temporal as automobiles for instance, serving their purpose for a time and then requiring the owner to move on. It is no surprise that this sentiment yielded a move towards minimalist housing, unencumbered by historicism, personal or otherwise. The interwar period in Europe proved fertile ground for such ideas to germinate and actualize. Housing was in exceedingly short supply due in part to the damage brought on by war, but more significantly as a result of the de facto 'moratorium' on construction during those years of war. Isolated prefabricated housing structures sprang up across Europe with various levels of prefabrication and to disparate public responses.[10] Understandably, the Second World War exacerbated the prewar housing shortages in Europe and therefore dense, multi-family housing remained a necessary topic of conversation.

Communist East Germany was no exception and faced its own verifiable housing crisis. Erich Honecker, the leader of the GDR from 1971 until shortly before the fall of the Wall in 1989, took it as a challenge and subsequent initiative to solve the housing problem by 1990. In effect, this meant making three million apartments habitable in whatever way possible – either by renovating existing stock or building new. The latter was the preferred option, especially in the early days of the programme.[11] As the GDR set about achieving its ambitious goal, it was destined to become a numbers game with fast and efficient construction setting the rules. New, modern technologies put housebuilding on the assembly line: prefabricated pieces and parts arrived on greenfield sites requiring only a minimal team to assemble them. With apartment sizes based on family size instead of earning power, the *Plattenbauten* helped to advance one of the tenets of the socialist agenda: a dissolution of class hierarchies.

Out of this mass onslaught of construction, a landscape developed that changed the face of major cities, and even some minor ones. In the interest of economy of scale, modern city planning aspects were put into effect: towers widely spaced to allow air and light into each housing unit, as well as broad, grand boulevards for convenient automobile circulation and large swaths of greenery for gathering, playing and enjoying nature. In reality, however, the widely spaced towers resulted in over-scaled megaliths dwarfing the streetscape, the broad boulevards became parking lots for heavily polluting *Trabant* cars, and so-called 'green spaces' were often neither green nor inviting due to constant construction, lack of maintenance and overall neglect. All of these realities are highlighted in a scene in which Daniel heads home at the end of a challenging day (see Figure 2.1). Also evident in this image is the monotony of the landscape. *Plattenbauten* took the form of only a handful of designs, typically either five or eleven storeys in height, fenestration on only two sides, with the other two sides solid concrete. Each elevation, however, bears the familiar stamp of prefabrication in the form of each panel's distinctive outline which can be seen in both Figures 2.1 and 2.2. The most widespread design utilized was the *WBS 70*[12]. Thomas Biewer sifts through extensive statistics in Christine Hannemann's *Die Platte – industrialisierter Wohnungsbau in der DDR* in his book review, and sums up the staggering numbers:

> There are 6.35 million apartments in the area comprising the former GDR, 2.1 million – so, nearly a third – of which have been built since 1955 using modern industrial methods. More than half of the urban population, which comprised 20 per cent of the total population, lived in industrial multi-family housing … This proportion grew steadily since 1955 reaching 83 per cent by 1985. A full 42 per cent of these modern industrial apartments were built within the *WBS 70* housing series.
>
> (1997: 250)[13]

Figure 2.1 Daniel walks along the wide gulf between the monotonous *Plattenbauten*. The streetscape, nearly empty of other pedestrians, displays the common Neubau hallmarks of lackluster landscaping, endless rows of parked Trabant cars, and a queue of people waiting. *Die Architekten* directed by Peter Kahane © DEFA-Stiftung 1990. All rights reserved.

With *Die Architekten* taking place in the late 1980s, by which point *Plattenbauten* had indeed become prevalent and truly developed an alternate urban topography, these numbers substantiate the collective's preoccupation with city building. They view their cultural centre as *the* entity which will turn a housing complex into a city, *the* building which will give people a destination, a place to gather, to bump into neighbours and such. The character of Martin Bulla (Jürgen Watzke), one of the collective's seven architects, summarizes the group's sentiments: 'I became an architect to build cities in which people can actually live. Not cemeteries' (*Die Architekten* 1990: 00:16:08). Equating the East German *Plattenbauten* blocks with cemeteries is not a bad analogy when one looks at the rows upon rows of cold hard towers, each unit assigned a name or family. The pared-down designs did not offer much more than a place to lay down one's head to rest at the end of a work-weary day.

The pervasive *Platte* – a typology emerges

The tedious topography is only half the story. As the film expounds, architects are in a position to offer creative solutions, to exercise their problem-solving skills. In short, architects have the ability to realize and capitalize on the power that a single unique building, in a sea of otherwise similar structures, has to transform not just a landscape but also a mentality. The *Platte* did more than dominate the scenery, it dominated lives. Its proliferation addressed critical shortages in the housing stock. In the postwar period, old tenement buildings offered inhabitants little in terms of comfort, space or sometimes even essentials. Most were lacking in physical condition, which meant drafty or damp spaces, with outdated utilities in the form of inadequate heat sources (typically localized coal-burning units) and no in-unit water closets as these were often located on common hallways and, hence, shared amongst multiple over-crowded units. The material improvements inherent in the *Platte* (new, clean apartments with central heat and in-unit toilets) garnered immediate interest and quickly became highly desirable, due mostly to their stark contrast with existing housing conditions. Within the communist system, where need pre-empted financial ability, people often married and had children not altogether irrespective of the beneficial impact these life choices had on their ability to secure coveted *Plattenbau* apartments. Additionally, the desirability of life in the *Platte* worked favourably for the government's overall agenda. 'The housing stock within the *Plattenbau* settlements primarily served the government-steered housing supply toward those employed in major industries, those belonging to the State's defence or security forces, as well as those involved in State administration'[14] (Biewer 1997: 251). Effectively, a large-scale rewards programme developed, encouraging citizens to expand their families, follow certain professional paths or, in general, to reinforce party politics.

   Plattenbau capitalizes on two main aspects of construction: method and material, specifically, prefabrication and concrete. Prefabrication offers resource efficiency and speed in construction. With regard to *Plattenbauten*, this meant concrete floor and wall panels which were poured in a factory, shipped to the site and set in place piece by piece with only the connections to be completed in the field. The bones of the entire building could be built in a fraction of the time that it would typically take to build formwork, pour concrete and allow for the requisite concrete cure times on a floor-by-floor basis (see Eli Rubin, *Amnesiopolis* 2016: 60–6). Additionally, inherent in prefabrication is a level of uniformity, repeatability and quality control that typically does not exist in the field[15]. Technological advances along the way, such as windows preinstalled in the panels, streamlined the process even further. Production lines of all construction materials which constituted the limited number of building designs[16] were optimized, saving time but, more importantly, saving money. Daniel bumps up against this hurdle when he visits the glass manufacturer to discuss the specific glass needed for the skylights. 'Of course, we can produce hail-proof glass. But why should we? … The technology requires revamping assembly lines. It's just not worth it for a few skylights. We can't raise prices' (*Die Architekten* 1990: 01:15:52). Because everything had become so systematized, even one small change or new idea is nearly impossible to bring to fruition as it would require a major interruption of process at the expense of all other production. Once again, Daniel is stymied in his attempts to break the mould.

Beyond method, mere materiality also comes into play in this emergent typology. Reinforced concrete changed the world, and not just aesthetically. Heavily utilized to reflect modern architectural ideas due to its expressive nature,[17] concrete is also deeply connected with socialist politics. Adrian Forty, who explored the material in all its forms and associations in *Concrete and Culture: A Material History*, identifies the political correlations of concrete as 'left-leaning', 'radical' and 'left-wing' stemming back to the early twentieth century. Beyond highlighting certain 'concrete "manifesto" buildings', he also traces its ideological expressions: 'The synthetic nature of reinforced concrete made it a symbol for Lenin's view of the "indissoluble unity" of the proletariat, formed through the process of revolution'; this quote by the main protagonist in Fyodor Gladkov's socialist realist novel, *Cement* (1925), follows: '"Cement is us, comrades – the working class"' (Forty 2012: 147–8). Although concrete in the form of prefabricated panels does not quite fit the analogy – panelized construction is essentially a kit of parts and not a fluid mass solidifying to become a single object – it does speak to the worker mentality, the abundant utilization of a largely unskilled labour force and the resultant 'machine' that developed out of the highly systematized construction industry. In 1954, Nikita Khruschev, first secretary of the Communist Party Central Committee of the USSR, illustrated the extensive virtues of concrete in a lengthy address to the All-Union Conference of Builders, Architects and Workers in the Building Materials Industry. His well-informed message resounded with purpose; first and foremost, concrete could help solve the housing crisis by means of prefabrication; prefabrication in concrete circumnavigated the skilled labour shortage as concrete does not require the same amount of training requisite of other trades; the lack of skilled labour all but drove out any remnant of ornamentation reminiscent of Stalin's preferred neoclassical style, thereby reinforcing a solid break in attendant political arenas (Forty 2012: 150).

Overall construction costs could be traced directly to process and so any improvements or efficiencies that could be attained anywhere along the assembly line led to money saved. Due to substantial subsidization of the end product, the individual *Plattenbau* apartments, the *Wohnungsprogramm* on the whole, however, lost considerable money. Indeed, Honecker's grand plan to solve the housing problem was a double-edged sword. On one side, the fact that more apartments became available reinforced the communist idea that the State provided for its citizens, which kept workers generally content and productive. On the other side, the more apartments the government built, the greater the financial burden. Constantly looking to reduce costs, the government further reduced variation amongst *Plattenbau* designs, hence the high prevalence of the *WBS 70* design. This lack of housing diversity did not pose a problem for those of strong ideological convictions, at least philosophically. 'The standardization of *Plattenbau* construction is not only cost effective in its implementation, but it also underscores the socialist vision: equal apartments for equal people. Dissolution of class and rank differences. In theory, the machinist lives next to the professor'[18] (*Von Plattenbau* 2020: 03:25). In reality, however, this repetition of housing units weighed heavily on the well-being of those that called the *Platte* home. The rhythm of same or similar towers caused a drab and anonymous topography to develop, but the litany of identical apartments themselves forced a further typology to emerge, one sardonically referenced as *Arbeiterschließfach* (worker-locker) or *Wohn-klo mit Koch-nische* (habitable bathroom with cooking niche)[19] (*Von Plattenbau* 2020: 05:10). Attempts at individualization are made in any way possible; for example, in the backdrop of Figure 2.2 where Daniel and his daughter Johanna (Judith Richter)

Figure 2.2 Daniel and his daughter Johanna ride their bicycles near the site of the future cultural centre; a *Plattenbau* apartment building looms in the background. *Die Architekten* directed by Peter Kahane © DEFA-Stiftung 1990. All rights reserved.

ride their bicycles across the site of the soon-to-be cultural centre, the balcony surrounds of each unit in the building are painted a different, bright colour. Additionally, as a result of the lack of variety in apartment layouts, other industries such as furniture also capitalized on efficiencies and tailored their production lines towards the specific needs, dimensions and/or limitations inherent in the *Platte*, further limiting opportunities for personal expression and originality.

Das Ende

In light of this film's uncanny timing, at the bitter end of the GDR, it comes up short in its original objective – to sympathetically highlight one man's struggles with the system and the heavy price he pays for having hope. One of the last films produced by DEFA, *Die Architekten* is regarded as unique among the hundreds of feature films accredited to the GDR's rather prolific film industry.[20] Simply terminating an impressive four-decade lifespan, however, is not its true contribution to DEFA history; for a film which seeks to elucidate the depressive melancholia attributable to its current urban condition, it was ironically outdated before it ever finished shooting. Initially written in 1987 by Thomas Knauf, the script underwent the typical DEFA and SED reviews to ensure adherence to policies and politics, was surprisingly approved by the studio with very little modification,[21] and initially scheduled to begin production in April 1989. Due to delays attributable to resource availability and the inner politics of DEFA, cameras did not start rolling until early October 1989, and filming would straddle the momentous events of 9 November 1989, when the Berlin Wall fell (Heiduschke 2013: 124–5). Post-production occurred during the ever-changing landscape which ensued after the fall, but prior to Germany's reunification on 3 October 1990. *Die Architekten* premiered June 1990, to a meagre audience, one most definitely preoccupied with matters of profound and life-changing impact. Kahane observes in the interview, *Ein ganz normaler DEFA-Film?* (*A Regular DEFA Film?*), that he believes the poor box-office numbers were the result of the currency exchange happening at the time. People traded in their GDR Marks into Deutsche Marks; it was a time of excitement at the new access to all things 'West', but also a time of great distress, financial and otherwise, not knowing how their livelihoods might be affected. He also acknowledges that 'nobody really was interested in delving into GDR history, especially recent GDR history. … A cinematic retrospective was just not necessary. There was just no interest, no public interest'[22] (*A Regular DEFA Film?* 2004: 11:46). This upheaval of the entire political system happened very quickly, and quite unexpectedly for most. Unrest had been growing and borders of other Eastern Bloc countries had already relaxed, but the sudden announcement of Germany's open border took all by surprise. Kahane was lucky in that his full team of cast and crew remained loyal to the project, given their newfound ability for unrestricted travel. For a film largely about context, about existing conditions both environmental and institutional in nature, it nevertheless chose not to respond to the ironic circumstances at hand. As events began to unfold, Kahane and team initially attempted to capture this shifting landscape, shooting additional scenes not in the original production plan. However, these were left on the cutting room floor as the realization crept in that 'keeping up with history was impossible' or rather, in Kahane's own words, 'a feature film can't stay on the heels of reality, less so in these weeks, than ever before'[23] (McGee 2003: 326).

The film's initial lacklustre public response preceded nearly fifteen years of near oblivion until it finally appeared on a German late-night television line-up to little fanfare. But it only started to gain traction as a film worth resurrecting when shown alongside twenty other DEFA entries during the New York Museum of Modern Art's 2005 'Rebels with a Cause' event (Heiduschke 2013: 129). With some time to let the dust settle, *Die Architekten* has less to do with giving voice to long held frustrations in the face of impenetrable government control, allowing audiences to root for an unlikely hero attempting to upend the system all around him, and has more to do with providing a true account of the life that so many led, one that did not gloss over the quiet but constant degradation of spirit. It also clearly delineates the socialist reverence towards the building trade and all who have a role in it. In a conversation in which Daniel's mentor, Professor Vesely (Joachim Tomaschewsky), tries to restore Daniel's faith in the profession by pointing out that nothing gets built without compromise, he explains, 'Construction is politics. The representation of power. Every building tells of relationships – intended or otherwise. They communicate prosperity or austerity, dreams or despair, economics and technology. And of course, also the clients' tastes' (*Die Architekten* 1990: 01:07:15). These lines are delivered as the two men look out the window with an impressive overview of the *Karl-Marx-Allee* (the central Berlin boulevard lined with large apartment buildings and punctuated with towers, formerly called the *Stalinallee*). A prime example of communist productivity hard at work, the *Stalinallee* rose out of the rubble to a monumental scale and magnificent grandeur unequalled anywhere in the country, a deliberate testament to the strength of the working class. If the *Stalinallee* building campaign is to be considered the GDR's first real display of communism's power to affect change, then the *Plattenbauten* can be seen as its second, and perhaps greater, act. Though extensive and constructed in record time, the *Stalinallee* is still just one street. The effects of *Plattenbau* touched nearly every aspect of East Germany, all in the name of public housing. Initially a much-needed and desirable solution, the *Platte* went the way of anything that is repeated *ad nauseam*: it led to widespread depression and dreariness. Stagnant designs do not accommodate the needs of a changing population. Though not unique to the GDR, nor to any political system, the association of *Plattenbauten* to socialism remains because it was seen as *the* answer and not just *an* answer to problematic housing deficiencies.

The Pritzker Architecture Prize, considered the highest international honour within the profession, was awarded in 2021 to Anne Lacaton and Jean-Philippe Vassal, partner architects at their eponymous firm based in Paris, France. Unlike other Pritzker laureates, Lacaton and Vassal have a body of work largely built on renovating existing buildings, predominantly those of social housing. Their interventions are grounded in an individual's well-being and attempt to inject a human touch to otherwise cold structures. Lacaton notes, 'Good architecture is open – open to life, open to enhance the freedom of anyone, where anyone can do what they need to do. ... It should not be demonstrative or imposing, but it must be something familiar, useful and beautiful, with the ability to quietly support the life that will take place within it' (*The Pritzker Architecture Prize* 2021). Decades after the proliferation of *Plattenbauten* as the solution to social (and socialist) housing, the world is starting to recognize that, 'by prioritizing the enrichment of human life through a lens of generosity and freedom of use, [architects] are able to benefit the individual socially, ecologically and economically, aiding the evolution of a city' (*The Pritzker Architecture Prize* 2021). If only this sentiment had echoed through the prefabricated concrete canyon Daniel Brenner called home.

Notes

1   *Plattenbau*, or panel construction, shares similarities with slab construction, but also has some notable differences. Both utilize prefabricated concrete components as structural elements, both enable large building endeavours (particularly with repetitive features) to be constructed efficiently, and both capitalize on a generally low-skilled labour force. Slabs however typically compose horizontal elements only, for example, floors, which would then be supported by structural columns and/or

load-bearing walls. *Plattenbau* elevates this notion to include vertical elements, for example, walls, which then become structural components often eliminating the need for columns.

2   'Socialism' and 'communism' feature heavily in this chapter; references to these terms imply the following interpretations. While both political/economical philosophies are based on the merits of shared resources and services to the benefit of the working class, their methodologies differ. Socialism can more easily be applied to individual enterprises while still allowing for private property and democratic governance whereas communism relies on a forceful, single party government to manage shared assets. Usage of the terms in this chapter strives to reflect this distinction. When 'socialism' is used within the context of East Germany, a communist state, the intention is to highlight the nature of the endeavour which could just as easily take place under different governance.

3   Although the film studio's name translates as German Film Joint Stock Company, 'joint stock' does not reference the open market, but instead the company's Soviet component. It was the only film studio active in East Germany, producing feature-length films, shorts, documentaries and children's entertainment and existed during the years 1946–94 (Allan and Heiduschke 2016: 1).

4   Throughout this chapter, East Germany is referred to as the GDR (German Democratic Republic, 1949–90) and denotes the country born out of the Soviet allocation of Germany after the Second World War.

5   It is worth noting that the word *Trabant* also denotes the most common and often only make of personal car available to East Germans and so this common term takes on a heightened meaning in the East in that these satellite cities were disconnected from city centres and far removed from common amenities.

6   *Ministerium fur Bauwesen* (1958–89): GDR governmental entity which functioned as 'client' insofar as determining what gets built, how it gets built, as well as controlling the allocation of funds; it operated in tandem with the *Abteilung Bauwesen des ZK der SED* (Construction Department of the SED), the ruling political party, which ensured that all endeavors adhered to communist ideology and standards (Biewer 1997: 250).

7   Original quote: 'Die ganze Würdigung der Bauarbeiter war mehr als nur die Würdigung einer praktischen Arbeit. Es war ein Stück der Ideologie. Es bezog sich auf den Gründungsmythos der DDR. Also, aus den Trümmern ist das Land entstanden'.

8   A unique German word which translates loosely as 'homeland' or just 'home' in general but extends beyond the physical to the emotional realm in that it also connotes a sense of belonging and arguably also pride.

9   Taking place predominantly at the beginning of the twentieth century, but with noted examples in the worlds of art and architecture reaching back into the latter

half of the nineteenth century, the modern era is characterized by 'a formalist, functional, and moral streak in architecture' (Kostof 1995: 547) in tandem with a clear rejection of previous schools of thought.

10 Spiro Kostof provides a general overview of the rise of industrial and prefabricated housing in his chapter 'Architecture and the State: Interwar Years' (1995: 695–707) which is sufficient to understand the social and artistic climates as well as concomitant politics which affected contemporary construction methods as it pertains to this chapter.

11 Brian Ladd addresses the GDR *Wohnungsprogramm* thoroughly in his chapter, 'Socialist Planning and the Rediscovery of the Old City in the German Democratic Republic' highlighting the initial preference to build new housing stock at the cost of renovating existing buildings. He subsequently illustrates the GDR's delayed initiatives to focus on the deteriorating buildings to restore city centres not just physically, but also emotionally (2001: 584–603).

12 WBS=*Wohnungsbauserie* (Housing series). Based on the authors' assessment of film footage, it appears the Brenners live in a *WBS 70 3-Raum-Wohnung mit Innenküche* (3 Room Apartment with Interior Kitchen) which had an area of 60.12 square meters or 647 square feet (Hannemann 1996: 143).

13 Original quote: '6,35 Millionen Wohnungen gibt es auf dem Gebiet der ehemaligen DDR, 2,1 Millionen davon – ein knappes Drittel also – wurden seit 1955 in industrieller Bauweise errichtet. Von den etwa 20 Prozent der Bevölkerung, die in Großsiedlungen lebten, wohnte über die Hälfte in industriell errichteten Mehrfamilienhäusern. ... Seit 1955 war der Anteil der industriellen Bauweisen am DDR-Wohnungsbau stetig gestiegen und hatte 1985 einen Anteil von 83 Prozent erreicht. ... 42 Prozent der industriell erstellten Wohnungen wurden allein in der Wohnungsbauserie (WBS) 70 ausgeführt'.

14 Original quote: 'Der Wohnungsbestand in den Großsiedlungen diente vornehmlich der staatlich gelenkten Wohnungsversorgung von Beschäftigten der Hauptindustrien, der "bewaffneten Organe" und der Angehörigen der Administration'.

15 Uniformity and quality control are inherent in prefabrication, at least in theory. Reality did differ somewhat as Eli Rubin outlines in *Amnesiopolis* (2016: 64–5). These characteristics are still valid to note however, as they influenced the decision to prefabricate, a decision based on conceptual findings, and not necessarily practical results.

16 E.g. *WBS 70*.

17 Reinforced concrete can be poured into any shape thereby blurring the line between common structural elements of columns (vertical) and beams (horizontal); early exploration of this new-found structural freedom can be found in the apartment building at 25 bis rue Franklin, Paris (built in 1903 by architect Auguste Perret); previous structural systems were primarily trabeated in nature,

stacking one structural element on top of another, transferring forces orthogonally from top to bottom. Ironically, *Plattenbau* did not take advantage of this modern technology.

18 Original quote: 'Die Normierung des Plattenbau sist nicht nur kostengünstig in der Umsetzung, sie unterstreicht auch die sozialistische Vision: Gleiche Wohnungen für gleiche Menschen. Aufhebung der Klassen – und Schicht-Unterschiede. In der Theorie, wohnt der Maschinenschlosser neben dem Professor'.

19 The term *Arbeiterschließfach* (worker-locker) implies that the entire building appears as a bank of lockers, in which each worker gets placed in his/her individual little box. The term *Wohn-klo mit Koch-nische* (habitable bathroom with cooking niche) puts a similar negative spin on the *Platte* offering nothing more than the essentials – a toilet and kitchen – in lieu of a 'home'.

20 In 'The State-Owned Cinema Industry and its Audience', Rosemary Stott gives a thorough account of the makeup of DEFA: its overall contribution to cinema; procedures by which screenplays underwent censure review; how directors were chosen and how funding was allocated. It is important to remember that cinema in communism is not driven by public interest and subsequent box office returns, but rather by government-directed tactics and ideology-reinforcing subject matter (2016: 19–40).

21 Heiduschke notes *Die Architekten*'s surprisingly minimal censorship. Whether this reflected an intended lapse in ideological rigour or was a side-effect of the current change in directorship at DEFA remains a point of discussion. However, as the GDR catapulted towards political ruin during the course of the year 1989, the reason quickly becomes moot (Heiduschke 2013:124–5).

22 Original quote: 'Keiner hatte eigentlich Lust sich mit der DDR, mit der jüngeren DDR Vergangenheit zu beschäftigen. ... So eine Art Rückblick wie er im Kino dann stattfand war gar nicht nötig. Es war gar kein Interesse, kein öffentliches Interesse'.

23 Original quote: 'Ein Spielfilm kann der Wirklichkeit nicht auf den Fersen bleiben, in diesen Wochen weniger en je'.

References

Allan, Seán and Sebastian Heiduschke (2016), 'Introduction: Re-imagining East German Cinema', in S. Allan and S. Heiduschke (eds), *Re-imagining DEFA: East German Cinema in Its National and Transnational Contexts*, 1–16, New York: Berghahn Books.

'Anne Lacaton and Jean-Philippe Vassal Receive the 2021 Pritzker Architecture Prize' (2021), The Pritzker Architecture Prize. Available online: https://www.pritzkerprize. com/laureates/anne-lacaton-and-jean-philippe-vassal (accessed 12 September 2021).

Biewer, Thomas (1997), 'Review of Die Platte Industrialisierter Wohnungsbau in der
    DDR by Christine Hannemann', *Zeitschrift für Unternehmensgeschichte* (*Journal of
    Business History*), 42 Jahrg. H.2: 250–2.

Corbusier, Le ([1931] 1986), *Towards a New Architecture*, trans F. Etchells, New York:
    Dover Publications.

Die Architekten (1990), [Film] Dir. Peter Kahane, Germany: DEFA-Studio für
    Spielfilme.

Forty, Adrian (2012), *Concrete and Culture: A Material History*, London: Reaktion
    Books.

Hannemann, Christine (1996), *Die Platte Industrialisierter Wohnungsbau in der DDR*,
    Braunschweig/Wiesbaden: Vieweg & Sohn Verlagsgesellschaft mbH.

Heiduschke, Sebastian (2007), '«Das ist die Mauer, die quer durchgeht. Dahinter
    liegt die Stadt und das Glück.» DEFA Directors and Their Criticism of the Berlin
    Wall', *Colloquia Germanica*, 40 (1): 37–50. Available online: http://www.jstor.org/
    stable/23981914.

Heiduschke, Sebastian (2013), 'Passed by History: Dystopia, Parable, and Bookend:
    Die Architekten (The Architects, Peter Kahane, 1990)', in Sebastian Heiduschke
    (ed), *East German Cinema: DEFA and Film History*, 123–9, New York: Palgrave
    Macmillan.

Kostof, Spiro ([1985] 1995), *A History of Architecture; Settings and Rituals*, New York:
    Oxford University Press.

Ladd, Brian (2001), 'Socialist Planning and the Rediscovery of the Old City in the
    German Democratic Republic', *Journal of Urban History*, 27 (5): 584–603. Available
    online: https://doi.org/10.1177/009614420102700502.

McGee, Laura Green (2003), '"Ich wollte ewig einen richtigen Film machen! Und als
    es soweit war, konnte ich's nicht!" The End Phase of the GDR in Films by DEFA
    Nachwuchsregisseure', *German Studies Review*, 26 (2): 315–32. Available online:
    https://www.jstor.org/stable/1433328.

A Regular DEFA Film? (2004), [Video] Dir. Lars Mikolai, Berlin: Studio Fünf
    Fernsehproduktion and DEFA-Stiftung. Available online: https://icpl.kanopy.com/
    video/architects (accessed 17 October 2021).

Rubin, Eli (2016), *Amnesiopolis: Modernity, Space, and Memory in East Germany*,
    Oxford: Oxford University Press.

Stott, Rosemary (2016), 'The State-Owned Cinema Industry and Its Audience', in Seán
    Allan and Sebastian Heiduschke (eds), *Re-imagining DEFA: East German Cinema in
    Its National and Transnational Contexts*, 19–40, New York: Berghahn Books.

Von Plattenbau und Wohnraumvergabe – Wohnen in der DDR (2020), [Video] MDR
    DOK. Available online: https://www.youtube.com/watch?v=pG0aTZBoa94
    (accessed 16 October 2021).

3

Architect and amateur documentarian, Yitzhaq Perlstein: Planning Israeli public housing (1960–70)

Daphna Levine and Liat Savin Ben Shoshan

Introduction: The Modernized Eye

In this chapter, we will examine the home movies made by Israeli architect and amateur filmmaker Yitzhaq Perlstein in the 1960s. Perlstein played a key role in the physical building of the state of Israel (established in 1948), and particularly in the planning and building of public housing. Through the building of public housing in Israel in the state's first decades (1950s–70s),[1] an entire research field developed, focusing on the living space, from apartment to neighbourhood to city (Shadar 2004, 2018; Hananel 2018; Shaham 2021). Public housing also played a key role in the social engineering of Zionist Israeli nationality (Kallus and Yone 2002). Perlstein's office, opened in the early 1950s, growing rapidly in the 1960s and active until a few years after his death in 1981, was central in forming the logic and visibility of public housing in Israel. Throughout the years, the office rigorously developed public housing units in a large variety of types and forms. Through its ongoing attempt to improve housing, by the mid-1960s the office planned 30,000 housing units, the highest number in the country (Groag and Harel 2016). Throughout these years, Perlstein was also an avid amateur photographer. The paper will examine his diary-like home movies shot in the 1960s, in which he documented personal and professional travels and, most significantly, the building of his office's projects of housing and town planning in Israel.

In the early 1960s, Perlstein bought a Canon 8mm movie camera and began filming. His films show incessant movement, as if attempting to capture everything possible, searching for both the new and the similar. He filmed houses, neighbourhoods, towns and infrastructures while moving from one place to the other. In what follows, we refer to films of new neighbourhoods planned by his office at the same time and in proximity to one another, during and after their construction, some of them built using precast materials, according to a system imported from France. Accordingly, we will refer to a Parisian suburb he filmed at the same time.[2] We will examine how Perlstein's perspective as a modernist functionalist architect is reflected in his movies, while also highlighting what the architect-planner chose to 'see' as well as to overlook; this will encompass how his perspective as a tourist, moving between countries and 'copying' from one place to the other reveals his understanding of his role as an architect within the larger project of Israeli public housing and state and nation building.

Our focus on Perlstein's home movies sheds light on an alternative source of information for understanding architecture and urban planning and the ideas behind it. As Patricia Zimmerman notes, amateur films provide a vital access point for academic historiography in their trajectory from official history to the more variegated and multiple practices of popular memory, a concretization of memory into artefacts that can be remobilized, recontextualized and reanimated (2007: 1). Like other types of historical evidence previously considered marginal, home movies promote new explanatory models of discerning significance within and between disparate events and artefacts (Zimmerman 2007: 1). Home movies represent unexplored evidence for film history, as well as for history in general, as a 'history from below' in that they 'present a materialization of the abstractions of race, class, gender, and nation as they are lived and as part of everyday life, much valorized by cultural studies as a site for agency, fissure, and resistance for dominant modalities' (Zimmerman 2007: 3). Péter Forgács proposes that the amateur film 'is an imprint of culture rewritten by motion picture that has a certain self-reflective impact on the overall face of culture' (2007: 48). He goes on to say that the 'maker of a home movie acts as the narrator, in a manner that recalls that of silent film. ... The home movie or private film, not unlike the letter and diary, is biographical. It is one of the most adequate means of remembrance. It is a meditation on "who am I?"' (Forgács 2007: 49).

By examining Perlstein's home movies we will attempt to understand the parallels between his perspective as a planner and his cinematic eye, his interest in the mechanization of architecture and his certain oversight of specific territory, history and identity of its future inhabitants, common to many modernist and Zionist planners and architects at the time. We shall also seek to understand through his films Perlstein's own personal and professional imprint on the wider historical circumstances.

Yitzhaq Perlstein: Zionism, modernism and architecture

Yitzhaq Perlstein was born in Tel Aviv in 1914, and his life and career were immersed in the city and state-building projects. His parents were among the founders of Tel Aviv in 1909; his father was a trader who was also involved in real-estate. Born and raised in Tel Aviv, which became in the 1930s an epicentre of modernist, International Style architecture imported by Jewish refugee architects, most of them, though not all, from Germany, young Perlstein was highly influenced by architectural modernism.[3] Perlstein came of age in a climate of urban and bourgeois Zionism, along with the influence of European architectural modernism. He was also a subject of the British Mandate in Palestine (1918–48).

Perlstein decided to travel to Great Britain for his academic studies and began studying architecture and town planning at University College, London in 1933. After receiving his degree in architecture, he studied town planning in what was one of the first Town planning departments in the UK. Perlstein excelled in his studies and was in close contact with the department's head, Patrick Abercrombie, a well-known and influential British town planner, who had also visited Palestine several times to advise local planners. Several of Abercrombie's planning concepts would be later integrated into Perlstein's planning.[4]

In 1949, the year after the State of Israel was established, young Perlstein was selected to be part of the prestigious Planners Team, headed by architect Arieh Sharon, which would subsequently provide the blueprints for the establishment of new settlements in the centre and peripheries of the new state, planned according to modernist principals, many of them almost identical to one another.[5] His experience in the Planners Team was a fundamental source for his professional knowledge and his future architectural designs.

The Zionist national housing project

Established in 1948, the State of Israel underwent a rapid process of development in the subsequent decades.[6] Zionism, as a nation-building project, was also concerned with land and housing development, considered by some a colonial enterprise. The arid land in the midst of an Arab world was seen in the eyes of the Jewish settlers, similar to the view of British Mandate officials who preceded the Israeli state, as underdeveloped and primitive. It had to be quickly and thoroughly developed, with modern housing built to settle hundreds of thousands of incoming Jewish immigrants (Levy 1997, 2001; Levin 2015).

The new state launched a series of development projects, including towns and settlements, rural, semi-urban, small and medium in size, as well as roads and transportation systems, pipelines and many public housing projects. The Ministry of Housing and the Planners Team aspired to 'make the empty land bloom', as the famous saying of the era went.[7] They worked towards two goals: to disperse the new immigrants throughout the country in order to prevent the congestion of existing cities, by sending (Jewish) immigrants from Arab countries, considered inferior to immigrants of European countries, to settle the peripheral territories of the new state and occupy territories whose Palestinian inhabitants were uprooted during the war of 1948, to prevent their return (Sharon 2006: 32–3). Public housing slabs and new settlements were spread throughout the country. All projects were planned with a double purpose: to apply sovereignty over the territory through the establishment of Jewish settlements and to construct the physical landscape by designing and building the living space (Kallus and Yone 2002: 155–6). The huge number of housing units that had to be supplied quickly demanded frugality and, consequently, the apartments were small and the buildings simple and low cost. The uniformity of the housing played a major role in Zionist nation-building, which aspired to constitute a modern Israeli citizen (Kallus and Yone 2002), free of the religious and social traditions of the past, socialist instead of bourgeois and Westernized rather than Oriental or Arab (Raz-Krakotzkin 1993).

The modernist principles of architecture applied in the construction of the housing and the new neighbourhoods and towns were imported from Europe.[8] A primary principle was *existenzminimum*: providing every human being with minimal conditions of decent housing – light and air, living space, washing and cooking facilities.[9] Another was standardization, in which apartments were built in repeatable structures, in a low-cost and efficient model of construction.[10] Finally, the new urban planning followed the modernist principle of functional zoning, the spatial separation of urban areas according to function: housing, transportation, work and entertainment (Mumford 2000).

Perlstein's neighbourhood planning and the serial building type

After the Planners Team was dismantled in 1951, Perlstein started his private office, and began receiving commissions from the Ministry of Housing. In 1956, he received a commission to plan new neighbourhoods in Bat Yam and

Holon, satellite towns south of Tel Aviv. The new projects were planned to be neighbourhood units. These were to provide their residents with peacefulness, greenery and all necessary services and amenities (Collison 1954; Gold 2000). They were meant to have a population of 2,000–3,000 residents. The neighbourhoods were built in series of identical buildings. Some were elongated or cube-shaped, made of factory-produced blocks and cement, plastered and painted white. These structures had three or four storeys, no elevators, sometimes with a red, green or blue concrete belt (exterior trim) across the top, as a constructional and aesthetic element. Fenestration was sometimes emphasized by protruding squares or rectangles of concrete or plastic (in colours matching the top belt). Apartments were small (two to four bedrooms, 30–70 square metres) and had windows with white plastic shutters and provided covered places to hang laundry nearby.

The neighbourhoods in Bat Yam and Holon were planned by Perlstein for the Ministry of Housing in a comprehensive plan approved in 1958. They were built on sand dunes that became state lands after the expulsion of Palestinians from the area in 1948. While Jessy Cohen was built in the 1950s as an immigrant neighbourhood, Ramat Yosef and Neot Rahel were designated for young families, each one surrounding a large commercial centre, and Ramat Hanasi was the last to be built, designated for the up-and-coming middle class. The four neighbourhoods were planned as autonomous residential areas – neighbourhoods that were part of the city but at the same time self-contained. They included public buildings, like schools, a synagogue, health clinic, commercial centre, all set in vast green areas and pedestrian walkways that served the needs of the neighbourhood residents.[11]

The methods of construction of these buildings and neighbourhoods were developed and improved as well. In 1960, Perlstein began collaborating with French Engineer J. Bory and imported his method of construction to Israel. The precast elements such as window frames in various forms and colours, facade parts like horizontal belts, vertical square and rectangular elements of the façade, small concrete balconies and laundry covers were designed in France and produced in a field factory at the building site. The modular planning expanded from the room to the apartment to the building, and the neighbourhoods were composed of combinations of these different elements (Groag and Harel 2016).

Perlstein's office planned these neighbourhood units as serial and often identical housing units throughout the country. It established a highly efficient work system that produced housing types realized by the Ministry of Housing and by public contractors. The need to build rapidly, along with the mechanization of design, led to uniform planning, sometimes in areas that were different climatically and culturally. For example, neighbourhoods in Southern cities like Dimona and Be'er Sheba in the Negev desert at the South were built identically to neighbourhoods in the Northern town of Kiryat Shmona, although the climatic conditions were completely different. This homogeneity, along with its population by poor immigrants and neglect by authorities, led later on to the negative stereotyping of public housing in Israel, as well as to its failure, as noted by Naomi Carmon: 'The failure of the housing projects was especially severe where the homogenous construction, incompatible with the specific needs and preferences of the residents and with local environmental conditions, was combined with homogenous inhabitation, usually of weak population groups' (2001: 15).[12]

In the 1960s, when Perlstein was preoccupied with planning an ever-growing variety of neighbourhoods throughout the country, he also began filming. The amateur films he made with his 8mm movie camera are a significant primary source for the study of his works.[13] In the following section, Perlstein's home movies will be examined with reference to documentary films about new Israeli towns made at the same time, as well as earlier films made in the 1920s–30s by modernist architects as professional instruments. Unlike Perlstein's amateur films, these films are intentional and meant for public view, while Perlstein's films are private notes and impressions. The first three films are Israeli propaganda films made by professional filmmakers for the government, to advertise and fundraise for the national project of housing for the large numbers of new immigrants, which was at its peak at the time. These films, like Perlstein's, explore the great modern project of housing with curiosity and admiration, expressed in the selection of objects filmed and in their camera work. In the professional films, this is accompanied by authoritative voiceover, while Perlstein's films are silent, his curiosity expressed in quick tilts, pans and zooms. Perlstein rarely films residents, while two of the other three films focus on the immigrant inhabitants. These relate particularly to the immigrants' difficulties in getting used to modern living environments, being careful not to express any criticism of planning and housing authorities, instead attributing these hardships to 'cultural' reasons. Together, the private and public films portray the official point of view of the time. The architects' films of the late 1920s share Perlstein's interest in construction and building details. In 1928, Siegfried Giedion, the historian of the modern architecture movement, wrote: 'Only film can make the new architecture intelligible. Still photography does not capture it clearly' (1995: 176). Perlstein's films as well as the architects' films express Giedion's words.

This is apparent in the camera movements and the selection of themes which are clear expressions of the style and logic of his architecture and, as will be seen, the camera is yet another tool for a deeper professional understanding of the construction and visibility of serial housing and of the organization of new neighbourhoods.

Professional and amateur filming of modernist architecture

The Zionist state and nation-building project and particularly its housing projects were shown in a variety of professional documentary films made in the 1950s and 1960s. One such example is *Housing and Building* (Yoram Gross 1960). It shows the rapid developments in planning and construction in Israel, in a film that is creative and artistic and, at the same time, applies a semi-propagandist authoritarian tone, which was common at the time. It documents the construction of the housing unit from the concrete and steel skeleton to the complete apartment, including minute details. It is accompanied by upbeat music and a voiceover that explains what is being seen – for example, a shot of architects seated at their drawing desks in a large hall. The film shows works of construction as well as the various factories that produce the basic elements necessary to a house, such as toilets, sinks and lightbulbs.[14]

In addition, two films made by Helga Cranston (later known as Helga Keller) documented the building and the populating of new towns by immigrants: *Ashdod* (1961) and *Dimona: The First Days* (1962). *Ashdod* shows the building of the eponymous new port city on the sands in the southern Mediterranean coast (the general plan and the design of some of the neighbourhoods of this port city were also prepared in Perlstein's office). *Dimona* shows the first days of a group of immigrants from North Africa arriving directly from the boat to a remote new town built in the Negev desert. Both films focus on the immigrants from North African countries, showing interest and sensitivity to their hardships, although not criticizing the housing policy. In these two films, there is a voiceover narration as well as diegetic sounds of people speaking about their difficulties and joys. Both show the moments of stress, excitement and disappointment when immigrants first arrive at their new homes in the identical housing slabs, described above, which were built all over the country. The film tells and shows us that these are the moments of encounter between a 'backward' population and progressive housing. The newcomers are not used to such a quality of life, and sometimes do not know how to use facilities such as taps and sinks with running water. Thus, these films, while giving voice to the new immigrants, nevertheless maintain the hegemonic beliefs of the Zionist institutions at the time.

These are joined by several additional examples of film as a professional tool by architects in the interwar period. These films, some of them made by professional filmmakers and others by amateurs, are significant since they used the camera to express the free-flowing movement inside modernist buildings, the penetration of light through horizontal windows and the focus and zoom to examine modern construction techniques and architectural details. Films relating to Le Corbusier's architecture are a prominent example, such as *L'architecture d'aujourd'hui* (Chenal 1930). This professional documentary explores three of Le Corbusier's villas, enabling the viewer to experience his architecture through the deliberate dispersion of a fixed point of view and the annihilation of perspectival space. The camera follows Le Corbusier walking around in his villas wearing a hat, giving him the appearance of a tourist, a visitor or like a rather mysterious figure in a 'film-noir' (Colomina 1996: 289). However, for Le Corbusier, the medium of film was not only used to solve the problems of visual representation, such as that presented by the so-called multi-perspectival character of modern architecture, but was also a means of promoting himself and his work (Koeck and Roberts 2010: 208). Ernst Weissmann, a collaborator in Le Corbusier's atelier, also made amateur films of Le Corbusier's works. He documented his visits to the Villa Savoye, Le Corbusier's most famous villa, during different stages of its construction in 1929–30 (Wouters et al. 2018). Like Le Corbusier, Perlstein is a tourist in his works, seeming distant from his houses and neighbourhoods, constantly moving from one to the other, never resting or stopping for conversation. It seems that, although these are future homes and neighbourhoods, Perlstein has no personal interest in any one of them, a fact that goes hand in hand with the seriality and lack of any singular attributes and personality of the national housing project. However, Perlstein does not share Le Corbusier's awareness of the media. His films are made for his own eyes, perhaps for the eyes of employees and colleagues, and express his lack of interest in self publicity.

By the time Perlstein began using his own camera in the 1960s, amateur filmmaking had become popular among less experienced users, mostly in booming postwar economies in the United States and parts of Europe, where it became an ideal for 'a middle-class male hobbyist' (Zimmermann 2007: 1). However, in Israel of the 1960s, where austerity was prevalent, a private film camera was still a rare sight. Perlstein as a filmmaker is not subversive or marginal, nor is he engaged in counter-narrative. Rather, his filming appears to be simple and direct. In his home movies, the newly built housing projects are shot during motion, on foot or from a passing car, as if he were a tourist or a visitor. His camera does not get close, never steps inside any of the houses and he never starts a conversation with a resident in the presence of the camera. The planner who is also a tourist, a foreigner, was common in the field of urban planning at the time. Zionism aspired to build a modern Western state, in a territory that was conceived of by state officials and urban planners as underdeveloped, primitive and mostly empty, overlooking the local Arab Palestinian population.[15] The perspective of the tourist has some resonance with the writings of Europeans who had toured Palestine throughout the nineteenth and twentieth centuries, Christians, as well as Jewish ones. Some of these tourists were architects and planners invited by Zionist officials to devise plans for the new Jewish settlements in Palestine, during the British Mandate.[16] The designs of the foreign architects-planners, some of them realized, introduced key concepts to the planning in Mandatory Palestine and later in the new state of Israel.[17]

Architect, camera, modernist housing

Perlstein uses the camera to study his own work and, at the same time, as an excuse to study the camera apparatus and the act of filming. It is an expression of a passionate pursuit of modern technology – in construction and in filming alike. The implied message of his silent films is a modest pride – of the construction of good and solid public housing, of the progressive usage of serial planning and building types and of precast construction technologies. The horizontal spread and seriality of the buildings are reflected in the horizontal movement of the camera. This is also an expression of Perlstein's keen awareness of motion, of pedestrian and vehicular traffic in the neighbourhoods. It is a basic similarity between his work as a planner and his eye as a filmmaker.

Perlstein, like his colleagues at the time, viewed the house as a functional object, a machine for living, required to supply the minimal living conditions as efficiently as possible. As such, its form, details and construction technologies could be borrowed and learned from other countries in which large-scale housing projects were built, like France, and Paris in particular. The massive construction of social housing, new neighbourhoods and infrastructure was at its peak in Paris of the 1960s. Paris and its region experienced administrative restructuring and large-scale construction work, including the Boulevard

Périphérique ring road, the first line of the future RER (regional express railway) and the beginning of five new towns (Paskins 2009: 1). Massive housing projects were built in the suburbs of Paris, called the 'grand-ensembles d'habitation'. Such was the scale of construction that by 1968, one in six residents of greater Paris lived in a grand ensemble (Newsome 2009: 109).

Perlstein's film of Parisian suburbs which are followed by his newly planned Israeli neighbourhoods (see Figure 3.1) shows filming as part of an act of architectural tourism, through which knowledge is transferred from one country to the other. The films he shot in Paris in the 1960s may be compared to a sketchbook, where Perlstein, now as the tourist planner, jots down his thoughts, ideas and impressions, creating a catalogue that will later be used in his own country. The film focuses on the construction methods that inspired him and which he imported to Israel. The footage begins with two impressive thirty-storey buildings in Place d'Italie, structures made of concrete with a grid of precast window frames and facade parts, which protrude to protect from the sun, all of which are transported to and fixed on site. The buildings were part of Italie XIII, a large urban project in Paris that started in the 1960s, interrupted by public criticism shared by politicians and experts, stopped in 1974 (Texier 2005) and never completed. In another part of the neighbourhood, the camera studies windows set between precast parts – grey horizontal belts and sand-coloured vertical elements

Figure 3.1 Neot Rahel Neighborhood, Holon, *c.* 1968, a film still from footage taken by architect Yitzhaq Perlstein. Photographer: Yitzhaq Perlstein © The Perlstein Family Collection. Used by permission.

that create a repetitive rhythmic facade, sometimes with a resident peeking out. Later, a field factory: piles of precast elements, cranes above, carrying parts, construction elevators moving alongside unfinished buildings. Perlstein's camera zooms in on the improvised shacks of the workers' families, quickly moving away. His interests lie in the building skeletons and the arrangement of the site, not in the construction workers; he studies precast window frames, balconies and brown laundry protectors, all the elements that create the repetition and rhythm, the 'music' of public precast mass housing facades.

On the same reel as the Paris film, are shots of neighbourhoods in the Israeli towns of Holon and Bat Yam. The neighbourhoods were built using French precast technology, and so the proximity of filmed materials is also of the architectural and constructional aspects. Filming a neighbourhood in Holon, the camera zooms in and pans across four-storey housing slabs. A zoom-out shows sand dunes in the background of the slabs, soon to be covered with more slabs, roads and streets. Residents are rarely filmed face to face, perhaps out of respect, or a lack of interest. Perlstein's camera is in incessant movement. He never stops to speak with residents, although such conversations may have existed, but not on film. The Ramat Yosef neighbourhood in Bat Yam appears in a separate film, viewed from above, from one of its high rises. The camera moves across the spacious green area in the centre of the neighbourhood, with its pedestrian paths and public buildings (see Figure 3.2), filmed from different angles. It

Figure 3.2 Ramat Yoseph neighbourhood, Bat Yam, a film still from footage taken by architect Yitzhaq Perlstein, 1963–64. Photographer: Yitzhaq Perlstein © The Perlstein Family Collection. Used by permission.

is a space where residents not only live, but also socialize (this design won Perlstein the Rokach Prize for Architecture, 1958). In a panning shot across the rooftops of Ramat Yosef, the construction of a new neighbourhood is seen in the background. Perlstein himself appears for a fraction of a second, in a celebration of the new neighbourhood's connection to the electrical grid. It is late afternoon, and the new slabs look gloomy, dark, disappearing. Though the excitement of the new and of modern technology is felt in the air – buildings, neighbourhoods, the movie camera – the darkness that falls on the neighbourhood makes it seem that their troubled future is already anticipated. The public housing slabs filmed in their nascent stages were duplicated throughout the country in new neighbourhoods and towns. Perlstein sees himself as he truly was, one of the builders, literally speaking, of the state. Just as The Parisian grand-ensembles were criticized by the public from the late 1950s[18] and were soon to become areas of neglect, segregation and poverty,[19] the Israeli public housing project, although smaller in scale, suffered similar problems. As early as the 1970s, it was criticized for being unidentifiable, impersonal and anti-social (Elmelech and Levin-Epstein 1998; Carmon 2001).

Conclusion

The home movies of Israeli architect Yitzhaq Perlstein are a piece of micro-history that function as a personal-professional archive within the grand narrative of the Zionist nation-building project. In his films, he gazes outwards to European building practices, revealing his keen interest in these methods, which enable the construction of hundreds of units a month, rapidly realizing the new nation-state. The covering of the territory with new housing, to settle incoming immigrants quickly and efficiently and the colonialist project of converting into Western standards as much territory as possible – as sandy and arid as it may originally have been – is something with which Perlstein the professional completely identifies. In Perlstein's home movies, the logics of building serial public housing and the camera come together, representing similar conceptions relating to the home, the neighbourhood and dwelling in general. They reflect the dominant point of view of the Zionist and colonialist urban planner in an era of nation building. His view reveals his conception of himself, facing the land, and his understanding of his part in the state building mechanism. This perspective becomes his own, and the two are inseparable. His camera eye is part of the collective of modernist architecture professionals and other social engineers, that turned a blind eye – as realized later – to public housing residents as individuals who may not easily assimilate into the project, and who were often alienated by it, coming from non-Western, Middle-Eastern or Asian countries of origin (Samocha and Peres 1974; Kimmerling 1993, 2008; Elmelech and Levin-Epstein 1998; Carmon 2001: 14–15).

Still, there is a certain power in Perlstein's perspective, revealed in his home movies. His relation to the place, the landscapes, is devoid of spiritual or religious ambition; it is also free of nostalgia or idealization. The local Arab architecture is no source of inspiration or interest for him, nor does he attempt to appropriate local vernacular forms. Instead, he has confidence and belief in the industrialization of housing as epitomizing progress and he enjoys experimenting with the camera as a tool for documenting his designs, for himself and for future generations.

Furthermore, though blind to cultural differences, Perlstein was attentive to inhabitants' needs in other ways. Even as the housing he planned was based on types repeated in many neighbourhoods, he worked constantly on improving his own plans, revising and updating them and, through modest circumstances, providing the best *existenzminimum* apartments possible. Changes were made to the directions that certain rooms faced, in order to provide better light and air to the interior; the shape and size of fenestrations were changed, as were finishing materials such as floor tiles and toilet parts.[20] The neighbourhoods he chose to film were ones he was proud of. They were planned for pedestrians and supplied places for social encounters; the ones he filmed were the ones he wanted to *remember* and to remind others to do the same. His shunning away from publicity and from the camera, his modesty and matter-of-factness expressed in his simple and clear conception of architecture, convinces of his belief in the agency of urban planning in creating better living environments, realized in his neighbourhoods throughout the years, despite social and economic transformations in Israeli society and the transition to a privatized economy, which began in the late 1970s and continues to this day (Mandelkern and Paz-Fuchs 2018: 2–3).

Moreover, the lack of face-to-face encounters of individual public housing residents could be a reflection of his avoidance of all forms of personal publicity throughout his life.[21] In this, Perlstein is the opposite of Le Corbusier, as described earlier by Colomina (1996) and Koeck and Roberts (2010). Le Corbusier appeared in his films several times, as a shadow, from behind, or through his hand pointing at an architectural model.[22] Perlstein, by contrast, wants to disappear and wants the architecture to be present and to speak for itself. The movement in the films is also a consequence of this attempt to disappear, to stay away from public attention, to become an eye that documents for experience and learning. From this perspective of present-absence, the amateur films we have discussed here could be considered a biographical message from Perlstein to future generations who may see his work – both built and filmed – and understand these as the architect's own 'words'.

Notes

1   The public housing stock was built to supply shelter for the hundreds of thousands of new immigrants and later provided affordable housing for low-income households. By the 1990s, public housing in Israel was privatized (Werczberger 1995). See more on the building of public housing in Israel and its privatization in Shadar (2018); Shaham (2021); Hananel (2018).

2   The massive housing and infrastructural projects built in the suburbs surrounding Paris in the 1960s are discussed in depth in Paskins (2009); Newsome (2009); Cupers (2010); Cupers (2011).

3   This refers to the design principles developed in the 1920s–30s and was closely related to Le Corbusier's principles of modern architecture: free plan, free facade, *pilotis*, horizontal windows and the garden. They were titled 'International Style' by Museum of Modern Art curators Henry-Russell Hitchcock and Philip Johnson in 1932 (Hitchcock and Johnson 1997).

4   One such principle, the Neighborhood Unit (Collison 1954) dividing the city into a hierarchy of urban social units, as they were titled in an earlier more socialist concept, in the dissertation of Arthur Ling (1938), supervised by Abercrombie (Gold 1995: 244).

5   Many peripheral settlements were populated by immigrants settled there by the government, not by choice (Elmelech and Levin-Epstein 1998). A majority were 'Oriental Jews', 'Mizrahim', immigrating from the Middle Eastern and North African countries. They were discriminated against by the Israeli establishment, seen as 'backward' if not 'primitive', compared to immigrants from Europe and North America (Samocha and Peres 1974; Kimmerling 2008).

6   The 1950s–70s were an era of rapid development in new social democratic welfare states. As noted by Escobar (1992: 132), 'planning techniques and practices have been central to development since its inception. … The concept of planning embodies the belief that social change can be engineered … the path of progress through planning has always been an indubitable truth [adopted by] development experts of most persuasions' (ibid).

7   See the report published by the Planners Team. It was titled the 'Sharon Plan' after the head of the National Planning Department Arieh Sharon (Physical Planning of Israel 1951).

8   They were imported by Jewish architects, most of whom had been educated at the Bauhaus and other European school and a few, like Perlstein, educated in British institutions. The Modernist principles were raised and developed at the meetings of CIAM – the *Congress Internationale d'Architecture Moderne* – the association of modernist architects (1928–59). CIAM arranged a series of events in the pre- and postwar-era Europe. The CIAM Congress on the Functional City took place aboard a cruise ship in the Mediterranean in the summer of 1933 (Mumford 2000: 73–90).

9   The term was coined by Ernst May and adopted by Walter Gropius, who lectured at CIAM II on 'The Sociological Foundations of the Minimum Dwelling' in 1929 (Mumford 2018). It was also developed by Karel Teige (2002/1932), who envisioned the minimum dwelling not as a reduced version of a bourgeois apartment or rural cottage, but as a wholly new dwelling type built with the cooperation of architects, sociologists, economists, health officials, physicians, etc.

10   Le Corbusier repeatedly referred to the notion of serial housing. In 1926, Le Corbusier was commissioned by industrialist Henry Frugès, to build a complex of worker housing, the Cité Frugès at Pessac, near Bordeaux. This became his first laboratory for residential housing: a series of rectangular blocks composed of modular housing units located in a garden setting. Pessac became the model for his later and much larger *Cité Radieuse* projects (Huxtable 1981).

11   Groag, S. and L. Harel (2016), *Ramat Hanasi Neighborhood Documentation File*, a survey done for the Department of Conservation, the municipality of Bat Yam, Israel (Hebrew). Levine, D. (2018). Sacred Masses: Religious Architecture in Bat Yam. Massa-Holy, 2, 38–49.

12   Most projects were designed solely for immigrants and were built near established settlements or in the State's peripheries, which were often dangerous frontiers where the Ministry of Housing could easily locate available land for mass construction (Carmon 2001: 13).

13   The films Perlstein made comprise an important primary source for the study of his works, since the majority of primary materials from his office was not kept.

14   The film uses theatrical gestures such as the pantomime actor dressed in white, who draws white lines on a black background, a reference to prewar modernist genres like Dadaism and Surrealism. *Housing and Building Operations* (1960) [Film] Dir. Yoram Gross, Israel State Archives, catalogue n. ISA-Collections-MiscFilms-0010xmo, https://www.archives.gov.il/archives/Archive/0b071706802fe50d/File/0b07170681087aa6 (accessed 4 May 2022).

15   Zionism has been referred to as a colonial project, in which the establishment of a Jewish state is a means of gaining political control over the Arab population, including the destruction of Palestinian villages and cities and replacing them with Jewish settler colonies, thereby exploiting the colonized people (see Ilan Pappe 2007). Others refer to Zionism as a Settler Colonialism, in which the colonization is achieved through settlers (see Salamanca, et al. 2012; Lloyd 2012).

16 These prominent figures included Patrick Geddes (Rubin 2013: 86–91), Patrick Abercrombie (Abercrombie was Perlstein's mentor, thesis supervisor and his employer; their professional connection began at the time of his studies in London 1933–9), and Clifford Holiday (Wilkof 2017: 141–2; Home 1994: 479–80; Kolodney 2010: 154–5).

17 Several sources relate to the involvement of British planning officials in Palestine, during and after the mandate period (see Rubin 2013; Welter 2009; Kolodney 2010: 151–4; Wilkof 2017: 141–2, 194).

18 As Cupers notes, the negative reactions of the inhabitants were due to the fact that they 'were forced to organize their everyday lives in an environment that was often neither finished nor accommodating to their way of life' (2011: 36). Cupers relates particularly to the suburb of Sarcelles: 'it was proclaimed as "Europe's largest construction site" and soon became notorious as journalists and sociologists flocked to it to gauge the future of urban France. From the late 1950s onwards, Sarcelles was the national staple for popular criticism about the grands ensembles' (Cupers 2011: 38).

19 Cupers, relating to Sarcelles, notes that just like in other new developments, the concentration of a homogeneously undesirable housing stock led to an increasing problematization in terms of social segregation. (Cupers 2011: 47) Another example is the Cité Balzac, a housing complex built in the 1960s in Vitry-sur-Seine. It has been initially occupied by an emerging middle class that left the apartments when private property became encouraged by a liberal government during the 1970s. In the 1970s, the social housing apartments were then occupied by impoverished immigrants and French citizens coming from former colonies and became stigmatized as a symbol of social problems and ethnic conflicts (Inglez de Souza 2022).

20 Based on interviews held with several architects, like Gobi Kertesz, Alex Kaminsky and Eli Mani who had worked in Perlstein's office, which were conducted between May 2020 and June 2021.

21 Information based on conversations with his family (2019–20) as well as on interviews with architects who worked in his office (2020–21).

22 For example, in scenes from *L'architecture d'aujourd'hui* (Chenal 1929).

References

Bullock, Nicholas (1997), 'Architecture, Reconstruction and the British Documentary Film Movement', in François Penz and Maureen Thomas (eds), *Architecture and Cinema: Méliès, Mallet-Stevens, Multimedia*, 52–61, London: British Film Institute.

Carmon, Naomi (2001), 'Housing Policy in Israel: Review, Evaluation and Lessons', *Israel Affairs*, 7 (4): 181–208.

Collison, Peter (1954), 'Town Planning and the Neighborhood Unit Concept', *Public Administration*, 32 (4): 463–9.

Colomina, Beatriz (1996), *Privacy and Publicity: Modern Architecture as Mass Media*, Cambridge: The MIT Press.

Cupers, Kenny (2010), 'Designing Social Life: The Urbanism of the Grands Ensembles', *Positions*, 1: 94–121.

Cupers, Kenny (2011), 'The Expertise of Participation: Mass Housing and Urban Planning in Post-War France', *Planning Perspectives*, 26 (1): 29–53.

Elmelech, Yuval and Noach Levin-Epstein (1998), 'Immigration and Housing in Israel: Additional Look at Ethnic Inequality', *Megamot: The Israeli Quarterly for the Behavioral Sciences* (Hebrew), 39 (3): 243–69.

Escobar, Arturo (1992), 'Planning', in Wolfgang Sachs (ed), *The Development Dictionary: A Guide to Knowledge as Power*, 132–45, London: Zed Books.

Forgács, Péter (2007), 'Wittgenstein Tractatus: Personal Reflections on Home Movies', in Karen I. Ishizuka and Patricia R. Zimmermann (eds), *Mining the Home Movie: Excavations in Histories and Memories*, 47–56, Berkeley: University of California Press.

Giedion, Sigfried (1995), *Building in France, Building in Iron, Building in Ferroconcrete*, Los Angeles: Getty Publications.

Gold, John R. (1995), 'The MARS Plans for London, 1933–1942: Plurality and Experimentation in the City Plans of the Early British Modern Movement', *The Town Planning Review*, 66 (3): 243–67.

Gold, John R. (2000), 'Towards the Functional City? MARS, CIAM and the London Plans 1933–42', in Thomas Deckker (ed), *The Modern City Revisited*, 81–99, London: Routledge.

Gold, John R. and Stephen V. Ward (2005), 'Of Plans and Planners: Documentary Film and the Challenge of the Urban Future, 1935–52', in David B. Clarke (ed), *The Cinematic City*, 59–82, London: Routledge.

Groag, Shmuel and Lilach Harel (2016), *Ramat Hanasi Neighborhood Documentation File, A Survey Done for the Department of Conservation, the Municipality of Bat Yam, Israel* (Hebrew). Available at https://issuu.com/vsitepro/docs/_____63_-_____ (Accessed 4 August 2023).

Hananel, Ravit (2018), 'Deserving and Privileged: The Social Construction of the Right to Housing in Israel', *Israel Affairs*, 24 (1): 128–49.

Hitchcock, Henry-Russell and Philip Johnson (1997), *The International Style*, New York: W. W. Norton & Co.

Home, Robert (1994), (Book Review) 'Bauhaus on the Carmel and the Crossroads of Empire: Architecture and Planning in Haifa during the British Mandate by Gilbert Herbert and Silvina Sosnowski', *The Town Planning Review*, 65 (4): 479–80.

Huxtable, Ada Louise (1981), 'Architecture View; Le Corbusier's Housing Project – Flexible Enough to Endure', *New York Times*, 15 March. Available online: https://www.nytimes.com/1981/03/15/arts/architecture-view-le-corbusier-s-housing-project-flexible-enough-endure-ada.html (accessed 3 March 2022).

Inglez de Souza, Diego (2022), 'The History of the Cité Balzac and the Vicious Circle of Social Housing', *Cidade, Comunidades e Territórios*, Spring Special Issue: 89–101.

Available online: https://journals.openedition.org/cidades/5289 (accessed 1 January 2023).

Kallus, Rachel and Hubert Law Yone (2002), 'National Home/Personal Home: Public Housing and the Shaping of National Space in Israel', *European Planning Studies*, 10 (6): 765–79.

Kimmerling, Baruch (1993), 'State Building, State Autonomy and the Identity of Society: The Case of the Israeli State', *Journal of Historical Sociology*, 6 (4): 396–429.

Kimmerling, Baruch (2008), 'State Building, Mass-Immigration and Establishment of Hegemony (1948–1951)', *Israeli Sociology*, 1: 167–208.

Koeck, Richard and Les Roberts (2010), 'Introduction', in Richard Koeck and Les Roberts (eds), *The City and the Moving Image: Urban Projections*, 1–18, London: Palgrave Macmillan.

Kolodney, Ziva (2010), 'The Politics of Landscape, The Production of Landscape in Haifa between the British Mandate and Sovereignty', Ph.D. diss., Technion Institute of Technology, Haifa.

Levine, Daphna (2018), *Ramat Hanasi Neighborhood Documentation File*, A Survey done for the department of Conservation, the municipality of Bat Yam, Israel (Hebrew).

Levin, Iris (2015), *Migration, Settlement, and the Concepts of House and Home*, New York: Routledge.

Levy, André (1997), 'To Morocco and Back', in Eyal Ben-Ari and Yoram Bilu (eds), *Grasping Land: Space and Place in Contemporary Israeli Discourse and Experience*, 92–108, Albany, NY: State University of New York Press.

Levy, André (2001), 'Center and Diaspora: Jews in Late-Twentieth-Century Morocco', *City & Society*, 13 (2): 245–70.

Lloyd, David (2012), 'Settler Colonialism and the State of Exception: The Example of Palestine/Israel', *Settler Colonial Studies*, 2 (1): 59–80.

Mandelkern, Ronen and Amir Paz-Fuchs (2018), 'Privatizing Israel: An Introduction', in Amir Paz-Fuchs, Ronen Mandelkern and Itzhak Galnoor (eds), *The Privatization of Israel: The Withdrawal of State Responsibility*, 1–18, New York: Palgrave Macmillan.

Mumford, Eric (2000), *The CIAM Discourse on Urbanism 1928–1960*, Cambridge: The MIT Press.

Mumford, Eric (2018), *Designing the Modern City*, Newhaven: Yale University Press.

Newsome, W. Brian (2009), *French Urban Planning, 1940–1968: The Construction and Deconstruction of an Authoritarian System* (Studies in Modern European History), Vol. 61, New York: Peter Lang, Inc.

Pappe, Ilan (2007), *The Ethnic Cleansing of Palestine*, New York: Simon and Schuster.

Paskins, Jacob (2009), 'Vague Terrain: Bidonvilles, Run-Down Housing, and the Stigmatization of (Sub)urban Space in and around Paris in the 1960s', *Moveable Type*, Vol. 5 'Mess': 1–19.

Raz-Krakotzkin, Amnon (1993), 'Exile within the Nation-State', *Theory and Criticism*, 4: 23–55.

Rubin, Noah Hysler (2013), 'The Celebration, Condemnation and Reinterpretation of the Geddes Plan, 1925: The Dynamic Planning History of Tel Aviv', *Urban History*, 40 (1): 114–34.

Salamanca, Omar Jabary, Mezna Qato, Kareem Rabie and Sobhi Samour (2012), 'Past Is Present: Settler Colonialism in Palestine', *Settler Colonial Studies*, 2 (1): 1–8.

Samocha, Sami and Yochanan Peres (1974), 'Ethnic Gap in Israel', *Megamot: The Israeli Quarterly for the Behavioral Sciences* (Hebrew), 20 (1): 5–42.

Shadar, Hadas (2004), 'Between East and West: Immigrants, Critical Regionalism and Public Housing', *The Journal of Architecture*, 9 (1): 23–48.

Shadar, Hadas (2018), *The Building Blocks of Public Housing: Six Decades of Public Urban Construction in Israel* (Hebrew), 2nd ed., Tel Aviv: The Ministry of Housing and Building.

Shafir, Gershon (1996), *Land, Labor and the Origins of the Israeli-Palestinian Conflict, 1882–1914*, Berkeley: University of California Press.

Shafir, Gershon (2012), 'Settler Citizenship in the Jewish Colonization of Palestine', in Caroline Elkins and Susan Pedersen (eds), *Settler Colonialism in the Twentieth Century: Projects, Practices, Legacies*, 55–72, London: Routledge.

Shaham, Israel (2021), 'Public Housing in Israel', in J.S. Fuerst (ed), *Public Housing in Europe and America*, 52–66, London: Routledge.

Sharon, Arieh (1951), *Physical Planning of Israel*, Jerusalem: The Government Printer Publishing.

Sharon, Smadar (2006), 'Planners, the State, and the Shaping of National Space in the 1950s' (Hebrew), *Theory and Criticism*, 29: 31–57.

Teige, Karel ([1932] 2002), *The Minimum Dwelling*, Cambridge: The MIT Press.

Texier, Simon (2005), *Paris Contemporain: De Haussmann à nos jours, une capitale à l'ère des métropoles*, Paris: Parigramme.

Welter, Volker M. (2009), 'The 1925 Master Plan for Tel-Aviv by Patrick Geddes', *Israel Studies*, 14 (3): 94–119.

Werczberger, Elia (1995), 'The Role of Public Housing in Israel: Effects of Privatization', *Scandinavian Housing and Planning Research*, 12 (2): 93–108.

Wilkof, Shira (2017), 'Urban Arcadias: Émigré Experts, Spatial Knowledge, and the Rise of Zionist-Israeli Planning, 1933–1953', PhD diss., Berkeley: University of California.

Wouters, Ine, Stephanie van de Voorde, Inge Bertels, Bernard Espion, Krista de Jonge and Denis Zastavni (eds) (2018), *Building Knowledge, Constructing Histories: Proceedings of the 6th International Congress on Construction History (6ICCH 2018), July 9–13, Brussels, Belgium*, Volumes 1 & 2, Boca Raton: CRC Press.

Zimmermann, Patricia R. (2007), 'Introduction: The Home Movie Movement: Excavations, Artifacts, Mining', in Karen I. Ishizuka and Patricia R. Zimmermann (eds), *Mining the Home Movie: Excavations in Histories and Memories*, 1–28, Berkeley: University of California Press.

4

Pier Paolo Pasolini's *Mamma Roma* (1962): INA-Casa public housing and remaking Rome's postwar social landscape

Alberto Lo Pinto

This chapter aims to demonstrate how Pier Paolo Pasolini employs cinema in its representational capacities to convey his political interpretation of the Roman built environment. I will use Pasolini's second feature film *Mamma Roma* (1962) as a case study, to showcase how he expresses his critique of INA-Casa, a postwar public housing project, through visual representation, narrative and character building. Pasolini considers the INA-Casa plan to be a manifestation of fascist and Christian Democratic powers, and *Mamma Roma* is his consummate polemic, providing an argument to that effect. This chapter is a critical continuation of John David Rhodes's *Stupendous, Miserable City: Pasolini's Rome* (2007) and its focus on the representation of INA-Casa Tuscolano II. Building upon Rhodes's study, this chapter explores the representation of INA-Casa by expanding the focus to two other villages and considering the public housing programme in relation to prewar and postwar power discourses. The architectural aspects of the INA-Casa public housing project will be examined as narrative elements within a larger critique of architecture's political role in a capitalist society.

Pasolini's second feature tells the story of a sex worker, Mamma Roma (Anna Magnani), who reconnects with her teenage son Ettore (Ettore Garofolo) whom she abandoned as a little child. Mamma Roma takes him from the small town of Guidonia where he grew up to her apartment in the working-class suburb of Casal Bertone in Rome. Soon after quitting her job as a sex worker, she decides to move into INA-Casa public housing, where she also finds a job as a market seller. She considers the new neighbourhood and employment as a fresh start for both herself and Ettore. But things degenerate quickly. The local boys Ettore befriends involve him in petty crimes, while Mamma Roma's former pimp

Carmine (Franco Citti) forces her back to the streets. Eventually, Ettore learns of his mother's work and, in despair, is caught stealing and put in jail, where he meets his death.

Mamma Roma, together with Pasolini's first feature film *Accattone* (1961), is one of the most vivid representations of postwar Rome and its suburbs in Italian cinema.[1] After portraying the proletariat life of the Borgata Gordiani shantytown in *Accattone*, Pasolini's attention moved to another very specific reality in the vast Roman suburbs, the brand-new INA-Casa villages. The INA-Casa villages were part of a state-funded nationwide initiative 'to increase workers' jobs through the construction of houses for workers' (*Piano incremento occupazione operaia* 1949). The plan, presented in 1949 by Amintore Fanfani, Minister of Labor in the centrist conservative party of Democrazia Cristiana (Christian Democracy – from now on 'DC'), sought to achieve two goals: curbing unemployment and providing housing for the poorest citizens. With two million people left unemployed after the war, most of whom were unskilled labourers, legislators decided to focus on building for the masses. The INA-Casa plan, named after the Istituto Nazionale Assicurazioni (National Insurance Institute) and developed in two septennia (1949–56; 1957–63), was one of the major public housing achievements of Italy's history (Beretta Anguissola 1963; Di Biagi 2010a; Pilat 2016; Sergio 2002). It envisaged the creation of two million apartments and employed a yearly average of 41,000 construction workers at 20,000 construction sites (Di Biagi 2010b: 17).

The architecture and urbanism of INA-Casa villages was affected by the historical context of postwar Italy. After twenty years of a regime that tried to promote its image by adopting a monumental style that was at times neoclassical, at other times rationalist, the postwar architectural scene moved away from its recent past to offer a more human-scale architecture. INA-Casa president and renowned architect Arnaldo Foschini and his collaborators favoured a humble architecture of low houses with few ornaments. This was a simple varied architecture, rich in communal public spaces among the buildings, combining housing blocks and towers, while avoiding the rigid alignments and repetitions of fascist public housing. The architecture and layout valorized the local urban setting, its history, orography and artistic heritage. Swedish and Scandinavian public housing was taken as inspirational sources, as attested in the four booklets, two for each septennium, that circulated among the designers.[2] Scholars of various disciplines have compared INA-Casa architecture to architectural neorealism (Conforto et al. 1977: 29–31; Poretti 2003: 13–16; Tafuri 1986: 23–5), the movement of organic architecture (Di Biagi 2010b: 24–5; Farabegoli

2002: 432–4; Pilat 2016: 60–5) and the Garden Cities and the Greenbelt Towns (Pilat 2016: 65).

This chapter addresses the extensive use of INA-Casa locations in *Mamma Roma*. The film's main location was in the southern suburbs, in and around INA-Casa Tuscolano II. INA-Casa Tuscolano consisted of three developments: Tuscolano I (1950–56), Tuscolano II (1950–56) and Tuscolano III (1952–6).[3] Architects Mario De Renzi and Saverio Muratori were both urban designers and lead architects of the design team of Tuscolano II. De Renzi and Muratori designed the most iconic buildings of the village, notably the V-shaped buildings in Largo Spartaco and in Via Sagunto (De Renzi; Muratori), and the star-shaped towers on Via del Quadraro (De Renzi). The V-shaped building in Largo Spartaco is the location of the apartment of Mamma Roma, while the star-shaped towers are frequently featured in the background of Ettore in the nearby green expanse punctuated by the aqueducts' ruins.

Although INA-Casa Tuscolano II serves as *Mamma Roma*'s primary setting, it would be erroneous to confine the discussion to this site alone without considering the relevance of two other INA-Casa villages – INA-Casa Torre Spaccata and INA-Casa Acilia – which appear briefly in the film.[4] INA-Casa Torre Spaccata (1958–60) had architect and urban planner Plinio Marconi in the role of urban designer, lead architect of one design team and coordinator of nine others. *Mamma Roma* featured the iconic market at the centre of the village designed by Marconi in the scene of the encounter between Ettore and Bruna, in which he gives her a necklace. The project of INA-Casa Acilia (1958–60) was coordinated by Cesare Valle, with Giuseppe Perugini and Attilio Spaccarelli as lead architects. Perugini's low-rise housing block forms the background of the inception of Ettore and Mamma Roma's motorcycle ride around the Roman suburbs.

Apart from Federica Capoferri's mention of INA-Casa Torre Spaccata (2017: 139–40), these two locations have yet to be considered in scholarship. Furthermore, no scholar has ever mentioned or discussed the presence of INA-Casa Acilia, which is not even listed in the film's locations (Pasolini 1991: 53). Despite their minimal presence in front of the camera, their inclusion is driven by both aesthetic and narrative concerns.

The presence of as many as three INA-Casa villages out of the nine built in Rome and the near absence of other recent residential developments highlight Pasolini's attention to the INA-Casa public housing plan, rather than in generic Roman suburbs. We should ask why Pasolini chose these three villages at the expense of the other six, and more importantly, from what sprang his interest in INA-Casa.

In addressing the first point, we can infer that Pasolini was impressed by the sheer size and monumentality of INA-Casa Tuscolano II, in particular the towers and the boomerang building, which are widely depicted in the film. This grandiosity is evident in all three villages, not only in the architecture of the buildings but also in their layout, the wide avenues and the large green spaces at their borders. The cinematography stresses this characteristic, by positioning either Mamma Roma or Ettore in wide streets bordered by imposing buildings or in neighbouring spaces whose background is defined by the profile of INA-Casa buildings.

The intent to represent and emphasize the grandiosity of the architecture also reveals the immense scale of these villages. As a matter of fact, out of the nine INA-Casa villages in Rome, INA-Casa Tuscolano and INA-Casa Torre Spaccata were the largest developments. INA-Casa Tuscolano spanned 35.5 acres and had 3,150 apartments, while INA-Casa Torre Spaccata extended for 31.2 acres, with 2,000 apartments (Segarra Lagunes, Guccione and Vittorini 2002: 51, 109). We can infer that Pasolini chose the two INA-Casa villages to showcase the grandiose scale of these two developments, as also suggested by Rhodes in regard to INA-Casa Tuscolano II (2007: 108–9).

Pasolini's choice of INA-Casa Torre Spaccata and Tuscolano II also stemmed from his knowledge of the southeastern sector of Rome, which he often visited and depicted in his literary and cinematic work of the time. We may also assume that the proximity of these two villages helped to reduce the production cost. Finally, in addition to economic reasons and personal fascination with the area southeast of Rome, I argue that the choice of these three villages is also related to the presence of vast terrain around them. As I will address below, these fields functioned as a counter-space to INA-Casa itself in a discourse on the influence of the bourgeois mentality over Ettore.

From a diegetic point of view, I argue that Pasolini chose these three villages for their urbanistic and architectural congruity, without wanting to distinguish one from the other. In fact, the three INA-Casa villages appear in the narration as part of the same cinematic space: the neighbourhood where Mamma Roma and Ettore settle. By being brought together, their forms are augmented and emphasized. Since the name of the INA-Casa villages is never mentioned in the film, mixing them became easier.

Having presented the three villages and the reason for their choice, it is now convenient to explain Pasolini's interest in INA-Casa and the use he makes of it in the film. Amongst all the Roman suburbs, Pasolini chose to portray INA-Casa, because it was a direct state intervention, promoted by the DC, whose politics he frequently condemned. Therefore, painting INA-Casa negatively ought to be seen as a direct attack on DC, and its social values. Pasolini's main accusation against the DC was that of seeking to gentrify the lower social class. Furthermore, in regard to public housing, Pasolini accused the DC of adopting very similar social policy measures to those implemented during fascist years. I would like to begin on this very point and then move later to the gentrification issue, which is related also to the use of INA-Casa in the film. In order to present the first topic, I would consider a literary text by Pasolini, namely a 1958 article, entitled 'Campi di Concentramento' ['Concentration Camps'], published in *Vie Nuove*, a weekly magazine of the Partito Comunista Italiano (Italian Communist Party). In this very critical contribution, Pasolini argues that postwar public housing was nothing more than a replica of fascist public housing, with the sole exception of a different architectural style. He believes that the overlap of fascist and postwar public housing could be found in: 'il rapporto che si istituisce tra Stato e 'poveri:' rapporto autoritario e paternalistico, profondamente inumano nella sua mistificazione religiosa' [the relationship between the State and 'poor people': authoritarian and paternalistic relationship, deeply inhumane in its religious mystification] (Pasolini [1958] 2000: 1461–2). Furthermore, in order to stress the relationship between fascist and postwar public housing, he names the latter, 'borgate democristiane' (Pasolini [1958] 2000: 1461). The *borgate* were fascist low-income residential structures located in suburban areas and connected with little continuity to other suburbs, to which they were adjacent. Pasolini's attribute 'democristiane' (linked to the DC) rather explicitly suggests the affinity between fascist public housing and the ones built during the postwar government led by the Christian Democratic party.

Pasolini never mentions the INA-Casa villages in this article but his description of generic postwar public housing here contains similar language to his depiction of the INA-Casa villages in *Mamma Roma*'s screenplay. The detail present in both descriptions that informs us that Pasolini in the article refers precisely to the INA-Casa villages is one architectural trait, the *spigoli*, the idiosyncratic sharp angular points of facades, peaked roofs, balconies and windows. In fact, Pasolini employed the term 'spigoli' both when describing generic postwar public housing – 'allineando spigoli anziché facciate' [aligning edges instead of facades] (Pasolini [1958] 2000: 1462) – and the INA-Casa villages – 'gli spigoli color polmone delle case iterate di Cecafumo'[5] [the lung-coloured edges of the iterated houses of Cecafumo] (Pasolini 1962a: 149); 'case dalla forma più assurda, dagli spigoli più vezzosi' [houses of the most absurd shapes, with the most charming edges] (Pasolini 1962a: 37). Furthermore, the 'aria romantica e civettuola' [romantic and gracious look] (Pasolini [1958] 2000: 1462) of the postwar public housing featured in the article fits well with Pasolini's description of INA-Casa in the 'Diary of Mamma Roma', a recollection of events and memories from the set of the film inserted in the volume in which the screenplay was published. In fact, in the 'Diary of Mamma Roma', Pasolini describes INA-Casa villages as an enchanted place, made of houses 'rosa, giallo, come di latta, come di zucchero ... in mezzo a un prato ... tutto fiorito di piccolo fiori' [pink, yellow, like tin, like sugar ... in the middle of a field ... blooming with small flowers] (Pasolini 1962a: 37).

Once we have established with a fair amount of certainty that the public housing referred to by Pasolini in the article are INA-Casa villages, we can add that the similarity Pasolini noted between the fascist public housing and INA-Casa villages has a foundation of truth. Giorgio Ciucci and Francesco Dal Co noticed that several points of the law for INA-Casa resembled the regulations of the 1938 royal decree on economic public housing (1991: 41). For Lando Bortolotti, a 1939 proposal by the Fascist National Party for the construction of worker houses resembled the ones proposed in 1949 by Fanfani (1978: 167–8). It is hard to assess whether Pasolini had knowledge of these earlier attempts at similar low-income development planning during the fascist regime of the 1930s. Nevertheless, references to the recent fascist past, and especially to social housing, scattered throughout both *Mamma Roma* and the eponymously titled volume suggest his knowledge of the subject.

In *Mamma Roma*, the link between fascist and INA-Casa public housing is found in two instances. It can be argued that the choice of INA-Casa Acilia (see Figure 4.1) is related to the fact that the town of Acilia was funded as a fascist *borgata*.[6] The position of Acilia in the eastern sector of the city chosen by the Governatorato satisfied the rhetoric that saw in the urban expansion towards the sea a parallel extension of the Fascist Empire towards the Mediterranean Sea, as with the Esposizione Universale Roma, a planned world's fair site and residential district in Rome designed in the late 1930s. Furthermore, the landscape of INA-Casa Acilia used for the extreme long shot of Mamma Roma and Ettore riding a motorbike contains one of the most emblematic examples of *spigoli*, especially in contrast to the uniformity of Rationalistic prewar public housing.

Another reference to fascist public housing in the film is in the first prostitution scene, in which Mamma Roma tells of her arranged marriage with an elderly builder who, during fascism, built very cheap public housing that even lacked bathrooms, called Pietrarancio. In writing this monologue, Pasolini makes two references to real fascist public housing. First, Mamma Roma's

Figure 4.1 Giuseppe Perugini's pitched-roof houses of INA-Casa Acilia. *Mamma Roma* directed by Pier Paolo Pasolini © Arco Film 1962. All rights reserved.

anecdote about her former husband building only the first house properly for the sake of Mussolini's visit, while neglecting the rest most likely derived from a real anecdote about the *borgata* Acilia: only the first structure was built with real bricks for Mussolini's eyes while the others were made with very weak wood fibre (Mancini 2011: 79). Second, the name Pietrarancio is a play on an actual fascist public housing development, Tormarancio. The *borgata* of Tormarancio is a sort of embodiment of Pasolini's link between prewar and postwar public housing, because it was replaced by a postwar public housing. Pasolini critiqued the fact that postwar government eliminated *borgate*, but then built similar public houses (Petaccia and Greco 2016: 107).

In the 1958 article, Pasolini noted that architectural style and urban layout were the only difference between prewar and postwar public housing: the latter was less severe and rigid in its design than the former. I believe that *Mamma Roma* critiqued the traditional, human-scale architecture of INA-Casa as something that covered up the same ideologies of the fascist regime. The INA-Casa architecture has the narrative function of hiding the true authoritarian and paternalistic nature and the capitalist and petite bourgeois world at the foundation of this public housing initiative. Pasolini's rejection of INA-Casa architecture was quite surprising. In fact, the repudiation of fascist monumentalism and neoclassicism as well as Rationalism's serial repetitions and rigid grid plans was a way to redeem the city's recent involvement with the regime, representing an act of resistance against and opposition to the recent past in proposing postwar housing that was free of any political connotations. Nevertheless, Pasolini saw in the picturesque, village-like brick-and-masonry image of an INA-Casa village only an empty exercise in style, far from the ideas and aspirations of the architects and planners of these public housings to realize the best possible environmental conditions for the life of the citizens – large green spaces and buildings of various heights, colours and forms.

Introducing the architecture of INA-Casa as a veil behind which an authoritarian relationship between social classes is concealed has the narrative goal of making the protagonist Mamma Roma believe that moving to this neighbourhood represents an opportunity for social mobility. As a matter of fact, Pasolini also saw the INA-Casa public housing as the site designated by the DC for class advancement. Acting as a paradigm of postwar urban transformation, INA-Casa public housing embodied in Pasolini's eyes the evolution of the subproletariat into the middle class. The depiction of INA-Casa villages in *Mamma Roma* constituted an indictment of this social advancement. Pasolini condemned this evolution, assigning the blame to the DC, who promoted and funded the plan. In fact, in building the suburbs, and therefore the city as a whole, the DC used INA-Casa to attract the middle class, the same middle class regarded as its main electorate. INA-Casa represented for the Christian Democrats a showroom where the new values of the middle class were put on display. Therefore, Pasolini saw the INA-Casa villages as the site of the *petite bourgeoisie*, rather than public housing built for and inhabited by the working class (Pasolini 1962b: 443). Pasolini's depiction of INA-Casa's social transformation has been confirmed by several historians. Marialuisa Sergio has argued that in its later years the INA-Casa plan was revised to fit middle-class aims (2002: 61). For Sergio and Paola Bonifazio, the transformation of the proletariat into the middle class was defined as a method of political control of the working class by the ruling class (Sergio 2002: 61; Bonifazio 2014: 95). Therefore, *Mamma Roma* pointed especially to what these public housing developments signified in the urban agenda of that time. One can argue that Pasolini directed his critique to what INA-Casa had become during the intervening fourteen years since it was built, and not as a plan to help the subproletariat.

Pasolini's considerations of the influence and control exercised by the DC towards the INA-Casa plan find a narrative and stylistic transposition in the different, if not opposite, ways in which Mamma Roma and Ettore experience the INA-Casa villages. The following analysis aims to show how the INA-Casa built environment is an agent in the unfolding of events and acts as a commentary on the actions of the main characters. The spatial location and movement of the two protagonists within the cinematic space help us to understand the relationship between them and the INA-Casa villages. For Mamma Roma, INA-Casa is the social and economic turning point for her and her son, the realization of the dream of living in a 'quartiere di gente per bene' [neighbourhood of good people] and of having a job that she should not be ashamed of. Mamma Roma is in a way blinded by the lights of the petite-bourgeois ideology embodied by the INA-Casa which pushes her to live in a well-to-do neighbourhood (Pasolini 1962b: 440). By contrast, Ettore experiences an unnamed sorrow, a melancholia, in inhabiting the space of the INA-Casa, which he tries to overcome by befriending the boys of the neighbourhood and hanging out with the market vendor Bruna (Silvana Corsini). Like Mamma Roma, Bruna is, in Pasolini's words, 'corrotta dalle influenze della piccola borghesia' [corrupted by the *petite bourgeoisie* influence] (Pasolini and Halliday 2014: 130). She has many traits in common with Mamma Roma: both women are sex workers and market vendors, and each takes care of a child that later dies.[7] Ettore tries to resist Mamma Roma's and Bruna's attempts to convince him to be part of the middle class, but his failure to adapt to the new petite-bourgeois value system will lead to his tragic death.

Given the protagonists' opposing ways of relating to the INA-Casa, two different perspectives can be observed: Mamma Roma exhibits (as the name itself suggests) an urban point of view, while Ettore an anti-urban one. On the one hand, Mamma Roma follows the movements and novelties of contemporary Rome by moving into a newly built public housing. On the other hand, Ettore shuns the INA-Casa to experience the green areas outside them where ruins attest to an urban past that nature has taken over. The undeveloped land outside the three INA-Casa villages in which Ettore takes refuge, with a particular emphasis on the remnants of several Roman aqueducts in front of INA-Casa Tuscolano II, functions as a narrative device, namely a counter-space to the INA-Casa villages. If Ettore's urban context looks like a prison (Brunetta 1970: 107), the unbuilt environment surrounding the INA-Casa is a space of freedom where he can express his feelings. It is a world long gone, a 'versione antiretorica di Eden' [anti-rhetorical version of Eden] (Capoferri 2017: 91–2), represented by the ruins of aqueducts and medieval buildings.

The difference between Ettore and Mamma Roma's relationship to INA-Casa becomes clear when considering the film's most featured buildings: iconic Tuscolano II's V-shaped building by Muratori and star-shaped towers by De Renzi. These structures are respectively characterized by the presence of Mamma Roma and Ettore. On the one hand, Mamma Roma binds herself to the V-shaped building, where her apartment is located, which is the embodiment of her desire to join the middle class. The V-shaped building takes on the features of scenic backdrops that are not transgressed by Mamma Roma to avoid breaking the illusion of a neighbourhood of good people. This is made explicit by the scene of her arrival when she and Ettore, once they get to the apparent entrance to the V-shaped building, decide to turn right, suggesting that if they had entered, they would have seen the real nature of the neighbourhood. On the other hand, Ettore defines his relationship with the INA-Casa by placing himself in opposition to the towers. Their contrasting modes of relating to the INA-Casa buildings are made explicit by Mamma Roma's centripetal movement towards the heart of INA-Casa Tuscolano II, the V-shaped building, and by Ettore's antithetical centrifugal move away from the outskirts of the INA-Casa villages.

Cinematography effectively reveals these two interactions with the INA-Casa built environment. The camera moves on a dolly in both scenes in which the V-shaped building appears, while it is stationary when shooting the star-shaped towers. The camera's movement is a metaphor for Mamma Roma's climbing the social ladder, while the fixed camera symbolizes Ettore's disinterest in class mobility. The protagonists' contrasting positions are also reiterated by the distance from which these buildings are filmed, which attests to the different feelings that the two characters have towards them. The V-shaped building is shot from a short distance, the camera almost enters it at the end of the walk by Ettore and Mamma Roma upon their arrival in the INA-Casa village, while the star-shaped towers are shot from the faraway green area of the aqueducts' ruins. The contrast between INA-Casa and the green expanse around it is implemented stylistically by the Director of Photography, Tonino Delli Colli. He achieves a tension between antiquity and modernity by sharply contrasting the film's black and white, using 50 ASA camera lenses (Bertini 1979: 203–4). These lenses make the disparity between the white plaster sun-drenched facade of the building and the shaded dark bricks of the ruins more visually evident.

The star-shaped towers and the ruins stand in contrast to each other. In the first shot of Ettore's second scene among the ruins, the triangular shape of the star-shaped towers' perforated gable roof, as well as that of low-rise buildings, is repeated upside down in the ruin on which Ettore rests his head (see Figure 4.2). The perforated gable roof is a central element in the architectural style of Tuscolano II and in general of the INA-Casa villages (Mornati and Cerrini 2003: 125). Of the many ruins around Tuscolano II, it is no coincidence that Pasolini chooses the one that repeats the gable's triangular shape. This similarity suggests that the nature of the ruins is opposed to that of the new neighbourhood. Ettore's haptic gesture in finding relief on the ruin suggests the beginning of a bond that

Figure 4.2 Mario De Renzi tower of INA-Casa Tuscolano II in the background; Ettore and the triangular shape ruin in the foreground. *Mamma Roma* directed by Pier Paolo Pasolini © Arco Film 1962. All rights reserved.

is established between him and these objects, symbols of the past, which assume the role of confidante for the young man's sufferings.

Ettore empathizes with the ruins because they allow him to escape the real, to stand outside of the modern social and economic system embodied by the INA-Casa, to hide from a system of production that excludes him based on his inability to adapt or adhere to the value system of the *petite bourgeoisie.* The 1950s gave rise to a consumer society that erased traditions, previously established values and former social and political norms. Since the ruins are an architecture that has lost its original function, they are excluded from the productive order of modern society. Therefore, Ettore comes to view the city from the perspective of the ruins, identifying with them because they embody an antecedent world untouched by the capitalistic society he longs to escape.

The illusory freedom offered by the ruins, divorced from productive society, allows for Ettore's temporal and spatial liberation. In the 1911 essay 'The Ruin', Georg Simmel talks about ruins in relation to nature and man, suggesting that ruins stand as the symbol of the temporary triumph of nature over the will of man, expressed by architecture. The object, now that it has become ruins, has freed itself from the intentions of its maker. No longer constrained by the architect's idea, ruins become uncertain objects, in endless becoming and change (Simmel 1965: 259–61). This indefiniteness attracts Ettore, as is evident in the scene where he plays next to them. The surrounding undeveloped area and its ruins are an extra-urban space, not defined by imposed urban or architectonic paradigms, and therefore possess a certain anarchic character. The ruins, along with Ettore, escape spatial constraint because they have lost their architectural functions and have no real use in the present. Their instability leads Ettore out of the present world, as he aspires to detach himself from it to inhabit an imaginary reality. This is made evident when he shows off his skills as an equilibrist. Here, the ruins come to life: the mise-en-scène presents Ettore under an arch with a crumbling wall to his right. Elisabetta Sartoni sees in three broken holes on this wall the two eyes and mouth of a human face (2017). As the architectural form dissolves, the weathered ruins invite interpretation; the ecstatic face produced by the ruins beside Ettore seems to comment on his equilibrist skills. Ettore wishes to mould the ruins to his own will. Positioning himself in the vault of a ruin suggests Ettore's desire to become one with it.

Ettore's desire to abandon INA-Casa and live in the green space outside them is made manifest by three attempts to move away from the bourgeois world of INA-Casa. Mamma Roma and Bruna, in their influential roles as mother and lover respectively, sabotage Ettore's efforts, because they want him to embrace their bourgeois mentality. Each of these acts of fleeing features a gift-giving, which I read as their beguiling act of corruption towards Ettore. The three escape attempts are individually shot in each of the three INA-Casa neighbourhoods featured in the film, suggesting how the public housing seems to influence the protagonists' actions. In all three scenes the iconic architecture of each of the three INA-Casa villages is underlined: INA-Casa Acilia's gable roofs houses by Perugini, INA-Casa Torre Spaccata's tower and market by Marconi, and INA-Casa Tuscolano II's star-shaped towers by De Renzi. In the first instance, Ettore walks away from INA-Casa Tuscolano II in the direction of the ruins, where he bumps into Bruna and presents a keychain to her. In the second instance, Ettore walks among the buildings of INA-Casa Torre Spaccata in the direction of another green field, then he sees Bruna, and gives her a gold locket with a cameo of the Virgin Mary. In the third instance, Ettore and Mamma Roma leave behind INA-Casa Acilia on the motorbike she has just given him as a present. The motorbike gift is an attempt by Mamma Roma to convince Ettore to behave according to her ideology. As a matter of fact, during the ride, while he is extremely grateful for the gift, she encourages him to avoid embracing the wrong values: 'Look, we ain't gonna get along if you're acting like a comrade (communist)'[8] (*Mamma Roma* 1962: 01:12:24).

In the first two scenes, Bruna distracts Ettore and directs his attention to her; she uses Ettore's sexual drive towards her in order to receive presents from him and stop him from leaving INA-Casa. In fact, after Bruna shows interest in a keychain worn by one of Ettore's new friends, Ettore gives her a keychain and the locket, with the hope of a carnal encounter. Bruna appears while Ettore is outside the INA-Casa villages or moving away from them, as to stop him from abandoning the bourgeois world. In the keychain scene, she catches him while he is resting next to a ruin. In the locket scene, she blocks his walk towards the green expanse by sitting on a concrete barrier at the end of the main artery of INA-Casa Torre Spaccata. Both the barrier and the neckline of Bruna's dress function as an impediment for Ettore in moving towards the vast green expanse behind her. Furthermore, in both of these encounters between Ettore and Bruna, death is present. In their first encounter, Ettore's gift is a keychain in the shape of a gun while, in the second, he tells Bruna he nearly died when he was a child. Both scenes foreshadow Ettore's demise, suggesting that Bruna's love will lead to his eventual death.

Only Ettore's death will make Mamma Roma question her desire to belong to the bourgeoisie world. At the news of his death, she runs towards the V-shaped building and to his room. Mamma Roma's suicide attempt by jumping from Ettore's bedroom window testifies that the only liberation from INA-Casa is *through* the V-shaped building which embodies the petite-bourgeois mentality that led to the tragic event. Mamma Roma's exit takes place at the scenic backdrop of the neighbourhood and signals her recognition of Ettore's anti-urban perspective.

If INA-Casa influences her choices and her thoughts in adopting a petite-bourgeois mentality, the pitch darkness of the dark streets she walks as a sex worker gives her a mental freedom, allowing her to re-examine the choices she has made for herself and Ettore. The dark mise-en-scène, defined by Pasolini as a 'fondo astratto' [abstract background] (Pasolini 1962b: 443), propped up by the lights of the street lamps and the bridge, is an expression of her liberation from the clout of the INA-Casa, similar to Ettore's condition when he inhabits the spaces outside the INA-Casa villages. Furthermore, in inhabiting this dark space, Mamma Roma seems to be lucidly aware of the political context of public housing in Rome, as exemplified by her anecdote on how the administration of Rome during fascism failed in building public housing for the less well-off classes by erecting poorly built villages. Sadly, Mamma Roma's acknowledgement of her choices for Ettore and the injustice of public housing in Rome takes place while she is forced by her former pimp to walk the streets. The aimless walk that leads nowhere signifies Mamma Roma's impossibility of escaping her social status.

Mamma Roma's erroneous conception of INA-Casa public housing as a tool for social climbing instead of an inclusive and connected horizon of social relations attests to the emergence of a sociopolitical scenario characterized by the exploitation and marginalization of the subproletariat, which is consigned to the suburbs and so excluded from the city. The long and extreme long shots of the vast terrain outside the three INA-Casa villages so frequent in the film substantiate the banishment of the subproletariat. Furthermore, these shots also underline how these INA-Casa villages were built outside the urban context, going against the urban policies of the time and favouring real-estate speculation (Bortolotti 1978: 249; Tafuri 1986: 23). The exclusion of the INA-Casa villages from the city is resolved in the film by banishing their inhabitants from the city. Indeed, Mamma Roma's employment is at the local market at the INA-Casa Tuscolano II, while Ettore's experience as a waiter in a Trastevere restaurant ends very quickly.

Mamma Roma's emancipatory impetus found an obstruction in the same political realities she believed in and she, overwhelmed by the dominant society, like the whole subproletariat, failed to integrate within the city, both at the micro-level of the INA-Casa public housing and at the macro-level of the city. Ettore, in his efforts to question dominant ideas, could not resist the social processes and mechanisms of the Italian culture of the time where political agency was restricted to a small part of the population, failing to find interlocutors of his kind and therefore losing control of his own identity. In trying to overturn bourgeois order, Ettore declined to work and consume, but nonetheless was unable to initiate rebellion in a liberal and capitalist democracy. His contemplation of public housing from afar was a futile attempt to neutralize the capitalism with which he was still involved.

Eventually, the INA-Casa built environment takes on the features of a third character, one which acquires an agency of its own and whose physical and architectural characteristics act as a magnet that attracts anyone towards it. As *Mamma Roma* shows, the social climbing of a *petite bourgeois* took place on a politically designated site: INA-Casa. Ettore's tragic death is a revelation for Mamma Roma on how the relocation to INA-Casa public housing fails to bring about a new start for her family. Mamma Roma's passion for the bourgeoisie expresses the erosion of the city's historical character and the emergence of a global wealth and the commodification of culture. In *Mamma Roma*, Rome failed to turn into a paradigmatic modern city that had succeeded in incorporating its history into its modernity. Instead of being ideologically and formally coherent, the city's growth and expansion were driven by the need to accommodate its postwar economy. INA-Casa public housing was too much intertwined with prewar political realities, retaining and reinforcing their established patterns and characteristics, with the result that formal and ideological views overlapped.

Mamma Roma's release coincided with a pivotal moment in Italian urbanism. In fact, six months after the film's release in February 1963, the government passed law number 60, *Liquidazione del patrimonio edilizio della Gestione INA-Casa e istituzione di un programma decennale di costruzione di alloggi per lavoratori* [Liquidation of the building stock of the INA-Casa Management and establishment of a ten-year housing construction program for workers], which ratified the termination of the INA-Casa plan. The conclusion of the INA-Casa plan represented the end of a crucial phase of reconstruction and direct State intervention in public housing. The new plan, GESCAL (GEStione CAse per i Lavoratori) [Management of Houses for Workers], allocated new funds for the construction of public housing for workers. INA-Casa had already been substituted by law 167 of 1962, *Disposizioni per favorire l'acquisizione di aree fabbricabili per l'edilizia economica e popolare* [Provisions to encourage the acquisition of building areas for economic and social housing], which incentivized the construction of cost-effective public housing, this time without state management or direct oversight. In many Italian cities, law 167 developments were staging grounds for grandiose future projects. In the late 1960s, architecture and urban planning adopted a wider view of the potential of monumental structures, the *nuova dimensione* ['new dimension']. One reason for this change was the new emphasis on 'thinking big' for the first time after fascism, on designing urban space without masking it in anti-urban styles such as the architecture of INA-Casa. Another reason was the State's inability to bring urban planning to fruition, in part because of the ineffectiveness of the regional legislations.

Mamma Roma was thus conceived at a transitional stage in the way architects and urban intellectuals thought about the city. In the fourteen years of the INA-Casa plan, Italy moved from the period of reconstruction to the economic miracle. The INA-Casa villages, whose construction resolved housing problems and created jobs immediately following the war, were themselves embedded in the new society's capitalist system, and sat uneasily at the interface of two epochs of modern Italian history. Mamma Roma's quest for a house in an INA-Casa village hides her desire for integration into a new community. Her failure resembles the failure to create a house, to quote Ludovico Quaroni, one of the main architects of INA-Casa, 'che non fosse solo una materiale difesa dagli agenti atmosferici, ma rappresentasse veramente, per ogni famiglia, la materializzazione quasi del loro impegno morale verso la vita' [that was not only a material defence against atmospheric agents, but could truly represent, for every family, the almost materialization of their moral commitment to life] (Quaroni 1960: 113).

During the initial stages of Rome's postwar urban reconstruction, *Mamma Roma* stands as a prime visual representation of the contestation around social consolidation and class mobility. In the context of neoliberal socio-economic transformation, social restructuring by leading political forces generated a contentious new spatial environment for middle-class reshaping. The INA-Casa villages stood as urban enclaves, in which social groups essential for the city's liveliness were marginalized while higher classes were increasingly exerting wealth and power. This dual structure weakened social and spatial mobility, leaving on the ground a ruinous battlefield of marginality and segregation.

Notes

1   For a general introduction to *Mamma Roma*, see among others Capoferri (2017); Rhodes (2007); Zabagli (2019).

2   Piano incremento occupazione operaia case per lavoratori, *1. Suggerimenti, norme e schemi per la elaborazione e presentazione dei progetti. Bandi dei concorsi*, Roma (1949); *2. Suggerimenti, esempi e norme per la progettazione urbanistica. Progetti tipo*, Roma (1949); 3. *Guida per l'esame dei progetti delle costruzioni Ina-Casa da realizzare nel secondo settennio*, Roma (1956); 4. *Norme per le costruzioni del secondo settennio estratte da delibere del Comitato di attuazione del Piano e del Consiglio direttivo della gestione Ina-Casa*, Roma (1956).

3   For a general overview of the INA-Casa villages in Rome, see Segarra Lagunes, Guccione and Vittorini (2002).

4   Pasolini shot two scenes in Torre Spaccata. One of them was removed in postproduction. In the screenplay, it was titled *Alla fontanella* (*At the water fountain*). The scene, which follows the one in which Ettore is attacked by the boys of the neighbourhood because he doesn't want to share Bruna with them, sees Ettore wiping his face from the blood of the fist fight at a drinking fountain. There he meets an old homosexual who gives him compliments that Ettore doesn't like and for which he pushes him away. Roberto Chiesi puts forward the hypothesis that this scene may have been censored, see Chiesi 2019.

5   Cecafumo was the name for the area where the INA-Casa Tuscolano was later built.

6   Though historians always considered Acilia among the fascist *borgate*, recent scholarship argues that Acilia was not a *borgata* but simply a village. See Petaccia and Greco (2016: 107–8).

7   Bruna tells Ettore about her son who fell sick at an early age and passed away soon after.

8   All film dialogue from *Mamma Roma* (1962) is translated from the original Italian by the author.

References

Beretta Anguissola, Luigi (1963), *I 14 anni del piano INA-casa*, Roma: Staderini.

Bertini, Antonio (1979), *Teoria e tecnica del film in Pasolini*, Roma: Bulzoni.

Bonifazio, Paola (2014), *Schooling in Modernity: The Politics of Sponsored Films in Postwar Italy*, Toronto: University of Toronto Press.

Bortolotti, Lando (1978), *Storia della politica edilizia in Italia: proprietà, imprese edili e lavori pubblici dal primo dopoguerra ad oggi (1919–1970)*, Roma: Editori Riuniti.

Brunetta, Gian Piero (1970), *Forma e parola nel cinema, Il film muto, Pasolini, Antonioni*, Padova: Liviana.

Capoferri, Federica (2017), *La Roma di Mamma Roma*, Roma: Palombi Editori.

Chiesi, Roberto (2019), 'La censura occulta e i boicottaggi', in Franco Zabagli (ed), *Mamma Roma: un film scritto e diretto da Pier Paolo Pasolini*, 158–79, Bologna, Pordenone: Cineteca di Bologna; Cinemazero.

Ciucci, Giorgio and Francesco Dal Co (1991), *Atlante dell'architettura italiana del Novecento*, Milano: Electra.

Conforto, Cina, Gabriele De Giorgi, Alessandra Muntoni and Marcello Pazzaglini (1977), *Il Dibattito Architettonico in Italia, 1945–1975*, Rome: Bulzoni.

Curl, James Stevens (2006), *A Dictionary of Architecture and Landscape Architecture*, Oxford: Oxford University Press.

Di Biagi, Paola (2010a), *La grande ricostruzione: il piano INA-Casa e l'Italia degli anni Cinquanta*, Roma: Donzelli.

Di Biagi, Paola (2010b), 'La «città pubblica» e l'INA-Casa', in Paola Di Biagi (ed), *La grande ricostruzione: il piano INA-Casa e l'Italia degli anni Cinquanta*, 3–31, Roma: Donzelli.

Farabegoli, Johnny (2002), 'Oltre Il Neorealismo. Il Piano Fanfani a Roma', in Paola Di Biagi (ed), *La Grande Ricostruzione*, 431–41, Roma: Donzelli.

Mamma Roma (1962), [FILM] Dir. Pier Paolo Pasolini, Italy: Arco Film.

Mancini, Giulio (2011), *Tra Roma e il mare: storie di Acilia e dintorni: Casalbernocchi, Malafede, Casette Pater, San Giorgio, Casalpalocco e Axa, Infernetto, Dragona, San Francesco*, Ostia Antica (RM): Publidea95.

Mornati, Stefania and Filippo Cerrini (2003), 'Il quartiere Tuscolano a Roma (1950–1960)', in Pier Giovanni Bardelli, Rinaldo Capomolla and Rosalia Vittorini (eds), *L'architettura INA CASA (1949–1963): aspetti e problemi di conservazione e recupero*, 122–39, Roma: Gangemi Editore.

Pasolini, Pier Paolo (1962a), *Mamma Roma*, Milano: Rizzoli.

Pasolini, Pier Paolo (1962b), '"Mamma Roma", Ovvero, Dalla Responsabilità Individuale Alla Responsabilità Collettiva', *Filmcritica*, XIII (125): 440–50.

Pasolini, Pier Paola (1991), *Le regole di un'illusione: i film, il cinema*, Roma: Associazione 'Fondo Pier Paolo Pasolini'.

Pasolini, Pier Paolo (2000), 'I campi di concentramento', in Walter Siti and Silvia De Laude (eds), *Romanzi e Racconti, Vol I (1946–1961)*, 1459–62, Milano: Mondadori.

Pasolini, Pier Paolo and Jon Halliday (2014), *Pasolini Su Pasolini. Conversazioni Con Jon Halliday*, Parma: Guanda.

Petaccia, Paolo and Andrea Greco (2016), *Borgate: l'utopia razional-popolare*, Roma: Officina Edizioni.

Piano incremento occupazione operaia: Case per lavoratori. Legge Fanfani del 28-2-49, n.43. 1, 1 (1949), Roma: F. Damasso.

Pilat, Stephanie Zeier (2016), *Reconstructing Italy: The Ina-Casa Neighborhoods of the Postwar Era*, London: Routledge.

Poretti, Sergio (2003), 'Dal Piano al Patrimonio INA Casa', in Pier Giovanni Bardelli, Rinaldo Capomolla and Rosalia Vittorini (eds), *L'architettura INA CASA (1949–1963): aspetti e problemi di conservazione e recupero*, 8–17, Roma: Gangemi.

Powers, Alan (2009), 'Organic Architecture', in Patrick Goode, Stanford Anderson and Sir Colin St. John Wilson (eds), *The Oxford Companion to Architecture*, 678–9, Oxford: Oxford University Press.

Quaroni, Ludovico (1960), 'L'abitazione per Le Famiglie a Basso Reddito in Italia', *Urbanistica*, 31 (7): 106–13.

Rhodes, John David (2007), *Stupendous, Miserable City: Pasolini's Rome*, Minneapolis: University of Minnesota Press.

Sartoni, Eleonora (2017), '(Mamma) Roma between Archaic and Modern Italy: Urbanisation and the Destruction of Poetical Dwelling', *Senses of Cinema*, 77. Available online: https://www.sensesofcinema.com/2015/pier-paolo-pasolini/mamma-roma/ (accessed 1 March 2022).

Segarra Lagunes, Maria Margarita, Margherita Guccione and Rosalia Vittorini, eds. (2002), *Guida ai quartieri romani INA Casa*, Roma: Gangemi.

Sergio, Marialuisa Lucia (2002), 'Le organizzazioni economiche e la società civile', *Fanfani e la casa: gli anni Cinquanta e il modello italiano di welfare state: il piano INA-Casa*, Roma: Rubbettino.

Simmel, Georg (1965), 'The Ruin', in *Essays on Sociology, Philosophy, and Aesthetics*, 259–66, New York: Harper & Row.

Tafuri, Manfredo (1986), *Storia dell'architettura italiana, 1944–1985*, Torino: Einaudi.

Zabagli, Franco (2019), *Mamma Roma: un film scritto e diretto da Pier Paolo Pasolini*, Bologna: Cineteca di Bologna.

5

Aerial transitions: Drones and domestic space in the *banlieue*

Isabelle McNeill

Introduction

In J. G. Ballard's 1975 novel, *High-Rise*, the character Richard Wilder, a television producer, imagines how he will film his documentary about the vast, 'Alcatraz blocks' of the high-rise building in which he lives, using a helicopter to film the exteriors: 'in his mind's eye he could already see a long, sixty-second zoom, slowly moving from the whole building in frame to a close-up of a single apartment, one cell in this nightmare termitary' (2014: 52) Indeed, the commanding vertical structure of high-rise buildings seems to call out for aerial photography to capture it in the frame, enabling full apprehension. Yet Wilder also imagines the possibility of zooming in to the single 'cell' of this complex social enclosure: the tower block is shown to elicit a desire for intimate knowing within the apparent impersonality of its geometric architecture, a desire to master its imposing scale by focusing in on just one of its 'termite' dwellings.

In the high-rise, a mass of existence is implied by the stacked layers of windows. Intimate and individual lives proliferate within the multiple, uniform boxes of the block structure, triggering a desire to see and know. In this, it seems that the verticality of high-rise architecture heightens a broader urban phenomenon, since cities typically encompass a density of human lives that are both proximate and separate: glimpsed yet unknown. Cinema, with its capacity to juxtapose scale and proximity through camera movement and editing, is therefore particularly well-suited to the visualization of urban life. As Pamela Robertson Wojcik has noted of the genre of film she calls 'the apartment plot', there is a tendency 'to use aerial shots or other mechanisms to lay out a larger urban space before narrowing to focus on the apartment as a microcosm of the city', thereby suggesting 'that each story is one among the millions possible' (2018: 4). In reflecting upon such transitions from aerial urban shot to intimate interiors, I will consider the example of a particular example of high-rise block, namely the French HLM, or 'habitation à loyer modéré' (low-rent social housing), notably as it is filmed by drone shots. Where Ballard's novel is set in housing designed for middle-class occupants (with a finely grained hierarchy) and Robertson Wojcik's 'apartment plot' may take place in any urban apartment, my focus is on social housing in the low-income, postcolonial neighbourhoods of the Parisian *banlieue*.

When reflecting on the *banlieue*, the question of desired knowledge, sought through both the elevated overview and singular domestic life evoked in Ballard's text, takes on a critical urgency. As I will outline below, the context of French colonial and urban history, including the history of post-Second World War urban development in France, is essential for situating relations between architecture, vision and knowledge in the *banlieue*. Discursively overdetermined and stigmatized, the so-called *banlieue* is subject to both State and media surveillance. Beyond the visual connection between the aerial view and the high-rise evoked above, the *banlieue*'s association with a threatening alterity and its media representation as a 'battleground' also suggests a connection with the military history of drones.

This connection is made explicit in Olivier Babinet's 2016 documentary *Swagger*, on which this chapter focuses. The film documents the thoughts and testimony of young people attending the Collège Debussy in Aulnay-Sous-Bois, a commune of Seine-Saint-Denis outside Paris. The opening drone shots gliding between tower blocks in nearby Sevran, where one of the film's subjects lives, are later echoed in a dystopic sci-fi sequence where police drones send multiple surveillance probes into the towers. Through a collaboration with young inhabitants of the *banlieue*, the film makes us reflect critically on the presumed necessity to know and control the interior spaces of *banlieue* housing. In so doing, the film pays homage to yet also moves away from Mathieu Kassovitz's canonical *banlieue* film, *La Haine* (1995), which also features creative use of an aerial transition between airspace and HLM domestic space. I will argue that *Swagger* proposes a different relationship to community, where the film and its fantastical elements both arise from collaboration between the filmmaker and the young inhabitants of the *banlieue*, who are shown to be articulate experts in *banlieue* life and architecture.

Beginning with reflections on the non-human – or inhuman – gaze afforded by drone cameras, this chapter will then analyse the relationship between surveillance, freedom and community in cinematic depictions of aerial movements in the *banlieue*. With reference to *La Haine* and *District 13: Ultimatum* (Patrick Alessandrin 2009), amongst other works, I will contextualize my reading of *Swagger* in cinematic traditions of the drone shot in urban spaces and the *banlieue* in particular.[1] While the invasive potential of drone vision recalls a long scholarly association between elevated perspectives and mastery or policing, I will suggest that *Swagger* evokes alternative possibilities in the fluid movements between *banlieue* airspace and HLM interiors.

Drone visions

Drones are incorporated in multi-faceted ways in *Swagger* and I will return to aspects of these sequences throughout the essay. As context for a discussion of drone visuality, however, I outline here some key elements of the drone shots in the film. The opening pre-title sequence presents us with a nocturnal, lateral, aerial view over Aulnay-Sous-Bois, gliding backwards to take in HLM towers in Sevran known as the Tours Marron. Floating through air between these 1970s housing blocks and their illuminated windows, the camera eventually homes in on a specific window, where we see a young man sitting at a sewing machine. Eventually the camera moves through the open window into the interior space. A few sequences later, after twelve-year-old Naïla has spoken about some of the problems she sees with vertical architecture in the *banlieue*, another drone shot starts at a teenage boy's bedroom and slowly glides out into the air, eventually taking in the whole estate (the 'cité haute') of the Tours Marron. Much later still, after the shy Aïssatou ponders dystopian futures, comes the sci-fi sequence which brings drones themselves into our field of vision. This scene depicts articulated drones, with robot-like 'heads' and police insignia, arriving in the area of the Tours Marron and circling around the towers, while other towers in the background are shown with plumes of smoke rising from their structures. At one point a control interface overlays the image, giving the impression that we are looking from the point-of-view of the drone, or drone operator.

In *Swagger*, therefore, drones offer specific ways of seeing, as well as being seen as objects in themselves. They enable us as viewers to travel fluidly between and into the high apartments of the tall buildings but also to visualize drones as invasive agents of State control, whose gaze we may share as viewers. This means thinking about the mobile, machine vision that drones make possible whilst also considering drones as a visual and conceptual object. The sci-fi elements also provoke reflection on both the military origins of drones and their diversified use in what Lisa Parks has termed the 'vertical field', which is 'an extensive realm of movement, occupation, appropriation, and demonstration ... a dynamic field of power and mediation' (2018: 3). The unique visual possibilities of drones include but go beyond aerial perspectives, making possible a heightened and fluid mobility that, amongst other possibilities, can transition between exterior and interior space in cinema without requiring a cut. As Anthony McCosker argues, '(t)he drone's *motility*, its "autonomous" or self-sustaining vertical and lateral movement differentiates it from fixed surveillance devices ... and the mobility of personal mobile phone cameras' (2016: np). Drones are not only flying cameras. Contemporary drones are semi-automated, connected at a distance to both satellites and human operators, and rely for their performance on multiple sensors, wireless networks, software and algorithms. They are hybrid machines; Adam Rothstein calls them 'aerial robotics platforms' (2020: 75), pointing out that they share technology with numerous other systems: surveillance, algorithmic, military and robotic. Yet the presence of a camera remains a defining feature of the drone, which leads McCosker to argue that they are the locus of a new, emergent visuality (2016: np), a new kind of 'camera consciousness' that he explores further with Rowan Wilken in *Automating Vision* (2020). This camera consciousness implies the adoption of drone visuality into a popular and regulatory imaginary, as part of a wider posthuman shift in which vision and other data run through and between humans and technology, since drone operation also depends, of course, on human skill and labour.

Drone visuality perpetuates the relation between seeing and control evoked, among others, by Michel de Certeau in *The Practice of Everyday Life* – where the view from above or 'map view' aligns with the controlling gaze of governance, making space legible (1984: 92). Furthermore, as Stephen Graham has argued, the military development and deployment of drones move us towards an even more violent situation, where 'weapons and imaging systems are so totally integrated that the acts of seeing and killing become effectively one and the same' (2018: 68). Cormac Deane has looked at drones from the perspective of the 'control room' – a real and fantasized military setup that has become increasingly panoptic with its augmented mobility, highlighting how, post-Second World War, 'conflict readiness is always switched on' (2016: np). *Swagger* imaginatively manifests these conceptions of drone visuality as an instrument of vertical, military control. In its police drones sequence, we hear a loudspeaker announcement that a 'state of emergency' has been declared, authorizing house searches to take place at any time. Evoking sci-fi and action movies, such as those in the Marvel franchise, the sequence also presents us with a 'fantasy user interface' (FUI), with a viewfinder, scrolling figures and radar grid reference apparently detailing the destination of the search probes.[2] This implies the perspective of all-seeing drones with the capacity to process and marshal vast reams of data. For Deane, the FUI is 'a cybernetic system that includes humans and machines', creating an aesthetic rendition of 'the process in which a system takes on properties (such as future-vision) in an autonomous fashion that it did not previously have' (2016: np). Deane contextualizes these cinematic developments in present-day military use of computing and communications technologies, whose continual data processing means that, 'even if war is not actually engaged, it is permanently virtually engaged, and as a result the legal-political exception becomes the norm' (2016: np). The sci-fi drone sequences in *Swagger* therefore reflect a tendency in military and technological development towards highly fluid, supple surveillance and control mechanisms. Imagined within the French context, this drone visuality evokes the *banlieue* and its housing blocks as a volatile terrain of conflict, in which military response is always ready to be 'switched on'.

Swagger's use of drone shots outside of the sci-fi sequences, however, contrasts the authoritarian police drones with images that unfold unexpected and unusual visions of both exterior and interior *banlieue* space. Moreover, as I will discuss below, the sci-fi drones are integrated into documentary space, making us question the supposed transparency of documentary representation, and consequently any secure sense of 'knowing' the *banlieue* through media imagery. Scholars such as McCosker and Joanna Zylinska have noted that, despite their military use and origins, drones may offer alternative and creative possibilities. Drones create, as McCosker says, 'a heterogenous assemblage that places perception outside of a singular, fixed perceiving subject' (2016: np). Its multi-directional movement and implication in non-human networks (including dissemination on social media) open drone vision up to protestors, artists and activists as well as the military and police. This ambivalent potential is taken up by Zylinska to support her argument for the creative power of non-human photography, which she views as a mode, full of vitality, that is liberated from certain habits of the human 'I/Eye' (2017: 17). While she focuses on photography specifically as a cut in duration (and distinguished, therefore, from the moving image) Zylinska's argument will inform my reading of *Swagger* in her suggestion that the non-human might afford ways of seeing and thinking beyond the power-steeped myopia of the human gaze: 'by tearing the myopic eye from the perspective-driven bipedal body and embracing the distributed machinic-corporeal vision, it may be possible to see the drone as more than just a killing machine – although, of course, there are no guarantees' (2017: 79). I will suggest that despite the apparently invasive aspect of drone shots that traverse *banlieue* airspace and enter the domestic space of public housing, *Swagger*'s use of drones does indeed contribute to alternative ways of seeing and feeling the *banlieue*.

Banlieue visions

The term *banlieue* in French refers simply to the suburbs or outskirts of a city. In the case of Paris, this means any part of its wider area that is outside the tight circle of the ring road or 'périphérique'. However, as Alec Hargreaves points out, 'popular usage of the word has been reconfigured and narrowed to denote certain types of highly stigmatised working-class neighbourhoods' (2013: 212). In his 2007 study of French urban policy, Mustafa Dikeç demonstrated how the term *banlieue*, 'stands for alterity, insecurity and deprivation' (2007: 8). It has become a term to designate zones often perceived as threatening – a threat specifically associated with immigration and ethnic otherness. The history of these neighbourhoods and their tower blocks of cheap social housing is indeed bound up with French colonial history, since amongst their uses, these HLM blocks, first constructed from the late 1940s to the 1960s, were to replace the appalling shanty towns that had previously housed migrant workers from the colonies, brought over as cheap labour following the Second World War. The enduring legacy of colonialism and French anxieties about national identity both feed into and are shaped by mass media representations of the *banlieue*, which in turn legitimizes State policy, in a process that Dikeç terms 'spatial injustice' (2007: 155). In her 2019 book, *Identités Françaises*, Mame-Fatou Niang has rigorously traced these interconnections and shown the process by which the so-called *banlieue* has become perceived monolithically as racialized, other and separate, through what she describes as a discursive 'hyperfocalisation' (3). Niang characterizes the *banlieue* as 'un espace symbolique dans lequel le réel, les représentations et les projections s'entremêlent et se valident par la répétition du discours' (30–31) [a symbolic space in which reality, representation and projection mingle and become validated through discursive repetition].[3] The idea of 'projection' is especially significant, since it evokes a conjunction of the voyeuristic desire to see and know this 'threatening' space with preconceptions and stereotypes that reiterate reassuringly familiar images. Indeed, that the *banlieue* functions as a focal point of both curiosity and anxiety is in keeping with a colonial logic of murderous fascination with otherness. The *banlieue's* multi-ethnic populations are often discussed in terms of French national identity, which they are thought to threaten; the supposed policy of integration therefore repeatedly manifests in segregation. As Achille Mbembe has argued in his book on *Necropolitics*:

> Colonizing broadly consisted in a permanent work of separation: on one side, my living body; on the other, all those 'body-things' surrounding it and 'flesh-meats' exist for me … the Others that I can bring to myself but with whom I can never genuinely entertain relations of reciprocity or mutual implication'.
>
> (2019: 46)

This segregation is often rehearsed in film imaginings of the *banlieue*, which oppose it to the supposedly civilized or white (and therefore supposedly 'properly' French) centre of Paris. One of the most spectacular fantasies articulating this colonial separation can be found in the two Luc Besson-produced *District 13* films. Made in 2004 and 2009, these films imagine a near-future in which the *banlieue* has become so unstable that it has been enclosed behind a wall. It is significant that walls, for Mbembe, are the epitome of the contemporary normalization of enmity and powerfully destructive fears of annihilation (2019: 43). Behind this wall, these films depict the *banlieue* as having degenerated into warring internal factions, fighting for control of drugs and weapons trades, in a hyperbolic version of news media images of riots and burning cars. Indeed, a dizzying, simulated drone shot in *District 13: Ultimatum* (2009) takes the viewer on a high-speed tour, rising up and over the wall then down between the tower blocks, to explore voyeuristically and fluidly a dangerous space marked by its otherness to traditional, white, French culture. The hyperbolic voyeurism of this sequence evokes the violent separation and attendant fascinated gaze of postcolonial necropolitics. Crucially, Niang's work demonstrates how representation of the *banlieue* is dominated by 'outsider' voices, rather than those who live there, signalling, 'l'urgence de mettre leurs résidents au centre de la production de discours sur ces quartiers' (61) [the urgent need to place residents from these neighbourhoods at the centre of discursive production about them].

Olivier Babinet's film *Swagger* is an attempt to do just that, since the documentary is driven by the voices and ideas of young people attending the Collège Claude Debussy in Aulnay-Sous-Bois. Babinet undertook two projects with the school pupils, over a period of two years, that included filmmaking workshops and resulted in a music video, *Life on Earth* (for a song by the band

Tomorrow's World, 2014), images from which are re-used in *Swagger*. Although Babinet is a white director who does not originate from Aulnay-Sous-Bois, nor Sevran, his motivation for making *Swagger* came from working with the young people, whose often difficult lives reminded him of his own youth in a neighbourhood of Strasbourg (Pacaud 2021). He describes in an interview his desire to convey the heterogeneity of a *banlieue* youth often reduced to menacing stereotypes, observing that news media often shoot briefly and from far away. Babinet explains that he wanted to go closer, spend longer, and show us the human beings 'behind the hoodie' (Ben-Youssef 2018). The film's use of surreal and incongruous imagery evokes Babinet's signature as an auteur, notable from work such as the situationist TV series *Le Bidule* (1999–2000) and ecological fable *Poissonsexe* (2019). Nevertheless, the film's collaborative origins are manifest, both because the young people are given space to speak – we hear their voices, not the director's – and because the editing positions their ideas as prompts for the subsequent shot, driving the film's direction, as subsequent analysis will show. In this, the final edit reflects the process behind the film: the sci-fi elements emerged from a prompt that Babinet set eighth-grade students (age 13–14) to imagine Aulnay-sous-bois in 100 years' time (Pacaud 2021).

The opening drone shots are crucial in the way they reframe a vision of the *banlieue* and encourage an act of listening to the voices of *banlieue* inhabitants. These drone shots are devoid of diegetic sound. Instead, we hear the dreamy electronic arpeggios of music composed for the film by JB Dunckel (often associated with his former band, Air) and the voice of Régis – though we have not yet learned his name. Régis is speculating about Aulnay: 'I don't know if it existed before, or after, I don't know. I have no idea. Maybe it was a forest, I dunno. Then they built the city' (*Swagger* 2016: 00:58-01:11). As he evokes the forest, the drone camera moves backwards, and the Tours Marron come into view. The familiar geometry of these 1970s tower blocks is abstracted from conventional media imagery in which the view from on high tends to map the segregated space of the *banlieue*. For example, in a France 3 reportage from 1994 on Aulnay-3000 (an HLM housing estate), a high-angle pan across the area cuts to a shot of a map, with a man's finger showing motorways that cut off the inhabitants of the estate from the surrounding city (Figure 5.1). While sympathetic to the plight of the inhabitants, such a mapping gaze aligns with the perspective of authorities and outsiders, viewing the 'problem' from a distance. Transforming the urban site into 'a text that lies before one's eyes', as de Certeau puts it (1984: 92), this legible audio-visual presentation of a problematic spatial separation here reinforces that separation, through 'the imaginary totalizations produced by the eye' (1984: 93).

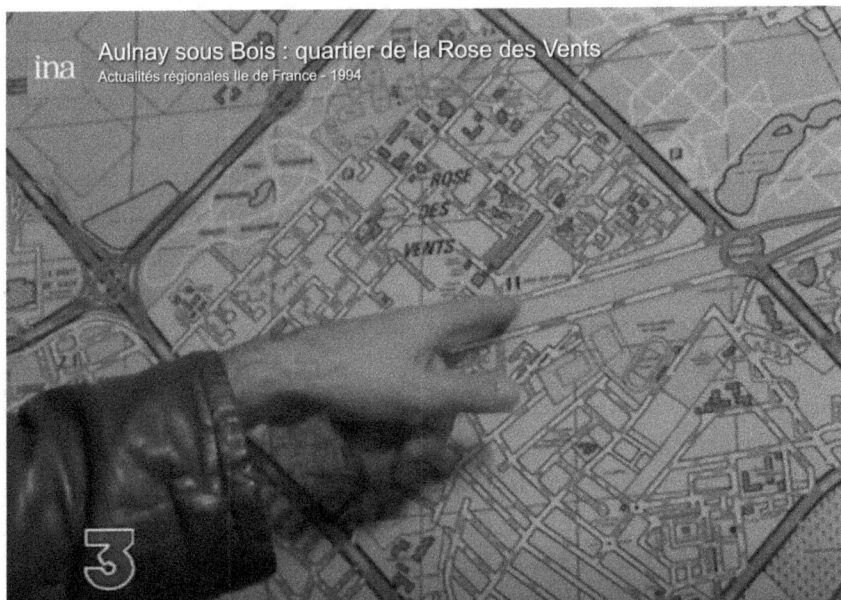

Figure 5.1 'It's a bit like borders. There is a feeling of ghettoization'. 'Aulnay sous Bois: quartier de la Rose des Vents', Actualités regionales Île de France. France 3, 19 October 1994 © INA.fr. All rights reserved.

The hand of Luc Jerabek, a public service officer for the local area, acts as a guide from the perspective of local authorities, explaining that the motorways create a feeling of 'ghettoization'. These indications distance the viewer from lived experience of the estate, as Jerabek suggests that the motorways act as *frontières*, or 'borders'. This produces a self-confirming 'knowledge' of life in public housing in the *banlieue* as an inaccessible territory (behind 'borders'), undesirable and deprived. In addition to this totalizing and distant perspective, media imagery of large-scale housing in the *banlieue* tends to focus on its monotony, greyness and imposing size, as Camille Canteux's study of media representations of large-scale social housing in France has shown (2014: 198–9).

In the drone shots at the start of *Swagger*, by contrast, the space is not immediately mapped in relation to borders and segregation, while the Tours Marron appear neither overwhelming nor monotonous. The dreamlike music and Régis's commentary, in substituting for diegetic sounds of urban space, defamiliarize our gaze over the towers as the drone camera glides fluidly past. There is 'synchresis' – as Michel Chion puts it, 'a spontaneous and irresistible weld' (1994: 63) – between the nocturnal image of the cityscape speckled with lights, the jewel-like illuminated window squares of the Tours Marron and the sparkling arpeggios of Dunckel's synthesizer score. An imagined past is evoked in Régis's mention of forests, further distancing us from default associations with tower blocks and urban life. Even the timbre of Régis's voice has a slight echo, appearing without a framework of recognition; only later might we connect this vocal apparition with the charismatic teenager. In these first shots, the *banlieue*, which Rosemary Wakeman has described as an 'overdone, over-imagined, over-cinematized space' (2013: 84) is insistently unknown (Régis repeatedly emphasizes a lack of knowledge of Aulnay's past). Instead, the *banlieue* and its high-rise HLM tower blocks become sites of multiple possibilities. The drone shot is crucial to this renewed vision since its nonhuman 'eye' detaches us from habitual perception.

The first thirty seconds of the film, therefore, prompt new ways of seeing the HLM structure. We are distanced from pre-existing imagery and knowledge of such places and instead notice aesthetic beauty in these windows glowing yellow, blue or pink against the shadowy forms of the tower blocks. However, the film quickly takes us from this dreamy perspective into a political reflection. The voice of Naïla (again, we do not know her yet) takes over from Régis to give her idea about the social history of Aulnay. Naïla, who we later learn is twelve, explains that in the past lots of 'people of French origin' lived here, but they moved away when the 'Blacks and Arabs moved in' (*Swagger* 2016: 01:40). Her commentary manifests an awareness of the racialized otherness of places like Aulnay-Sous-Bois and Sevran. She evokes the 'white flight' racism connected to the representational history of HLMs, which, during the 1970s, became increasingly associated with immigrant populations in media discourse (Canteux 2014: 281). Rather than plunging us back into stereotype, however, Naïla's commentary ensures that the aerial images are not framed as purely aesthetic or open. Heard in context of promotional materials and posters for the film, which focus on images of Black or Arab schoolchildren, we understand Naïla's words as coming from the perspective of a non-white inhabitant of Aulnay, which is important given Niang's point above about how outsider discourse tends to define and restrict these spaces. Yet by focusing on her words, not a visual image of her, her agency as a speaker and thinker is emphasized, putting her in a position of knowing an urban environment that we have just begun to 'unknow'. That Naïla's commentary is socio-political is especially significant, given that, as Dikeç argues, 'the status of *banlieues* as well-delimited spaces with negative connotations undermined the possibilities of opening up spaces of politics in such areas' (2007: 17). Dikeç here draws on Jacques Rancière's concept of the 'distribution of the sensible', in which the boundaries of meaningful discourse are already shored up by the powerful and authoritative, those with 'legitimate' voices: 'Such distributions define legitimate interlocutors, make sensible certain issues while making other imperceptible, distinguish voices from noises' (2007: 20). The two voices we hear on the soundtrack at the start offer divergent understandings of *banlieue* history, both of which are disconnected from media images of the *banlieue* youth as primarily associated with delinquency, radicalization and violent anger (see Niang 2019: 54). Combined with a shift outside 'human' perception in the floating drone shot, this opening sequence of the film expands the viewer's perceptive field, enabling an active listening to alternative voices who tend not to be legitimated within hegemonic discourse.

Transitions into domestic space

As mentioned above, the drone shots in *Swagger* do not only glide over the towers, they also enter – and depart from – domestic space inside the HLM. These transitions between inside and outside, made possible by drone cameras, recall the cameraman Richard Wilder's fantasy in *High-Rise*, cited at the start of this chapter, in which the wider structure of the building is contrasted with the individual 'cell'. While they might, therefore, appear as another manifestation of an intrusive outsider gaze on the *banlieue*, their use in *Swagger* in fact contributes to the expansion of the perceptive field begun in the very opening shots of the film. I will consider three features of these transitions, to show how *Swagger* creatively deploys drone visuality to counter the hyperfocalized discourse (to return to Niang's term) that has accrued around *banlieue* housing and its inhabitants: the interweaving of documentary and fantasy, the citation of cinematic memory, and the evocation of community through connections and networks.

The transitions from airspace into interiors focus on Régis, whose voice is also the first we heard on the soundtrack. The first of these passages occurs shortly after the opening shots discussed above. The drone camera approaches one of the Tours Marron and we notice an open window, through which we glimpse a figure operating a sewing machine. As the camera drifts closer, we begin to hear the diegetic whirring of the sewing machine alongside Dunckel's music – notable because of the absence of other diegetic sounds. The camera finally enters the open window and draws closer to a Black youth (Régis, as we later discover) who is sewing a piece of brightly-patterned yellow, red and black Ankara fabric by the light of a desk lamp; he does not acknowledge the appearance of a drone camera in his room. We stay with him for a fleeting moment as he sews before cutting to a shot of a full moon in the night sky. This movement into Regis's intimate interior and private activity seems to set up a documentary procedure akin to Richard Wilder's, a shift from an ensemble view of the buildings to a singular individual dwelling. This impression is reinforced to an extent by the following sequence, in which we see several of the other children featured in the film in their bedrooms, though this time shown through a series of cuts. The drone's motility, enabling a fluid camera movement between exterior and interior space, thus underscores the power of cinema, as a technology of vision, to document and expose lives inside HLM housing that we might not otherwise know. In this sense, the traversal of the window frame makes emphatically visible the process constantly at work in editing, which also permits entry through the cut.

Yet the interweaving of fantastical images into the film troubles any secure sense of documentary knowledge of such intimate spaces and makes us critically aware of the act of looking. The sci-fi sequence is not segregated from the 'documentary' shots of the *banlieue*, but instead both echoes them structurally and seeps into them through editing and sound design. Hints of the sci-fi drones' arrival appear in previous shots, blurring the boundaries between documentary and fantasy. As Abou Fofana speaks, filmed from a low angle at the Collège Claude Débussy, drones are glimpsed passing over the skylight above his head, their movement underscored by a whooshing sound, which continues in the next shot of a mysterious circle of stones under a motorway overpass. During the main sci-fi sequence, we once again find ourselves in Régis's domestic interior (this time through a cut). The image has been colour graded to match the warm, amber glow of the futuristic shots of drone policing, suggesting diegetic simultaneity. As Régis perfects his make-up in the bathroom mirror, his mother's voice calling for him to hurry, one of the miniature spider-like robot probes we have seen launched by the drones scuttles up the wooden frame of his mirror, presumably gathering surveillance data.[4] In this sequence, the police drones' dissemination of these miniature probes into people's dwellings both echoes and contrasts with the actions of the film's own drone camera. Both sequences operate a movement between aerial shots of the HLM buildings and an optical penetration of domestic space. However, the drifting motion and ethereal soundtrack of the opening drone shots discussed above are markedly contrasted with the stressful sirens, loudspeakers and mechanical noise of the drones in the sci-fi sequence. Yet, just at the end of the opening sequence, as the film's title appears, we hear the same sounds of shouting (given in subtitles as 'cop cars coming!' but rather unintelligible in the original French) and sirens that underpin the sci-fi sequence, creating a blurring of boundaries between documentary and fictional space. Such seepage elicits a critical reflection on the practice of documentary in the context of the *banlieue*, drawing attention to the problematic connection between media hyperfocalization, police surveillance and filmmaking set in the *banlieue*.

At the same time, the status of our knowledge of the film's subjects and their intimate lives is called into question by this foregrounding of artifice and its embedding in the documentary image. Instead, this hybrid imagining of the *banlieue* offers a different kind of knowledge, one that illuminates the creative and political imagination of the young HLM inhabitants. The film is edited to indicate that the sci-fi elements (among other incongruous images) arise from the subjectivity and critical reflection of the young people documented in the film. Immediately before the main sci-fi sequence, for example, Aïssatou expresses her doubts about the future, speculating that, 'maybe the future will already be the end of the world', evoking a dystopic vision of decimated buildings and raging fire, 'like in war films' (01:00:38-1:00:52). The images depicting the *banlieue* as a war zone therefore seem to arise from Aïssatou's thoughts. It is not a question, however, of the filmmaker displaying his creativity by visualizing Aïssatou's ideas, since other voices also frame and articulate the sci-fi scene. The shot of Régis tracked by a miniature robot in his bathroom is immediately followed by Naïla describing her idea of what surveillance will be like in the future: 'drones will be so small, they'll be as tiny as insects ... and then in the place where you spend the most time, it will spy on you' (01:01:44-01:02:00). Here, the film's genesis as a collaborative project, between the young people and Babinet, is materialized as fictional images emerge from and return to the voices of the Collège Claude Débussy pupils. A collaborative creativity and agency are therefore brought to the fore, resisting any conception of documentary as voyeuristic capture of the lives inside the HLM.

The movement into and out of domestic interiors in *Swagger* uses subtle clues to echo an earlier, iconic sequence of movement between HLM interiors in Mathieu Kassovitz's famous *banlieue* film, *La Haine* (1995). Although the 'unmanned helicopter' – a proto-drone camera – does not physically enter the housing blocks in *La Haine*, the sequence stages a connection between interior spaces and airspace that is recapitulated in *Swagger*. It is the sound of a helicopter's whirring blades that cues a connection between aerial sequences in the two films. In *La Haine*, the sequence begins inside a young man's bedroom, the character Hubert, who is smoking a spliff whilst listening to music. A shout from outside catches his attention and he goes over to the window. As he gets up, a cut takes us to a perspective outside his bedroom, with a mobile camera approaching his window (like the approach to Régis's bedroom window in *Swagger*). Hubert opens the window, and the camera comes to rest on a close-up as he leans out to gaze down into the courtyard. The shots that follow could be read as Hubert's point of view, though they do not align spatially with his perspective. In a high-angle shot, we catch sight of two of the other protagonists, Saïd and Vinz, walking across the courtyard. Rather than following them, however, the camera lets them walk out of the frame and then moves in the opposite direction, showing various young men hanging out in the courtyard, and kids on a playground structure, before finally rising to take in the windows of the houses on the other side of the central courtyard. Here we see another man framed by the window, swivelling a large sound system speaker to direct it over the housing estate. When the camera moves over the youths and kids in the courtyard that we hear the distinct sounds of helicopter blades, ominously suggesting police surveillance of an area where riots have recently taken place. A cut takes us into the room where the sound system was set up, and here we see the real French-Moroccan DJ Cut Killer preparing his set. As he begins his virtuosic mix, a cut takes us out into the courtyard again, where the unmanned helicopter shot glides over the scene below in an overhead shot that eventually takes flight up and over the rooftops of the HLM buildings, seeming to follow the soundwaves out into the air. It is as though the music has substituted for the sound of the helicopter's machinery. In separating the helicopter's aerial vision from its ominous sound, *La Haine* anticipates *Swagger's* opening and its use of dreamlike music to reframe the gaze from above.

In *Swagger* too, however, we hear helicopter blades. They are anticipated in the sound of Régis's sewing machine as the drone enters his room, but heard distinctly when, in a later shot, the camera moves out from his room into an aerial view over the Tours Marrons estate. Music is crucial here too, as I have shown elsewhere: the shot of Régis adjusting his bowtie in the mirror (setting up a theme of Régis's attention to fashion and style that will be resumed in the sci-fi sequence) is accompanied by a 1956 Polish jazz song that aptly evokes glamour whilst also creating spatio-temporal dislocation, since the music comes from another place and time (McNeill 2020: 331). Unlike in *La Haine*, however, the music is gradually swallowed by the sound of the rotor, as the drone camera moves smoothly out of Régis's room and into the air above the high-rise buildings. As the reverse shot of the earlier traversal of the window frame, this shot takes on a more sinister aspect as once again the helicopter sound draws attention to the use of aerial photography in surveillance and control. As the camera moves out, Régis is framed in the open window, the glass panels on either side reflecting the suburban cityscape surrounding him (Figure 5.2), and he finally disappears into anonymity in the aerial shot of his estate.

This shift away from Régis's creative world, returning to the distanced, mapping perspective discussed above, is only temporary, however, and serves as a reminder to critically reflect on the potential for projected stereotypes discussed by Niang. This is why the subtle evocation of cinematic memory, in an allusion to *La Haine*, is significant, as it sets the film's playful depictions of life in the HLM (e.g. the repeated trope of Régis preening in front of a mirror, with his mother's voice chivvying him) into relation with media imagery of the *banlieue*, such as that seen in canonical films like *La Haine*. More than this, in their resonance with one of the most creative sequences of *La Haine*, the drone shots prompt us to revisit the earlier, fictional film from a new perspective, in which alternative visions of the *banlieue* are possible. For Niang, *La Haine* has played a key role in the crystallization of *banlieue* imagery, as a profoundly violent film that has taken on a 'documentary value', depicting 'social facts' that symbolize the 'problem' of the *banlieue* and its disaffected, poorly integrated youth (2019: 86). *Swagger* proposes a critical reflection on the way that inhabitants of the *banlieue* are constructed through media technologies, at the same time as moving away from the stereotypes encoded in *La Haine* (and other *banlieue* films) with its multiplicity of voices. With this in mind, we might return to the Cut Killer

Figure 5.2 Régis is framed by reflections of banlieue space as the drone retreats from his room. *Swagger* directed by Olivier Babinet 2016 © Amazon Digital UK Ltd. All rights reserved.

sequence in *La Haine* and notice its staged quality (as a literal performance), and its momentary and unexplained drift away from the film's main protagonists as it draws out audiovisual connections between different cultures and spaces: famously it combines US and French hip-hop tracks with Edith Piaf's *Je ne regrette rien* (1960), a landmark of French *chanson*. As in *Swagger*, the mobile, aerial gaze expands our perceptive field, rather than fixing it into legibility.

This expansion of the perceptive field rests upon a creative agency, distributed between different subjects and gazes contributing to the film, as opposed to the singular control of an author-filmmaker or panoptic surveillance. This is particularly important in the context of *banlieue* stereotyping which reduces the '*banlieue* youth' to a fixed image of an angry young man (Niang 2019: 70). Instead, *Swagger* offers a vision of connected difference. Indeed, one of the most striking aspects of *Swagger* is the way it creates a sense of heterogeneous community. Notably, shots of one child speaking are often intercut briefly with an image of one of the other children. This gives the impression that they are listening to one another, whilst the mise-en-scène clearly indicates that they are in separate places. This asynchronous and constructed 'conversation' serves to emphasize the individuality of each of the young people, whilst also reminding us that they are part of the same school community. This connectivity is echoed in the fluid transitions between exterior and interior space, akin to the aerial drift in *La Haine* that evokes the housing estate as the locus of a disparate community. In *Swagger*, the drone movements into and out of bedrooms resonate with other connections between the HLM dwellings, such as a series of shots showing Régis and Salimata communicating with each other on social media, each separately in their bedrooms, yet sharing a moment of connection. In such sequences, film editing, rather than being an intrusive and violent 'cut' into an individual's privacy, instead becomes a means of bringing individuals together whilst also respecting their separateness. This is manifest in a poignant sequence incorporating a drone shot of HLM buildings, in which we learn of the death of Mamadou Fofana. While this sequence doesn't take us into domestic interiors, it nevertheless creates a movement between an aerial view of *banlieue* housing and the intimate lives of its inhabitants. In alternating shots, seated in school classrooms, Salimata and Astan recount the tragic accident in which Mamadou was stabbed trying to break up a fight. While Astan explains how it happened, Salimata expresses emotion bodily as she breathes in a pained whisper, 'he hadn't done anything' (00:50:00-00:50:13). As she says this, a low musical note on the soundtrack seems to be leading us into melancholy reflection, but this is interrupted by a cut to rap music accompanying a drone shot floating up over unnamed HLM housing blocks. The rap is uttered in the distinctive voice of a child, one of the members of MGS Spartiate, a youth rap collective based in Aulnay-Sous-Bois. As his flow continues, we cut to a shot of a red balloon floating upwards in a grey sky, its gold ribbon shimmering as it moves, followed by a shot of children playing during a school break. This last shot of the sequence moves away from the children chatting and chasing each other and grazes over the ground before finally coming to rest on a plaque commemorating Mamadou, wreathed in red carnations and white chrysanthemums. This sequence offers a different way of engaging with violence in the *banlieue*, focusing on affective connections between members of a community rather than moralizing discourses of criminality and delinquency. The brief drone shot of dingy housing blocks certainly recalls media imagery of rundown *banlieue* areas, but the focus here is on Mamadou as a friend and fellow school student, rather than a '*banlieue* youth'. Framed by the voices of different young people (not only Astan and Salimata, but the young rapper too), and images of school life, the drone shot establishes a heterogeneous space in which love and friendship flourish alongside precarious housing and knife crime. The floating balloon and ground-level plaque, with their echoing notes of red, mark out a decidedly non-military 'vertical field', in which the potentiality of a child's life cut short is allowed to resonate. Significantly, the plaque proclaims that Mamadou left his mark on the school, reinforcing the way this sequence of shots – like the film more broadly – traces connections between different school children in the local community.

I would like to conclude through a sideways look at the potential of drone vision in an urban context. One of the most famous aerial sequences in European arthouse cinema is the opening of Wim Wenders's *Wings of Desire (Der Himmel Über Berlin*, 1987), a film that follows angels watching over the inhabitants of Berlin. Beginning with a former angel arriving in Berlin by aeroplane, the helicopter shot takes us above and through the clouds before circling around the radio tower Funkturm Berlin, apparently picking up a jumble of broadcasts on the soundtrack. Emphasizing airspace as a realm buzzing with communications, the shot passes over the 100 motorway and approaches the Dernburgstrasse from the West, looking over its tall blocks of postwar flats before eventually entering one of the windows (using a dissolve and backwards dolly shot). We come to understand that this is the perspective of the film's angels; the film's soundtrack will continue to 'pick up' voices as the angels listen to the city dwellers' thoughts, compassionately and without judgement. Although in an entirely different cultural context, this earlier example of an aerial transition hints that we might perceive, in *Swagger*'s drone shots, a tender rather than controlling gaze. Instead of proposing a voyeuristic spectacle, the drone's disconcerting motility might instead blur the boundaries of social segregation. In working collaboratively with Régis, Salimata, Astan, Aïssatou, Naïla and others, Babinet creates a film that both deploys and subverts drone visuality to propose alternative assemblages, emerging through the agency of the *banlieue* inhabitants themselves.

Notes

1   The drone imagery in *Swagger* could be productively considered alongside a subsequent film, *Les Misérables* (Ladj Ly, 2017), in which a young inhabitant of the *banlieue*, experimenting with his drone camera, films police brutality towards another child. A brief exploration of the thematization of drone imagery as the site of a struggle for control over representation in *Les Misérables* can be found in McNeill (2021).

2   Here I refer to *Iron Man* (Jon Favreau 2008) and its sequels, in which we are shown a fantasy, point of view perspective of the graphic interface, with its data and diagnostics, that is seen and used by Tony Stark from inside his high-tech flying suit.

3   Translations from the French are mine throughout, including film dialogue.

4   This scene evokes the 2002 Steven Spielberg sci-fi film, *Minority Report* (based on Philip K. Dick's 1956 novella), in which autonomous insect-drones – 'Spyders' – are tossed by police into an apartment building where they crawl into every individual dwelling and forcibly perform eye scans on the inhabitants.

References

Ballard, J.G. ([1975] 2014), *High-Rise*, London: Fourth Estate.

Ben-Youssef, Fareed and Oliver Babinet (2018), 'Swagger: Interview with the Filmmaker', Dialogues (NYU Shanghai video series), *YouTube*. Available online: https://www.youtube.com/watch?v=MB4BBZ2pG5M (accessed 27 September 2021).

Canteux, Camille (2014), *Filmer les grands ensembles: Villes Rêvées, Villes Introuvables, Une Histoire des Représentations Audiovisuelles des Grands Ensembles*, Paris: Creaphis Éditions.

Chion, Michel ([1990] 1994), *Audio-Vision: Sound on Screen*, trans. Claudia Gorbman, New York: Columbia University Press.

Deane, Cormac (2016), 'The Control Room: A Media Archaeology', *Culture Machine*, 16. Available online: https://culturemachine.net/vol-16-drone-cultures/the-control-room/ (accessed 22 September 2021).

De Certeau, Michel (1984), *The Practice of Everyday Life*, trans. Steven Rendall, Berkeley and Los Angeles: University of California Press.

Dikeç, Mustafa (2007), *Badlands of the Republic: Space, Politics, and Urban Policy*, Oxford: Blackwell Publishing.

District 13: Ultimatum (2009), [Film] Dir. Patrick Alessandrin, France: EuropaCorp.

Graham, Stephen (2018), *Vertical: The City from Satellites to Bunkers*, London and New York: Verso.

Hargreaves, Alec (2013), 'Banlieue Blues', in Anna-Louise Milne (ed), *The Cambridge Companion to the Literature of Paris*, 212–27, Cambridge: Cambridge University Press.

La Haine (1995), [Film] Dir. Mathieu Kassovitz, France: Les Productions Lazennec.

Mbembe, Achille (2019), *Necropolitics*, Durham, NC: Duke University Press, doi: 10.1215/9781478007227.

McCosker, Anthony (2016), 'Drone Media: Unruly Systems, Radical Empiricism and Camera Consciousness', *Culture Machine*, 16. Available online: https://culturemachine.net/vol-16-drone-cultures/drone-media/ (accessed 22 September 2021).

McCosker, Anthony and Rowan Wilken (2020), *Automating Vision: The Social Impact of the New Camera Consciousness*, London and New York: Routledge.

McNeill, Isabelle (2020), 'Music and Spatial Injustice in *Banlieue* Cinema', *French Screen Studies*, 20 (3–4): 317–35.

McNeill, Isabelle (2021), 'Precarious Tactics of Habitability in the Banlieue', *Mediapolis: A Journal of Cities and Culture*, 5 (6): np. https://www.mediapolisjournal.com/2021/12/precarious-tactics/ (accessed 2 March 2023).

Niang, Mame-Fatou (2019), *Identités françaises: Banlieues, féminités et universalisme*, Leiden and Boston: Brill Rodopi.

Pacaud, Julie (2021), 'Entre clichés et fantasmes, la lente évolution de la représentation de la banlieue au cinéma', *France Culture*, 18 August. Available online: https://www.franceculture.fr/emissions/le-reportage-de-la-redaction/entre-cliches-et-fantasmes-la-lente-evolution-de-la-representation-de-la-banlieue-au-cinema (accessed 27 September 2021).

Parks, Lisa (2018), *Rethinking Media Coverage: Vertical Mediation and the War on Terror*, Abingdon and New York: Routledge.

Rancière, Jacques (2000), *Le Partage du sensible: esthétique et politique*, Paris: La Fabrique.

Robertson Wojcik, Pamela (2018), 'What Makes the Apartment Complex?' in Pamela Robertson Wojcik (ed), *The Apartment Complex: Urban Living and Global Screen Cultures*, 1–20, Durham, NC: Duke University Press.

Rothstein, Adam ([2015] 2020), *Drone*, London: Bloomsbury Academic. Available online: https://search.ebscohost.com/login.aspx?direct=true&db=nlebk&AN=1717217&site=ehost-live&scope=site (accessed 22 September 2021).

Swagger (2016), [Film] Dir. Olivier Babinet, France: Faro.

Wakeman, Rosemary (2013), 'Independent Filmmakers and the Invention of the Paris Suburbs', *French Politics, Culture & Society*, 31 (1): 84–95.

Wings of Desire (1987), [Film] Dir. Wim Wenders, Germany: Road Movies Filmproduktion.

Zylinska, Joanna (2017), *Nonhuman Photography*, Cambridge, MA, and London: The MIT Press.

Part Two

Spatialization of race, class and gender

6

Precarious homes in Britain and France – girlhood, escape and dance in *Fish Tank* and *Divines*

Anna Viola Sborgi

Introduction

Post-2008 transnational cinema has increasingly depicted girlhood stories in lower-income, working-class environments, often in public housing, a site which exposes contemporary patterns of socio-economic inequality. Director Andrea Arnold's depiction of girlhood in a London council estate paved the way for later representations of young women in European cinema such as *Girlhood* (Sciamma 2014), *Rocks* (Gavron and Henrique 2019), as well as *Divines* (2016). At the same time, these resonate with American films set in comparable environments, like *Precious* (Lee Daniels 2009), located in Harlem, and *Rise Up* (2016), a short documentary written, produced and shot by four young African American high-school girls in Chicago's projects.[1] Within broader representations of girlhood, these public housing films are part of what I identify as a 'transnational precarious home' genre, which, beyond the national specificities, develops in relation to transitional housing spaces and tightly intersects with the stories of the working-class, gendered and racialized people who inhabit them. While adult women are at the core of many precarious home narratives and several recent films – for instance, *Maid* (2021), *Herself* (2020) and *Rosie* (2018) – take the perspective of young mothers and their housing struggles, girlhood narratives in public housing occupy a subset of their own.

Reflecting on what they identify as broader transnational girlhood film genre, Fiona Handyside and Kate Taylor-Jones argue:

the linkage of contemporary girlhood to questions of risk and possibility means that the figure of the girl on screen both reflects and projects the shifting terrain of gender roles in a neoliberal postfeminist culture that emphasizes agency, choice, and empowerment for all, failing to take into account structural and institutional obstacles.

(2016: 3)

Public housing-set girlhood films certainly participate in postfeminist gender models and their contradictions. However, precisely because they take place in spaces that have been transformed by decades of disinvestment under neoliberalism, these narratives reflect and at least partly respond to the structural patterns that shape gendered and racialized inequality.

To demonstrate how space and spatial relationships are crucial to this argument, I will analyse two films produced seven years apart in Britain and France, Andrea Arnold's *Fish Tank* (2009) and Houda Benyamina's *Divines* (2016). These films share similar themes, narratives and a public housing environment. The council estate in the former and the *banlieue* housing project (the HLM, or *habitations à loyer modéré*) in the latter provide the setting for these two 'troubled' girlhood stories, dealing with the difficulty of fitting in, burgeoning sexuality and a disheartening relationship with adults. The girls' identity in transformation is mirrored by the places they inhabit, similarly in transition. These two films taken together, therefore, prompt us to interrogate the shifting place of home in contemporary European society against the backdrop of a crisis in public housing generated by decades of disinvestment and exacerbated by the economic consequences of the 2007–08 global financial crash.

Through a spatial analysis of the two films, I argue that setting them in dialogue with each other provides a wider understanding of representations of public housing on European screens and of the gendered and precarious mobilities these spaces allow. Different types of movement within the films – walking, dancing and escaping, or at least attempting to – shape the constrained mobility experienced by the main female characters in each film. Dance is a central representational mode in both films as it provides a dream of upward mobility which is ultimately never fulfilled. Despite these limits, I propose that dance represents a crucial way to appropriate the space of public housing, granting agency to the characters over their environment, if only temporarily.

Housing on screen: Comparative, transnational, intersectional

Despite differences between national systems, contemporary global landscapes of housing are shaped by an affordability crisis. Home, conceived as a real estate asset, ties to fluctuating global capital flows as housing provision becomes increasingly privatized. Within Europe, these processes are particularly striking in those countries where a once solid public housing system has undergone a deeper erosion from the 1970s–80s to the present (Watt 2017: 2). While housing practices in the UK and France have their differences, each is the product of a postwar wave of state intervention in the housing sector, which aimed to build homes for a large portion of the population. In France, this investment was propelled, among other factors, by the consistent migration from the country's former colonies; in the UK, it was part of a larger postwar reconstruction plan which prioritized mass state housing provision. Public housing in Britain was originally planned with the intent of accommodating large sectors of the lower middle class and the working class, as shown by classic documentaries such as Paul Rotha's *Land of Promise* (1946) but also, as we will see, in *Fish Tank*. Council housing in London was built within the inner city in the attempt to create a socially and culturally mixed environment. Public housing in Paris developed at the outskirts in the *banlieue*, a peripheral, segregated space which is vividly portrayed in *Divines* (see also McNeill, this volume). Despite these comparative differences in the spatial distribution of state-subsidized housing within the urban environment, both systems originally reflected a universalistic approach to housing that has gradually deteriorated in the past half-century, leading to further residualization and segregation of the populations that inhabit these spaces.

These two European films, set in London and Paris, reveal patterns of spatial segregation in the context of the global history of displacement rooted in coloniality. *Divines*, specifically, reflects a set of post-imperial legacies written into the fabric of the urban environments (and racialized female bodies) it depicts. While *Fish Tank* does not concern itself directly with discourses of coloniality, it is set and filmed in East London, strongly associated with those shipping routes along the Thames that trace Britain's history of imperial exploitation.

The presence of young women within this environment and their attempts to appropriate the space needs to be understood intersectionally in both films, affected as it is by the spatial and institutional frameworks of oppression they experience around gender, race and class. Building on the spatial bearings of Kimberlé Crenshaw, Massood, Matos and Wojcik argue that 'all spaces are intersectional. Insofar as people inhabit and use spaces, those spaces are available to be inhabited by intersectional identities; to show intersections among and between people; and to address issues of privilege, oppressions, and resistance' (2021: 7). Despite the urban planning goal of inclusion in welfare-based societies, these spaces have become unequal and segregated. So, both off and on screen, public housing is a particularly suitable space for intersectional analysis of characters' mobility in and around their precarious homes.

Precarious spaces, precarious mobilities

In *Cruel Optimism*, Lauren Berlant theorizes 'a cinema of precarity' in which 'attention to a pervasive contemporary social precariousness marks a relation to older traditions of neorealism, while speaking to the new social movements that have organized under the rubrics of "precarity" and the "precarious"' (2011: 7). Berlant's view was adopted in recent analyses of contemporary European and global cinema (Bardan 2013: 69–90; Sticchi 2021; Cuter, Kirsten and Prenzel 2022). Within this framework, I wish to build on Berlant's work to focus specifically on contemporary cinemas of housing precarity which, I argue, feature recurring types of spaces, such as the ones exemplified in these two films – the council estate and the *banlieue* projects – which are themselves precarious, in transition and inhabited by subjects, mostly women, leading equally in flux and precarious lives.

At the same time, these films are in dialogue with a longer history of representation within their two national cinemas. *Divines* belongs to a cycle of French *banlieue* films emerging in the mid-1990s of which Mathieu Kassovitz's *La Haine* (1995) is the most well-known example. While still helpful in some respects, this category has often and rightly been problematized. As Philippe Met and Derek Schilling argue, the Parisian suburbs do not just include public housing and high rises, but also other kinds of architecture, such as middle-class villas, which are at the centre of very different narratives (2018: 6). More importantly, according to Carrie Tarr (2005), a distinction needs to be drawn between two trends in French cinema from the 1980s to the early 2000s: *cinéma beur* (made by directors of Maghrebi descent) and *cinéma de banlieue* (filmed in housing estates often by white filmmakers) as they relate to issues of race, nationality and gender. *Divines*, whose director Houda Benyamina is of Maghrebi descent, sits in between these two trends, while at the same time converses with transnational representations of girlhood.

Fish Tank echoes the concerns of *banlieue* cinema with its revision to traditions of British 'kitchen sink' and social realism. This lineage was problematized in the work of Clive Nwonka, who argued that the emphasis on Mia's individual experience comes at the expense of a more sustained class and socio-economic analysis and produces an 'evasive attitude to sociopolitical engagement' (2014: 204). However, I argue that, while it is true that contemporary realist films miss out on representations of collective action, it is precisely the combined focus on marginalized, gendered individuals within the equally marginalized and transitional spaces of public housing that allows political reflection, through girlhood in motion. As Lucy Bolton also observes, Mia's story exemplifies a shift in focus from the stereotyped depictions of women in public housing to more in-depth and nuanced character studies, noting that Mia fits within

> examples of British films concerned with a young woman as a character in a story revolving around her, as differentiated from a girl as emblematic of social ills or who 'challenged conventional morality'.
>
> (2016: 76)

Similarly, *Divines* meets the trend towards female-centred *banlieue* narratives contrasting with the previous dominance of male-driven films like *La Haine*, as outlined by Ginette Vincendeau (2017: 90). In this way, *Fish Tank* and *Divines* rewrite these genres by tightly intertwining marginalized, precarious spaces of public housing with the limited mobilities afforded to their female inhabitants.

Movement

Both *Fish Tank* and *Divines* feature four interconnected types of movement: movement across the spaces of public housing, escape, social mobility and dance. Urban mobility has often been framed around masculinity: not only *flânerie*, following on Walter Benjamin's *The Arcades Project* (1927–40), but also contemporary practices like *parkour*. The association between masculinity and exterior public space is often counterpointed by the contested relationship between women and the private domestic interior. Instead, feminist scholarship has shifted attention to the ways in which women inhabit the city, rewriting their presence in exterior public space (Friedberg 1993; Bruno 2002; Elkin 2017). The two films in this chapter place female characters and their movements at the centre of their own stories, as they physically engage with their surroundings beyond the domestic, which is made less visible, especially in *Divines*. When interiors are used, the porosity between outside and inside is emphasized by the girls' restless movement between the different spatial dimensions and planes of the urban environment they inhabit – vertical, horizontal, interior and exterior. Boundaries between them blur as the girls expand their spatial trajectories through movement, in particular walking and dancing.

As we watch the main female characters transition from one space to another in *Fish Tank* and *Divines*, we also see them encountering limitations connected to their gendered, classed and racialized identities. The concept of home inside public housing is therefore framed as a space of restricted mobility and sometimes of entrapment. In transnational cinema, housing is always in transition, inhabited by precariously mobile subjects. Limits on characters' movements are not only physical but also reflect a lack of social mobility rooted in structural inequalities. The temporary nature of these spaces echoes the characters who make their homes there while also signifying a larger urban trend.

The transitional spaces of public housing

Fish Tank follows the vicissitudes of Mia Williams (Katie Jarvis), an unruly teenager who lives in a messy maisonette in East London's Mardyke Estate, with her mother, Joanne (Kierston Wareing), and her younger sister, Tyler (Rebecca Griffiths). Mia has a tense relationship with both of them but also with the other girls and boys on the estate and spends most of her time on her own, working on her dance routine, until she bonds with Connor O'Reilly (Michael Fassbender), Joanne's new boyfriend. A brief romance between the two escalates in a series of confrontations until Mia discovers he has a family. Eventually, Mia escapes the estate for Wales with a local Traveller, Billy (Harry Treadaway).

Divines is centred around the interracial friendship between Dounia (Oulaya Amamra, Benyamina's own sister), a girl of Maghrebi descent who lives in a Roma encampment on the outskirts of Paris, and Maimouna (Déborah Lukumuena), a young Black woman from a large housing project adjacent to the camp. Dounia, like Mia, has a conflictual relationship with her mother, Myriam (Majdouline Idrissi). Maimouna, the daughter of the local imam, comes instead from a more stable, tight-knit family. Dounia leaves school determined to join the ranks of drug dealer Rebecca (Jisca Kalvanda) and drags Maimouna into a series of illegal activities until tragic events lead to the latter's death by fire, with neither girl ultimately escaping the *banlieue*.

Fish Tank was shot on location at the Mardyke Estate, in the outer borough of Havering in Rainham, East London, a site which illustrates wider patterns of urban change.[2] The estate was built in the 1960s and demolished between 2009 and 2010, replaced by the renamed Orchard Village. The estate was therefore on the cusp of regeneration during filming, shaping the transitional nature of its onscreen spaces. Where Mia lives is peripheral to the rest of London and disconnected from its surrounding social city-space in contrast to most inner-city estates that are more integrated, as is common in Britain's social housing. Although these areas can be denoted as peripheral, the landscape in which Mia moves around – a part of the Thames Estuary being regenerated and renamed as the Thames Gateway – is also in transition, as much as Mia herself. This regeneration of East London, put in motion by the 2012 London Olympics, has connected the area to the city and altered the parameters of its relationship to what were once considered the margins, while also transforming its larger social makeup.

One aspect of this transition may be seen in *Fish Tank*, in which the housing site's state of disrepair is visible in its abandoned flats, one of which Mia takes refuge in for her dancing practice. However, dereliction is not the primary lens Arnold uses to frame the story and the setting. The estate is also depicted as a home, with people going about their lives, kids playing, little girls sunbathing, teenagers hanging out between fights and neighbours looking on from their balconies – the lives of the tenants are spatially interconnected, by gazes, movement and architecture. From the start of the film, Mia is in restless motion across the interiors and common areas of the Mardyke Estate, movement emphasized by what David Forrest, discussing Arnold's work in this film, calls the 'relentless mobility of the participatory, mobile camera' (2020: 84). Mia's seamless movement across different spaces of the estate contributes to establishing their spatial porousness. In her flat, for example, the walls are characterized by sound permeability, a recurring problem in postwar British housing and here is exploited to frame Mia's perceptions of home through sound – her reactions to the music played by her mum or to the noise of Joanne and Connor having sex. At night, we see how the interiors are also permeable by light – in warm yellow or blueish hues – coming from the estate's exterior. Characters are often framed against windows, particularly Mia who, in one shot, sits on her bed with the high-rise tower blocks visible behind her. The flat's door is often left open onto the shared balconies of the estate, a design meant to facilitate air circulation but also to encourage communal life on the estate. Plants, bright-coloured laundry on the lines and other everyday objects identify this as a shared, lived space and a reasonably peaceful one, in contrast to the stigma often associated with public housing. Mia repeatedly traverses these spaces – the open interiors and exteriors, the stairwells, the external balconies and the courtyards.

Meanwhile, the action in *Divines* takes place in two primary contiguous spaces: the housing project and the Roma camp next to it, a spatial configuration that is not uncommon in today's France. While the geography of *Fish Tank* is quite precise, the *banlieue* housing project in Montreuil (Seine-Saint-Denis), where *Divines* is shot, is left unnamed. In several shots across *Divines*, the buildings of the housing project are framed at low angles to emphasize their size, a recurring type of shot often employed in movies set in housing blocks to convey their imposing size and anonymity. Commenting on the image of a broken window to indicate the state of disrepair and neglect in the housing complex, Isabelle McNeill observes: 'The way that the block-like housing frames exterior space underpins the protagonists' desires for escape, contributing to a justification of their operations outside the parameters of law and order' (2021). With the housing complex left in this state, the inhabitants must fend for themselves. However, rather than portraying a united community fostering relationships of care, the film shows Rebecca's drug dealing gang as the centre of human relationships and as a possible means of escape.

Although *Fish Tank* employs a series of strategies to humanize the space where Mia lives, such as framing the estate's residents going about their daily lives, *Divines* instead presents public housing as an isolating and often violent environment. Benyamina stages positive human interactions only in the adjacent Roma camp, an even more marginal space, yet one in which Dounia seems well-integrated: we see her talking to her neighbours, helping her undependable mother (who has been fired for drinking on her night club job), as well as bringing shoplifted food to children in the camp. While Dounia's friend Maimouna is welcomed at the Roma encampment, seen in mobile phone footage of the two girls dancing at a party and riding a small bike with the kids there, Dounia's movement through the two spaces remains difficult. Despite being an outsider in the housing project, she is nevertheless determined to carve out a role for herself within its criminal underworld to ameliorate her economic situation.

A sequence early in the film captures Dounia's spatial in-between status. Carrying a bag with her shoplifted food, she moves through the edgeland between the housing project and the Roma camp, only accessible by crossing over a barbed-wire fence. Instead of choosing the girl's point of view here, Benyamina films her in a long shot, emphasizing her smallness in relation to the *banlieue* structures behind her, suggesting her struggle to belong in either world. Dounia's position is further complicated by her association with the travellers' community, whose mobility is often stigmatized as rootlessness.

At the same time, much of the action takes place in similarly liminal spaces. The girls often hide their money in the fly tower and catwalk backstage at a local theatre – from there, they spy on Djigui (played by dancer Kévin Mischel) rehearsing on the stage below for his audition to join a local dance production. This in-between space is where the girls are free to plot their escape while watching the dancers below, often mocking their self-important attitudes. This is also the space where Dounia discovers that Djigui (employed as a security guard in the supermarket where the girls shoplift) is also a ballet dancer. Following a series of interactions between them, largely regulated by Dounia's elevated gaze framing Djigui as an object of desire, they dance together on the empty stage and later in the closed supermarket. Their reciprocal attraction eventually leads to the boy's proposal to Dounia to leave Paris with him. In contrast to the edgeland where Dounia's struggle to belong is spatialized, these performative spaces represent the possibility of escaping to a different world.

However, despite the attempts by the characters to gain mobility and tactical control of the urban environment, this possibility is ephemeral at best. That the control of space is mostly a fantasy is demonstrated in a later sequence in *Divines*. While waiting for potential drug customers among the concrete debris in the housing project, Maimouna gets bored and Dounia pretends they are in Phuket, Thailand, driving a Ferrari and handing out money to passers-by. Benyamina films the two friends with a free-floating mobile tracking shot in a vacant lot, surrounded by high-rise towers, as they spin around in their dream car. We hear the non-diegetic sound of its motor, and the wind blows their hair as they blissfully imagine an alternative life of luxury (see Figure 6.1). Although

Figure 6.1 Dounia and Maimouna pretend they are driving around in Phuket, from *Divines* directed by Houda Benyamina © Easy Tiger 2016. All rights reserved.

this fantasy space is important, the reality of their socio-economic inequality keeps it out of reach.

Unlike *Fish Tank*, whose narrative is enclosed in the spaces of East London and Essex, a choice that isolates this area of London as a world of its own, *Divines* expands to include a foray into the heart of historical 'landmark' Paris, thus more clearly establishing the *banlieue* as its periphery. One night, Dounia and Maimouna dress up and venture to the city centre, sent by Rebecca to a nightclub where Dounia is to seduce shady businessman Reda (Farid Larbi) and steal the 100,000 euros he hides in his modern luxury apartment. One of Rebecca's dealers, Samir (Yasin Houicha), drives them there in a convertible and, in an exhilarating sequence, the two girls perch high atop the back seat of the car, arms thrust skyward, screaming and giggling as they pass in front of the Arc de Triomphe, a symbol of the city but also of France's expansionist past. Both Dounia and Maimouna as racialized inhabitants of the *banlieue* and as colonial descendants are at the margins – and often the victims – of this history. How escape is temporary (or impossible) with respect to their segregation in the *banlieue* is made clear by the film's finale, as Maimouna perishes in a fire set by Rebecca. Because of the city's history with race- and class-based riots (notably in 2005) at this public housing periphery, firefighters may only enter it in the company of heavily armed riot police, a delay which dooms the Black girl from the *banlieue*.

This melodramatic crescendo shows that Maimouna's death is much more influenced by systemic forces than by individual choices. She could have been saved but she is not, largely due to the city's public perception of criminality associated with the *banlieue*. However, Mainouma is also trapped by her own body in the burning basement of the HLM tower block. The small window is sufficient for Dounia's slender frame to escape through, but Maimouma cannot fit, thereby annihilating any possibility of movement and mobility for her. This sequence stages the female Black body's suffering and death as a spectacle but, at the same time, leads in the following scene to a powerful moment of righteous anger, a cry of the *banlieusardes* against their marginalization and segregation by an indifferent system, exacerbated by the inescapable past and presence of French coloniality.

Escape and failed promises of social mobility

The trope of escape is central in both films, though with radically different outcomes. As we have seen, the girls in *Divines* encounter tragedy trying to escape while the ending in *Fish Tank* gives Mia the possibility to move on.

Escape routes are connected to aspirational trajectories of social mobility which, whether fulfilled or not, play out in both films and are tightly connected to gender, race and class. Movement stands more widely for social mobility or rather the precarious mobility that these characters are afforded. Mia's fantasies of escape and mobility are therefore tied to her dreams of dance. At the same time, they are also tied to her brief romance with Connor and, eventually, to her later relationship with Billy. Connor is the catalyst for Mia's sexual awakening and a promise of escape from her life on the estate. He encourages Mia's passion for dancing, sharing music and moves with her, watching her dance and gifting her a camera for filming her audition tape.

This potential trajectory of social mobility, however, is fraught from the start. Connor's availability to Joanne first and to Mia later is just an illusion, because he is married and the father of a little girl, Keira (Sydney Mary Nash). In one scene, Connor leaves the estate and Mia follows him to his home in Tilbury. We follow her on a long walk on the A13, one of the main arteries through East London. Though Tilbury was not at the time of filming a particularly affluent area of London and remains so today, the neighbourhood where Connor lives is a suburban, aspirational location with well-trimmed lawns and patios decorated with potted plants and flowers. Connor's living space is therefore in contrast to the cramped council flat where Mia, Joanne and Tyler live. After an animated discussion about the impossibility of their relationship, Connor drives Mia back to the Tilbury train station, coincidentally the actual station where Arnold's casting agent found Katie Jarvis, the non-professional actress who plays Mia. However, instead of going home, Mia returns to Connor's house, crosses over the fence into a well-tended garden and breaks in to find a tidy, curated interior. She sees a home movie camera in the living room and watches its footage of a little girl and a woman playing in the house's garden. As Connor also appears on tape, his secret becomes clear. An increasingly agitated Mia notices signs of the family's presence – a woman's cardigan on the sofa and a piece of sparkly tinfoil from the child's princess costume. The suburban idyll of this house is ruptured by Mia who, disgusted by her discovery, urinates on the carpet, rejecting Connor's broken family life disguised by his perfect home decor.

Arnold differentiates this domestic space from Mia's messy family flat, with its dirty dishes piled in the sink and walls in need of repainting. But Mia's home also includes pastel-coloured bedrooms and a tropical wall mural in the living room, along with decorative elements throughout, such as butterflies and hearts, cheerful improvised curtains and seashell windchimes. Rather than highlighting Mia's lack of social mobility relative to Connor, though, these details signal an attempt by Mia and her family to appropriate their environment and, more symbolically, to create a space of care that might otherwise go unnoticed in a narrative of tense domestic relationships.

Social mobility is also a central theme in *Divines*, notably conveyed outside of domestic space. Dounia vehemently resists conventional paths by storming out of the vocational school she attends with Maimouna and other local girls. She rejects what she sees as low-paid service work, hospitality and teaching, employment paths that are also often classed and gendered, as evidenced by the majority of female *banlieue* students in the classroom. In this scene and in others throughout the film, Dounia mimics rapper Lil Wayne by skimming banknotes off the top of an invisible pile of cash in her hand: 'Money, money, money!' (*Divines* 2016: 00:10:22). This fantasy of class mobility is staged as the visual pleasure conjured by images of wealth, such as the fancy clothes the girls wear for their night out in Paris, the videos Rebecca shows them of her crime-funded life in Thailand and the shower of banknotes that Dounia finds in the false ceiling of Reda's apartment. While in *Fish Tank*, Mia seems mostly interested in escape through dance and running away (symbolized by her repeated unsuccessful attempts to free a decrepit chained horse in Billy's Travellers' encampment), in *Divines* the fantasy of wealth and commodification is foregrounded, and it is determinedly pursued by Dounia despite its elusiveness.

Seduced by powerful girl boss Rebecca, Dounia drags the reluctant Maimouna into illegal activities with her, a cliché of the genre, though usually associated with male characters in *banlieue* films. Rebecca embodies in the eyes of both girls an image of power and aspirational wealth that is central to *Divines*. This embodiment is associated with her ease of movement, especially when compared to the film's other racialized characters who have limited mobility within the HLM housing project. She is the leader of her group, keeps a fit blonde male playmate in her flat and owns multiple forms of transportation, freedoms normally reserved for men in such films, going beyond a traditional association with the interior spaces of domesticity and femininity.

In addition, Rebecca demonstrates ownership of the exterior spaces of the *banlieue*. Her agency is exemplified in one sequence where she explains the ropes of the drug dealing business and its spatial logistics to the two girls, who trot behind her visibly fascinated by her confident trajectory across the site's bare lots and concrete walkways. Dounia's dream of escape is powered by her project of forging a power move of her own – first, mastering her driving skills with Rebecca's scooter (a fast and manoeuvrable getaway vehicle) and, later, planning for a covert escape by train with the male dancer, Djigui, and taking Reda's cash for herself (but setting in motion a betrayal of the *banlieue*'s dangerous girl boss). As in *Fish Tank*, romantic attachment seems to promise an escape route, but drug dealing and following Rebecca's model of female leadership have a stronger hold on Dounia, although they end up being equally illusory pathways.

Precarious spaces of dance

Movement and mobility emerge in the practice of dance in both films, representing a fleeting but important way to appropriate the spaces of housing and to grant temporary agency over the environment. Some characters are aspiring dancers (Mia and Djigui), while others dance only intermittently, like Dounia but, as I will show, they negotiate their presence in space by setting boundaries of looking and being looked at while dancing. Dance has also been a recurring element in recent international girlhood films, usually signalling a moment of bonding and friendship between a group of girls. One of the most well-known examples is the Rhianna-synched 'Diamonds' choreography in Céline Sciamma's *Girlhood*, but also the rooftop dance sequences in Sarah Gavron and Anu Henrique's *Rocks*. While the use of dance in these films emphasizes friendship and bonding as a group, for the girls in *Fish Tank* and *Divines*, dance is most often an individual rather than a collective experience. This is specifically articulated by Mia's relationships with dance, the spaces of the Mardyke Estate and the other women who live there. For example, while walking around the block, she sees a group of girls dancing in the courtyard to the Cassie song, 'Me & U' (2006) in front of a group of boys.[3] Mia quickly becomes confrontational with the other girls, mocking their seductive moves and their 'terrible dancing' and, as the girls react to her provocation by insulting her as 'skanky', she headbutts one of them and defiantly walks away (*Fish Tank* 2009: 00:02:55-00:03:05).

Mia's solo breakdance number to Eric B. & Rakim's *Juice (Know The Ledge)* (1991) (see Figure 6.2) is one of the most iconic moments in *Fish Tank*. It takes place in an abandoned flat in one of the estate's tower blocks, which Mia claims as her private rehearsal studio. While dance for her is a personal retreat, rather than a means of connecting socially, the way the sequence is filmed emphasizes the porousness between interior and exterior, as her dancing appropriates these spaces and blurs their boundaries. The camera frames her movements in front of an entirely windowed wall in an abandoned flat, with high-rise towers visible outside. Sunlight streams through the windows, crosscut with interior shots as she bounces around the room. This upper floor flat provides an expansive

Figure 6.2 Mia dances in the abandoned flat, from *Fish Tank* directed by Andrea Arnold © BBC Films 2009. All rights reserved.

viewing position over the estate, again emphasizing the interconnection between inside and outside, as well as high and low. Her elevated perspective here puts her in a position of spatial control. Despite being empty and disused, the flat does not look grim. Rather, it looks airy and full of light (the director includes bright lens flares in her shots). The walls of the flat where Mia dances are blue and resemble the water implied by the 'fish tank' of the film's title. While the image of a fish tank suggests a form of entrapment, the element of water itself evokes transparency. This is particularly evident in this sequence, where light and the external world filter through into the domestic interior.

This spatial integration and porousness are emphasized by the filming but are also distinctive of postwar British tower block architecture itself, which was originally conceived as a system where all the inhabitants could have equal access to light, air and a view. As Mia's body moves fluidly through her surrounding environment, it echoes this compatibility of elements. Here, dance provides Mia with a sense of spatial appropriation, however precarious – for these fleeting moments she seems to find her own place and to be in control.

In her analysis of the *Magic Mike* franchise, Martha Shearer observes an explicit preoccupation with real estate in recent musicals and dance films (2021: 43). Dance sequences in *Fish Tank* and *Divines* are also about ownership of domestic space. However, because they are set in a public housing context, they convey slightly different meanings. For instance, Mia's dance allows her to cling to a space that was originally planned for the working class she belongs to. This appropriation, therefore, briefly evokes the utopianism of the postwar housing project just before it is irredeemably lost and home is transformed into private real estate, a space for profit – as illustrated by the later regeneration of the Mardyke estate.

As the story progresses, though, dance turns out to be another false escape route. This becomes obvious when Mia sets out for a dance audition. After spending most of the film perfecting her dance routine in preparation for the audition, her attempt to fit into what she imagines to be an official competitive dancing space is thwarted by the realization that this is, in fact, an erotic dancers' club. In a series of intimate close-ups, we see Mia looking around and gradually understanding her mistake. When her name is called, she takes the stage and prepares to dance to Bobby Womack's cover version of 'California Dreamin'' (1969), one of Connor's favourite songs, its dreamy qualities at odds with the song the other girls seductively dance to, Jay Sean's 2008 hit, 'Ride It'. As she stands on the stage, the woman conducting the audition asks her to loosen her ponytail, so that she can look 'a lot more feminine' and noticing Mia's tracksuit she asks if she has any shorts or hot pants with her (*Fish Tank* 2009: 01:45:36-01:46:34). Despite her negative answer, the audition organizers are happy to have her try but, as the music starts, Mia leaves abruptly, rejecting their objectifying gaze.

This solitary behaviour extends throughout *Fish Tank*, as Mia does not bond with any of the female figures in the film: girlfriends, the girls in the club, her mother or her sister. At one point, she looks at her mother's friends dancing in the flat from an aloof distance. Only at the end of the film, when she is about to leave the estate, in a belated and precarious half-reconciliation with 'home', she dances with her mother and her little sister in their living room to Nas's 'Life's a Bitch' (1994). This brief moment of mutual recognition between her family, however, contrasts with the overall lack of actual solidarity between women throughout the film.

Centred on a female friendship, *Divines* offers a somewhat different reading of girlhood bonds. Even so, such a friendship ultimately fails its promise of solidarity when Dounia's self-obsessed trajectory to money and power endangers Maimouna. As in *Fish Tank*, movement and dance permeate the film. From their hiding place on the high catwalk over the stage of dancers, Dounia watches Djigui through a decidedly female gaze with the camera adopting her point of view in close-ups of his lean, muscular body. The girls in *Divines* experience this kind of official dance space mostly vicariously. Where they do exercise some element of control – Dounia especially – is in looking at Djigui's body, experiencing him as visual pleasure. Djigui manages to lure Dounia down from her hiding place to the stage and involve her in a passionate, even aggressive, dance session. As Connor does for Mia, Djigui fuels Dounia's fantasy of escape and social mobility when he asks her to leave Paris with him.

In addition to these crucial interactions with the male dancer, we also see that *Divines* is interspersed with other dancing moments: from Dounia and Maimouna dancing together at the Roma camp, to Dounia's mother doing a drunken dance in the club where she works, to the Paris nightclub where Dounia performs a seductive dance for Reda, to her tentative solo moves watching herself in the theatre's front window. Her nightclub dancing parallels in some ways Mia's audition scene, although it shows contrasting expressions of agency and choice by the girls. While Mia precisely rejects the aspect of seduction required by the erotic dance club, Dounia embraces it to pursue her dream of social mobility. However, as the chain of events unfolds, it becomes clear that, even in this film, dance only provides a precarious hold on spatial appropriation and does not fully constitute a route to liberation and empowerment.

Moving forward?

Despite their restless movement, the girls in *Divines* are not progressing. Rather, by the end of the film, they have both succumbed to the environment. Their mobility is precarious and constrained, with no escape. Their respective homes in and around the HLM have become figurative and literal forms of entrapment. At the end of the film, Dounia is looking backwards at the burning tower block where Maimouna has perished, unable to move forward from that space of loss. She is framed on the margins of the estate – almost like the edgeland she traverses between the Roma camp and the tower block, once again suggesting her inert and marginalized social status, based on her precarious association with home in either the Roma community or the public housing complex.

In *Fish Tank*, Mia's destiny is also uncertain but more hopeful, as the film's conclusion is open-ended and captures her ambivalent relationship towards her home. When she leaves with Billy, we follow her point of view but we do not see the open road in front of her, only her backward look at Mardyke Estate, where her young sister Tyler briefly runs after the car. The very last image of the film is an aerial view over the estate with a heart-shaped balloon drifting by. This shot offers a much warmer perspective of the world Mia is leaving behind than her confrontational stance throughout the film might have led us to imagine. Although this finale does not offer collective social action, it is through Mia's personal point of view as she leaves home and the reciprocal gaze she shares with her sister that we see a faint but still possible relationship between the individual and the public housing community.

Conclusion

Fish Tank's more optimistic ending illustrates the difference in tone between the two films. This is where the chronological distance between them matters, as the pessimism of *Divines* reflects a further exacerbation of inequality in France, but also globally in the intervening years. Moreover, its bleakness is driven by the racialized patterns of segregation in the *banlieue* made visible at its core, compared to *Fish Tank's* emphasis on marginalized white lower working-class characters in British social housing. In neither film does physical proximity – in the shared space of the council estate in *Fish Tank* or between the two friends' bodies in *Divines* – translate into lasting relationships of solidarity. This reflects the erosion of these spaces of public welfare, more than a judgement on the characters who inhabit them. The recurrent choice of precarious public housing settings frames these girlhood stories as a cohesive subset of a 'transnational precarious home' genre. While the transnational girlhood film and the cinema of precarity more broadly do not necessarily feature domestic space, the intersectional dynamics of gender, race, space and spatial relationships in public housing films is crucial to underscore an equally multileveled precarity: the girls are as much in transition as the homes where they live.

With dance offering only a fleeting sense of spatial appropriation, these films from Britain and France point to an awareness on the part of filmmakers, Andrea Arnold and Houda Benyamina (who both come from areas like those they depict onscreen), that personal agency for girls living precarious lives in precarious homes can be just as elusive, precisely because of structural inequality. In this sense, even if the films, like other contemporary precarity dramas are 'mostly pessimistic about the prospects for political opposition and change' (Hill 2022: 34), attention to girlhood (embodied here by the raced, classed inhabitants of public housing) and its spatial relations, aesthetics, and politics within a deeply unequal society, suggests the political urgency of even the briefest of dances.

Notes

1   Similar to the films I analyse in this chapter, *Rise Up* includes aspirational teen girl
    dance contexts. John Psathas (Director & Faculty mentor), Shawntel Smitherman
    (17, Director/Writer), Deja Flanagan (16, Writer/Producer), Tay'rece Wise (15,
    Writer/Producer), Franshay Lopez (17, Writer/Director of Photography); the film
    was sponsored by the Chicago Housing Authority and DePaul University's School
    of Cinematic Arts, within the Documentary Filmmaking for Girls programme.
    The girls recall the experiences of violence that have hit their families, while also
    discussing how boxing and dance have helped them build strength. Film available
    at https://vimeo.com/showcase/4113637/video/180353217.

2   *Made in Dagenham* (Nigel Cole 2010) was also shot here, prior to the estate's
    demolition.

3   The video for this song features Cassie rehearsing alone in a dance studio, similarly
    to what Mia does in one of the abandoned flats on the estate. A siren sound
    at the beginning of the video suggests an urban setting, possibly an industrial
    reconversion as the exposed concrete walls indicate. The girls in the courtyard
    mimic – quite unskilfully, Mia thinks – the same seductive moves Cassie practices
    in the video.

References

Bardan, Alice (2013), 'The New European Cinema of Precarity: A Transnational
    Perspective', in Ewa Mazierska (ed), *Work in Cinema Labor and the Human
    Condition*, 69–90, London: Palgrave.

Berlant, Lauren (2011), *Cruel Optimism*, Durham: Duke University Press.

Bolton, Lucy (2016), 'A Phenomenology of Girlhood: Being Mia in Fish Tank (Andrea
    Arnold, 2009)', in Fiona Handyside and Kate Taylor-Jones (eds), *International
    Cinema and the Girl: Local Issues, Transnational Contexts*, 75–84, London: Palgrave
    Macmillan.

Bruno, Giuliana (2002), *Atlas of Emotion: Journeys in Art, Architecture and Film*,
    London: Verso.

Cuter, Elisa, Guido Kirsten and Hanna Prenzel (2022), *Precarity in European Film:
    Depictions and Discourses*, Berlin: De Gruyter.

Divines (2016), [Film] Dir. Houda Benyamina, France: East Tiger.

Elkin, Lauren (2017), *Flâneuse: Women Walk the City in Paris, New York, Tokyo, Venice
    and London*, London: Penguin.

Fish Tank (2009), [Film] Dir. Andrea Arnold, UK: BBC Films.

Forrest, David (2020), *New Realism. Contemporary British Cinema*, Edinburgh:
    Edinburgh University Press.

Friedberg, Anne (1993), *Window Shopping: Cinema and the Postmodern*, Berkeley: University of California Press.

Handyside, Fiona and Kate Taylor-Jones (2016), 'Introduction', in Fiona Handyside and Kate Taylor-Jones (eds), *International Cinema and the Girl: Local Issues, Transnational Contexts*, 1–20, London: Palgrave Macmillan.

Hill, John (2022), 'Working-Class Precarity and the Social-Realist Tradition in British Cinema', in Elisa Cuter, Guido Kirsten and Hanna Prenzel (eds), *Precarity in European Film: Depictions and Discourses*, 325–46, Berlin: De Gruyter.

Massood, Paula J., Angel Daniel Matos, and Pamela Robertson Wojcik (2021), 'Introduction: Intersections and/in Space', in Paula J. Massood, Angel Daniel Matos, and Pamela Robertson Wojcik (eds), *Media Crossroads: Intersections of Space and Identity in Screen Cultures*, 1–20, Durham and London: Duke University Press.

McNeill, Isabelle (2021), 'Precarious Tactics of Habitability in the French *Banlieue*', *Mediapolis: A Journal of Cities and Culture*, 9 December. Available online: https://www.mediapolisjournal.com/2021/12/precarious-tactics/ (accessed 12 June 2022).

Met, Philippe and Derek Schilling (2018), 'Introduction', in Philippe Met and Derek Schilling (eds), *Screening the Paris Suburbs: From the Silent Era to the 1990s*, 1–9, Manchester: Manchester University Press.

Nwonka, Clive James (2014), '"You're What's Wrong With Me": Fish Tank, The Selfish Giant and the Language of Contemporary British Social Realism', *New Cinemas: Journal of Contemporary Film*, 12 (3): 205–23.

Shearer, Martha (2021), 'E-Q-U-I-T-Y: Generic Boundaries, Gender, and Real Estate in the Magic Mike Films', in Julie Lobalzo Wright and Martha Shearer (eds), *Musicals at the Margins: Genre, Boundaries, Canons*, 41–54, New York: Bloomsbury.

Sticchi, Francesco (2021), *Mapping Precarity in Contemporary Cinema and Television Chronotopes of Anxiety, Depression, Expulsion/Extinction*, London: Palgrave.

Tarr, Carrie (2005), *Reframing Difference: Beur and Banlieue Filmmaking in France*, Manchester: Manchester University Press.

Vincendeau, Ginette (2017), 'The Parisian Banlieue on Screen: So Close, Yet So Far', in Alastair Phillips and Ginette Vincendeau (eds), *Paris in the Cinema: Beyond the Flâneur*, 87–99, London: Bloomsbury.

Watt, Paul (2017), 'Social Housing and Urban Renewal: An Introduction', in Paul Watt and Peer Smets (eds), *Social Housing and Urban Renewal: A Cross-National Perspective*, 1–36, Bingley: Emerald Publishing Limited.

7

Cooley High, Cabrini-Green and early-onset rusting in Chicago

Michael D. Dwyer

Before it gained cult classic status on cable and home video, the coming-of-age comedy-drama *Cooley High* was a surprise hit for American International Pictures in 1975. The film chronicles a few halcyon days in the life of a group of Black high school seniors in 1964 – primarily basketball star Richard 'Cochise' Morris (Lawrence Hilton-Jacobs) and the romantic and aspiring writer Leroy 'Preacher' Jackson (Glynn Turman). Well before the name 'Cabrini-Green' became a national shorthand for the supposed failures of public housing in the United States, the film represented everyday joys and struggles of life in the Cabrini-Green Homes, a large-scale public housing project located on the Near North Side of Chicago. Directed by Michael Schultz and written by Eric Monte, who grew up in Cabrini-Green and attended the real Edwin G. Cooley Vocational High School, the film was produced for a modest budget of US$750,000 but returned over US$13 million in box office receipts. It also garnered generally positive response from critics in reviews from *Variety*, *The Washington Post*, *The Chicago Tribune* and *The New York Times* (Murphy and Staff 1975; Rosenbaum 1985; Siskel 1975; Trescott 1975). Many of these reviews, responding to the clear similarity of the concept and the not-so-subtle suggestions in the film's promotional material, compared *Cooley High* to *American Graffiti* (1973), the breakout hit that made George Lucas's career and popularized the 'Fifties' nostalgia wave of the era.

If the appeal of *Cooley High* was the nostalgic pleasures it offered, what was it, precisely, that the film's unexpectedly large audiences were nostalgic *for*? Certainly, Black audiences were not insensitive to the fact that 'the Fifties' was not an ideal era for all Americans. And yet, some contemporary critics claimed that *Cooley High* offered a glimpse at better days for which America yearned.

In his 1975 review for *The New York Times*, Jack Slater claimed that *Cooley High* 'documents perhaps that last moment in modern American history – 1964 – when it was possible for young blacks to see their color as simply one of the components of their personalities' (1975). Other reviews of the film in outlets like *The Los Angeles Times* also favourably compared it to the cycle of Blaxploitation films that, from the reviewers' perspective, relied too heavily on themes of sex and violence. Even screenwriter Eric Monte himself claimed that the film was partially intended as a corrective to dominant narratives about life in Cabrini-Green. 'I grew up in the Cabrini-Green housing project and I had one of the best times of my life, the most fun you can have while inhaling and exhaling', he later told a reporter (Mitchell 2006). In these formulations, *Cooley High* represents nostalgia for Black American life before the divisive politics of the late 1960s (even if that is more fantasy than history).

Elsewhere, I have explained how nostalgia can tell us more about the anxieties and desires of the moment than it can tell us about the 'good old days' for which it yearns (Dwyer, forthcoming). In my book, *Back to the Fifties*, I make the case that *American Graffiti* represented not so much a desire to return to the historical 1950s but rather a mourning of the idyllic vision of the nation and its future that Americans – particularly the young people that went to see the film in its theatrical run – associated with America prior to the political assassinations, civil unrest and political scandals of the 1960s (Dwyer 2015: 58–63). *Cooley High* may be an even clearer illustration of that point, because the nostalgia prompted by the film is clearly more complicated and politically adaptable than a simple desire to 'turn back the clock'.

Rather than a simple romanticization of high school days, *Cooley High* continually reveals and reflects upon the myriad ways that the residents of Cabrini-Green were forcibly and painfully confined – not by their consciousness or by their politics – but by the built environment that surrounds them. The shape of urban space in cities like Chicago was in the 1960s (and continues to be now) a physical manifestation of racist hierarchies, as well as capitalist projects of extraction and exploitation. *Cooley High* affords us an opportunity to see how the so-called 'urban crisis' of the 1960s was a cover story that allowed political and economic power brokers to pin the blame for massive divestment in northern industrial cities on their most vulnerable Black and brown[1] communities. Careful attention to a film like *Cooley High* not only renders visible the relationships between race and space, but also the centrality of the concept of the so-called 'failing public housing project' to the emergent concept of the Rust Belt city in decline.

Though the City of Broad Shoulders did lose hundreds of thousands of industrial jobs and saw over a quarter of its factories shuttered in the forty years following the end of the Second World War, it never experienced the dramatic population collapse that decimated neighbouring industrial Midwestern cities like Cleveland or Detroit during the same time period. Unlike those cities, which were often held up as objects of mockery, scorn or pity in US media, Chicago's public image in the late twentieth century was never wholly defined by its relationship to deindustrialization. Central to Chicago's ability to withstand the economic and cultural shocks that battered other Rust Belt cities was Chicago's success in confining the negative effects of deindustrialization to particular neighbourhoods, and in cloistering the benefits of Information Age investment (financial and otherwise) in others.

It should come as no surprise that the delineation between the sections of Chicago that 'rusted' and those that did not roughly aligns with the city's historically racialized borders and boundaries. In both academic histories and in the popular imagination, the 'Rust Belt' is largely understood as emerging in the late 1970s and early 1980s. But both the economic processes of deindustrialization and the political project of postindustrialism began decades earlier – felt first, and perhaps most dramatically, in Black communities. *Cooley High*, a film that predates the very term 'Rust Belt' by about a decade, provides evidence that Chicago's Black residents, disproportionately housed in projects like Cabrini-Green, experienced 'early-onset rusting' as early as the 1960s. Even within its nostalgic register, the film renders visible the ways that Black and brown Chicagoans were contained and constrained by industrialization, then subsequently blamed for the fallout from deindustrialization.

While Chicago is not as commonly associated (at least, among white Americans) with chattel slavery or Jim Crow legislation, any honest accounting with its history must reckon with structural racism. From its origins as nineteenth-century trading outpost, Chicago's housing, commerce and industry all developed with an intentional commitment to white supremacy, even as rapid industrialization made the Windy City a primary destination for Black Americans during the Great Migration. This has not only shaped the concrete, material shape of Chicago as a city, it has also helped to articulate a structure of feeling for Chicago, the product of tension and exchange between the city's Black and white cultures, institutions and people. The point of this chapter is to argue that industrial development and the racialization of space are not merely parallel or coincidental phenomena, but rather fundamentally intertwined. As numerous scholars have demonstrated, Chicago's housing policies (like those of nearly all American cities) were deeply invested in strengthening housing and educational segregation, through both officially and unofficially sanctioned practices of both private and state entities (Hirsch 1998; Hunt 2009; Rothstein 2017; Taylor 2019). And Chicago's success stories of renewal and renaissance have largely been written alongside, if not through, a renewed commitment to school segregation, racist policing and gentrification of working-class Black and brown neighbourhoods. George Lipsitz has argued that 'race is produced by space, that it takes places for racism to take place' (2011: 5). The legal processes that confined Black Chicagoans to distinct neighbourhoods and the real estate practices that inflated prices for substandard housing offer clear examples of the racialization of space that Lipsitz describes. In what follows, however, I want to consider specifically how the industrial development of Chicago produced racialized spaces like Cabrini-Green.

Manufacturing spatial segregation in Chicago

Throughout the nineteenth and twentieth centuries, Chicago repeatedly and deliberately re-engineered its own geography specifically to benefit industry and trade. In 1848, the Illinois and Michigan canal was completed, connecting the South Branch of the Chicago River with the Des Plaines River flowing southward. Because the Chicago River flowed into Lake Michigan, and the Des Plaines River flowed into the Illinois River, the canal effectively linked the Great Lakes with the Mississippi River and the Gulf of Mexico. While the canal briefly facilitated passenger traffic, its most important legacy was establishing Chicago as a key hub for industrial production and commercial distribution. Barges shipping lumber, coal and agricultural commodities travelled up and down the canal, and warehouses and mills alike popped up along the Chicago River's south branch. Union Steel, one of Chicago's first large-scale steel mills, was built along the river on West 31st Street in 1863. The Union Stock Yards, the massive, 375-acre meat processing facility that earned the city the nickname 'the Hog Butcher of the World' and became infamous in Upton Sinclair's *The Jungle* (1906) was constructed on the river two years later. The stockyards and steel mills were connected to the major railroad companies which had expanded into Chicago, each running their own lines northward into the city. Chicago didn't only become a place railroads went through – it rapidly became a key hub in a nationwide freight and passenger rail network, with an enormous array of warehouses, railyards, switching stations, roundhouses, car and machine shops, die and tool fabrication and other facilities for the production and maintenance of railroad equipment (Bensman and Wilson 2005).

The expansion of the city's population and commercial activity did not come without its costs – as both population and industry expanded along the river, the city's nineteenth-century infrastructure strained to keep up. Specifically, the volume of factory, animal and human waste flowing into the Chicago River rapidly became a public health concern, especially after multiple outbreaks of cholera, typhoid and dysentery. At the time, the Chicago River flowed eastward, emptying into Lake Michigan (from which the city drew its drinking water). In response, the city undertook one of the nineteenth century's greatest feats of engineering in a thirty-year process that began in 1871. Through the modification of the Illinois and Michigan Canal and the construction of several canal locks, the city reversed the flow of the Chicago River, sending the city's considerable pollution south and west (Salzmann 2018). While much of the Loop and the North Side were re-made after the catastrophic Great Fire of 1871, public health and safety-minded reforms were slower to arrive in South Side neighbourhoods where most Black Chicagoans made their home and would continue to do so after the Great Migration.

I take the time to recount all of this nineteenth-century industrial history to emphasize how individually but especially in the aggregate, the environment of the South Side was adversely impacted by the reconfigurations of space that facilitated Chicago's industrial growth. The smells of the stockyard and the polluted river, the noise from the railways, the soot from the factories and the smog from the foundries, factories and mills all disproportionately impacted the spaces where the city's Black residents were confined. Conversely, the Loop and the city's North side neighbourhoods were relatively insulated from the negative environmental impacts of industrialization. That is to say, aside from the quality and availability of housing stock, consider the myriad ways that Chicago's industrialization impacted the bodies of the Black residents of the South and West side: smog clouding their vision, the smell of the entire city's sewage and the nation's largest supply of slaughtered livestock filling their noses, the incessant noise of rail and barge traffic ringing in their ears and the smoke from blast furnaces and output from chemical plants, heavy manufacturing and the rendering of animal products filling their lungs. These conditions didn't exclusively affect Black Chicagoans, of course, but Black Chicagoans were the only residents of the city who were, through both de facto and de jure methods, precluded from escaping those conditions. The spaces of industrialization created an unequal distribution of environmental hazards, and both market and government practices assured that Black residents would be confined to the spaces most intensely damaged by industrial production, literally and figuratively on the 'wrong side of the tracks'.

Public housing in Chicago

Public housing efforts in the twentieth century were, at least in part, a recognition of these inequities. While they were never truly designed to entirely solve the problems of housing shortages, inflation and discrimination, federal housing agencies and public housing programmes did make some efforts to ameliorate the worst effects of rampant racial segregation in housing. However well-meaning they might have been and regardless of how limited their choices were, the leadership of public housing organizations failed to adequately challenge racist segregation and, in the process, reified it. In the 1930s, for example, the Public Works Administration (PWA) headed by Chicago NAACP (National Association for the Advancement of Colored People) President Harold Ickes agreed to abide by a neighbourhood composition rule in which federal housing would reflect existing racial demographics in whichever neighbourhood they were constructed – unsurprisingly, the sites for these projects were almost always in neighbourhoods that were already highly segregated. Ickes' four projects constructed in this period (the Trumbull Park, Lathrop, Ida B. Wells, and Jane Addams Homes) were all segregated by race (Rothstein 2017: 17–36). As Rothstein describes it, in its prioritization of expediency to produce more housing, 'the federal government's housing rules pushed these cities into a more rigid segregation than otherwise would have existed' (2017: 24). The same critiques could be levied at the Chicago Housing Authority (CHA), which was charged by the state of Illinois with the construction and management of public housing projects in the city – initiatives that, because of the racialization of Chicago's space, disproportionately concerned Black residents.

The Frances Cabrini Rowhouses and William Green Homes serve as an illustration of the strategies of containment and confinement that Chicago pursued in the twentieth century. Despite the good intentions of many of the social reformers who staffed agencies like the CHA, Hirsch argues, it was their efforts more than the individual expressions of racial animus that guaranteed that Chicago would become one of the nation's most segregated cities. 'Chicago's racial geography – the Black Belt's concrete northern end, the white thorn in its flank, and its newly occupied southern and western provinces', Hirsch explains, was largely produced 'through government action after World War II' (1998: 10). Ongoing practices of redlining and blockbusting both facilitated white flight to the suburbs and stoked racist sentiment across the region. The cumulative effect of these forces was that, while Black residents were no longer solely confined to the 'Black Belt' by the 1960s, the level of segregation across Chicago intensified, with neighbourhoods south and west of the Loop becoming overwhelmingly Black and Latino, and with neighbourhoods in the north, far southwest, and far southeast remaining over 90 per cent white.

The construction of public schools after *Brown v Board of Education* (1954) followed a similar logic, as the historian Matt Delmont has demonstrated: new public school construction projects were often strategically placed to maintain neighbourhood racial boundaries, and public school boards were non-committal if not outright hostile to the project of school desegregation (2012: 68). When Cabrini-Green's population swelled, for example, the parents of Waller High School in Lincoln Park and Wells High School in West Town nearby raised concerns about overcrowding. The pressure only increased after Washburne Technical High School (the city's vocational-technical school) moved out of the Near North Side and into the heavily Czech and Polish Little Village. Overcrowding was doubtless a serious and legitimate concern, but racist anxiety over the influx of thousands of Black students to white neighbourhoods surely played its part as well. The city quickly responded by founding Edwin Gilbert Cooley Vocational High School in the space of the old Washburne High. When the school opened in 1958, it was considered to be a relatively integrated school but, within a decade, the school's population had become almost entirely Black. Many local trade unions refused to place Cooley's Black students in apprenticeship – effectively locking them out of the pathways industrial employment offered into the middle class. As the steel and auto manufacturing industries began to prepare to withdraw from the industrial Midwest, institutions like Cooley High had already been victims of austerity and neglect. By the 1970s, the building's condition was rapidly deteriorating, and the school's academic performance was considered by the city and state as substandard. Consequently, the Board of Education voted to phase out the school in 1975, the very same year *Cooley High* hit theatres. Thus, the film's nostalgia can be understood at least partially as a desire for a world in which public institutions (like schools and housing) and domestic industrial economies offered some measure of security and stability to Black Americans.

The view of Chicago from *Cooley High*

Cooley High establishes itself from the very outset as a Chicago film. The opening montage, underscored by The Supremes' 1964 classic 'Baby Love', begins with some of the most iconic and recognizable landmarks of the city. The first shot offers a beautiful view of the city's skyline (including an anachronistic Sears Tower) across Lake Michigan and is then followed by a towering view of the Navy Pier. The camera pans to the left, coming to a stop as the Wrigley Building, Tribune Tower and Equitable Building set the frame for the northward reaching of the Magnificent Mile. Following a dissolve is another high angle shot, this one facing westward along the Chicago River and Wacker Drive, capturing the traffic passing over the Franklin, Wells, Lasalle, Clark and Dearborn Street bridges. The next two shots bring the audience down to ground level – first to the edge of the Outer Drive Bridge, which carries Lake Shore Drive across the Chicago River, and next to a low angle shot of two Chicago Transit Authority (CTA) trains moving in opposite directions across the elevated deck of the Wells Street Bridge, with the shot tracking the northbound train before it disappears behind the Merchandise Mart. The focus on public transit continues for an ensuing pair of shots – the first follows a train rounding a bend, the next pivots from an upward shot of the elevated tracks to reveal the towering 'Reds' (the high-rise units) of Cabrini-Green. The camera slowly pans across the vast expanse of one of the high rises, finally landing on a shabby stretch of North Larrabee. The sequence ends among the low-rise Cabrini Homes, tracking Cochise as he makes his way to the intersection of Locust and Mohawk, where Preacher's apartment is located (see Figure 7.1).

   Considering this opening sequence carefully is important for a few reasons. Most obviously, it is instructive to note the stark contrast between the images presented in the montage's first half (centred on the Loop) with its second half (located in Cabrini-Green). The picture-postcard images of the city skyline and the remarkable architecture of the Loop are not only important because of their aesthetics, but also because they showcase the might of Chicago's downtown interests. Lake Shore Drive, the Magnificent Mile and the Navy Pier are not just famous places – they represent Chicago's cultural and economic influence in ways that few others do. By contrast, the shabbiness and disrepair on display in Cabrini-Green highlight the effects of economic and cultural divestment in the city's Black neighbourhoods. The second noteworthy theme in the montage is its focus on traffic infrastructure – the bridges, roads and rails that carry Chicagoans into the heart of the city are prominently featured. Shots of the bridges that cross

Figure 7.1 An external view of Preacher's apartment in Cabrini-Green is a stark contrast from the glittering Chicago skyline of the film's opening shot. *Cooley High* directed by Michael Schultz © American International Pictures (AIP). All rights reserved.

the main stem of the Chicago River in the Loop remind us of the ways that even geographically proximate neighbourhoods are separated by boundaries that must be traversed.[2] Those familiar with the area would know that, even though the apartment that Preacher lives in with his family in Cabrini-Green is literally only a mile away from Wacker Drive and the Chicago Riverwalk, in a cultural sense these locations are light years apart.[3]

The elevated public train system (known locally as the 'L'), which appears prominently in the opening montage, has a particularly significant role in *Cooley High* – it is routinely utilized in establishing and transitional shots, provides the backdrop for some of the narrative's most crucial plot points and the sound of the train rumbling on the tracks is repeatedly inserted into the sound mix even in scenes in which no trains could be diegetically audible. *The AV Club*'s review of the film suggests that the repeated appearance of the 'L' in the film (as mode of transport, as a meeting place, as backdrop and as plot point) reveals the degree to which it is 'a film about Chicago, as opposed to one incidentally set there – a resident's vision of the city, rather than a tourist's' (Dowd 2017). But the omnipresence of the 'L' in *Cooley High* does much more than signify Chicago authenticity – it serves as a constant reminder of the ways that Chicago's built environment, regarded as one of the greatest examples of North American architecture and urban planning, is actively hostile to Black residents. Along with the city buses, the 'L' provides *Cooley High*'s main characters their primary mode of transportation, and yet it also figuratively and literally circumscribes their community. Indeed, Cabrini-Green in the 1960s was hemmed in on all sides. Steel mills, gas works and other manufacturing along the North Branch Canal served as a boundary on the western side, while the Brown Line of the CTA's train system wrapped around the northern and eastern sides, dividing the heavily Black neighbourhood from the tony Gold Coast and hip, nascently countercultural Old Town. In addition to serving as a symbolic barrier, Chicago's transit system also sets limits on when, how often and at what cost the film's protagonists are permitted to move within their own city. From its opening moments to its closing scene, the film highlights the processes through which its protagonists attempt to navigate both the natural and cultural divisions of Chicago. In fact, we might understand *Cooley High*'s narrative as a series of attempted escapes from, and returns to, Cabrini-Green.

Cooley High is a vocational high school, but the film never provides any insight into the kind of technical or vocational training its students get. History and gym are the only classes the protagonists ever attend and even in those courses we do not see any teaching. The only scholastic instruction the film does represent is the white homeroom teacher leading students in a recitation of the 'Cooley Code', a pledge that focuses on moral behaviour like being a good sport, following the rules, being punctual and respecting parents and teachers. Though it is seemingly incongruous, the Code includes a promise that students will not 'enter public transportation illegally', which indicates the centrality of public transit to these students' worlds (the 'L' runs directly in front of their school), and the emphasis Chicago institutions place upon the importance of obeying its regulations.

Preacher and Cochise do not say the pledge, of course, preferring to run a scam with their younger friend Pooter (Corin Rogers) to get out of class, meet up with another friend Willie (Maurice Leon Havis) and promptly hitch an illegal ride on the back bumper of a CTA bus departing from the school's front door. This scene represents the first time that the film's characters are able to leave their neighbourhood and, when the boys gleefully jump off the bus at the Lincoln Park Zoo, their enthusiasm is clear to see. They engage in various hijinks before making their way to the primate house, where they begin to playfully compare the monkeys and apes behind the bars to various classmates (and Pooter's parents). When the boys discover that an outer door to the gorilla enclosure is open, they begin mocking and harassing the caged animal. After Pooter stands up for the dignity of the lowland gorilla, the great ape pelts him with faeces. The scene is clearly played for laughs, but it also plays on a more sombre register – it has something to say about how the combination of confinement and spectacle produces a situation ripe for abuse, and for misdirected retaliation and resentment as well. Pooter is distraught and humiliated, insisting that he needs to get back to school in order to take a shower – suggesting that he has none at home, which was a sadly common design feature of Cabrini-Green's 'kitchenette' units.

In the next scene, we see that the sense of shame that drives Pooter's desire to return home is shared by his friends. Immediately following their encounter with the gorilla, the boys find themselves the object of surveillance and scorn. Hopping the turnstile of the 'L' to return to school, the all-white passengers on the train eye them first with suspicion, then later with disgust when Preacher loudly identifies the source of the smell emanating from Pooter's shirt. Again, there is comedy in Pooter's misfortune, but the pain on the faces of all the boys when they realize the ways that the train's white passengers see them – as uncouth, unwelcome and uncivilized – conveys pathos as well. In an interview with *Filmmaker Magazine*, director Schultz said that part of his strategy for the film was to encourage 'the audience to fall in love with the kids and their hijinks' by showing 'the heart of these guys in a way that hadn't been seen in the Blaxploitation movies' (Hemphill 2015). True enough, *Cooley High* resists depicting Black characters as single-faceted, or only in relation to race and racism – both critiques levied against 1970s Blaxploitation films. However, it would be an oversimplification to say that the film eschews or ignores engaging with the pervasive influence of race and racism on its characters' lives, and how it confines them to specific spaces. That is why, even though Cabrini-Green is depicted as a true community and not simply as a 'slum' or as a 'warzone', the boys yearn to get out, if only for a trip to the zoo.

Cochise's ticket out of the city is a basketball scholarship to Grambling University. When the offer arrives in the mail, the boys celebrate together with a jug of wine in a dark alley. They do this not only because they are genuinely happy for their friend, but also because they know how rare and special an opportunity Cochise has. When Preacher asserts that, upon graduation he will be setting off to chase his dream of becoming a Hollywood writer, the normally mild-mannered Pooter dismisses the notion out of hand. 'Your ass ain't goin' no place but jail' (*Cooley High* 1975: 00:24:03) he says derisively. Gesturing towards the garbage-strewn alley, Pooter adds, 'What kind of script is gonna come from somethin' like this?' (00:24:05). The mockery infuriates Preacher, who bitterly responds, 'You guys think it's so funny because I want to be something besides a factory worker' (00:25:02), before taking a swing at his friends. Given that Preacher is something of a stand-in for the film's writer, Eric Monte, this moment provides a bit of metacommentary on the merits of self-belief. Jackie Taylor, the actress who plays Johnny Mae (one of Cochise's many girlfriends in the film) who went on to form Chicago's Black Ensemble Theater Company, told NPR in 2015 that '*Cooley High* has such a strong message of positivity and breaking through barriers and becoming somebody no matter what your circumstances in life may be', but this scene, among many others, reveals that the characters clearly understand how 'somethin' like this', a place like Cabrini-Green, only serves to fill the alleys and prisons (John 2015).

Later that evening, when Preacher and Cochise are presented with another chance to get out of the neighbourhood, they jump at it. This time, it is in a Cadillac stolen by local toughs, Stone and Robert. As the boys gaze out the window at the glittering neighbourhoods of the Near North Side, they fantasize about a life outside the projects. However, it quickly becomes clear that there are more barriers to their entry to this neighbourhood than they have anticipated. Soon after the boys cross the DuSable Bridge and arrive in the Loop, they are pulled over by the police.

It is worth pausing here to consider the absence of the police to this point in *Cooley High*. From minor infractions (jumping turnstiles, gambling, underage drinking and marijuana use) to more significant offenses (prostitution, theft, robbery), crime is a regular occurrence. Worse yet is the constant threat of violence, whether it comes from local tough guy Damon (Maurice Marshall) losing his cool at a party or hostilities breaking out between rival gangs at the movie theatre. Clearly, crime and violence abound in the film. And yet, the first and only time the police appear in the film is to investigate four Black boys in a nice car in a white neighbourhood. The clear conclusion to be drawn here is that, within the film at the very least, the role of the police is to maintain the boundaries between places associated with whiteness and consumer capital like the Loop and racialized, industrialized spaces like Cabrini-Green. In the ensuing madcap car-chase, Preacher is able to lose the police cruiser in the warehouses on the Navy Pier, but the threat that the police represent hangs over the rest of the narrative – it is only through the intervention of history teacher Mr. Mason (Garrett Morris) that Cochise and Preacher avoid charges. Stone and Robert, who do not have a teacher to advocate for them, are not so lucky. Their suspicion that they were ratted out by Cochise and Preacher drives the film's final act.

Parallel to the action sequences featuring Stone and Robert, the film's romance plot follows Preacher's infatuation with Brenda (Cynthia Davis), his bookish and beautiful classmate. After starting off on the wrong foot ('Y'all need to go to church', [00:16:42] she scornfully tells him when she finds him shooting dice in the back of Martha's Diner), the two eventually bond over a mutual love of poetry. They share a date the night after the boys evade the police, taking a walk over the West Division Street Bridge to Goose Island (see Figure 7.2), the site of some of Chicago's first steel mills and gas works. The pollution from these factories is what led to the Near North Side becoming known as 'Little Hell' in the late nineteenth century. But by the time Preacher and Brenda are walking arm in arm along the railroad tracks, much of the heavy manufacturing on the island appears to have abated – the smokestacks are inactive, and the industrial rail lines are empty enough that the two stroll on them, unconcerned with any potential traffic.

Even though the term 'deindustrialization' was not a part of mainstream discourse at the time, Christine Walley argues that, by the 1960s, many profitable industrial firms had already begun reducing their investments in manufacturing and industrial production in cities like Chicago (2013). This is to say that, although Preacher asserts in the film that he has no interest in becoming a factory worker, in many ways that possibility has already been foreclosed. The budding love affair with Brenda affords Preacher a vision of an adult life that is outside the one that he and his friends have built for themselves within Cabrini-Green, and outside the exhausting work that his parents' generation found in the city. A literary life with Brenda offers him a glimpse of a life outside all of that.

Figure 7.2 Preacher and Brenda wander the industrial sites of Goose Island. *Cooley High* directed by Michael Schultz © American International Pictures (AIP). All rights reserved.

Life in Cabrini-Green (and loyalty to his friend) pulls Preacher back. In the film's tragic climax, Preacher is able to narrowly escape the wrath of Damon, Stone and Robert and gets on the 'L' with Brenda at Sedgwick Station, once again heading south towards the Loop. But when she tells him that Cochise had gone to look for him and could be in danger, loyalty to his friend forces him off the train at Chicago Station. When he finally finds Cochise under the 'L' near the intersection of North Orleans and West Hill (one of the locations from the opening montage of the film), he is too late – Robert and Stone had beaten him badly, and a punch from Damon sent his head flying into a beam supporting the train tracks. Preacher calls out for help, but his cries are drowned out by the screeching sound of the train above.

I read this scene as highlighting the violence of the city's racialization of space. The sounds of city infrastructure render inaudible the pain of Black residents. We learn from the film's epilogues that Stone, Robert and Damon are never held accountable for what is essentially a murder in broad daylight, which indicates the city's disinterest in protecting young Black men. In this way, one could argue that while Stone, Robert and Damon perpetrated the crime on an individual level, it was the neighbourhood itself that killed Cochise. For the other characters in the film, it is either escape from Cabrini-Green or death. Preacher, Brenda, Pooter and Damon make it out alive. Cochise, Stone, Robert and Tyrone are all killed in Chicago. As those groupings of characters indicate, the film refuses to suggest that some inherent goodness or morality or talent safeguards anyone from the violence inflicted upon residents through the racialization of space. Cochise dies over a mistake, while Tyrone is killed during the 1968 DNC (Democratic National Convention) protests in Chicago. Brenda, the most morally upstanding character in the film is rewarded with a respectable career, as is Damon, the person most directly responsible for Cochise's death. There is no rhyme or reason to this. As with Preacher at the back of Martha's Diner, it is often just a roll of the dice.

Cooley High demonstrates the material consequences of both the reification of racialized space and the erosion of industrial employment opportunities in the late twentieth century. As such, the film can be read as a symptom of 'early-onset rusting' that particularly afflicted communities of colour and as a prototype for 'Rust Belt' films of the 1980s, like *All the Right Moves* (1983) or *Flashdance* (1983) wherein youths stuck in deindustrializing communities dream of escaping them. Because the most dramatic economic consequences of deindustrialization had not reached white communities in cities like Chicago in the 1960s, the economic and material pressures that affected places like Cabrini-Green were considered 'race problems' rather than issues of national concern. According to Hirsch, the policies of racialized space that Chicago pursued made the city 'a persistent pioneer in developing concepts and devices that were later incorporated into federal legislation' (1998: xviii). It was these concepts and devices that Hirsch describes as producing the 'second ghettos' that are referenced in his book's title. In the context of this essay, I would add that the segregated neighbourhoods that served as the home base for Chicago's largest public housing projects continually served as buffer zones between Chicago's economic elite and the impact of their decision-making. Originally, these neighbourhoods physically separated the Loop from the environmental hazards of industrialization and, by the late 1970s, these same neighbourhoods, which were hardest hit by the impact of deindustrialization, were subject to economic divestment in order to finance the renewal of downtown commercial districts.

Tracy Neumann describes these processes as driven by an ideology of postindustrialism, through which 'government officials and civic leaders imbued their activities with a sense of public purpose by describing urban renewal as a way to meet public needs for adequate housing and commercial development' (2016: 17). But when the rubber hit the road, Neumann reminds us, 'the benefits of urban renewal primarily accrued to a small number of local elites and blue collar workers in the construction trades', while the negative consequences 'fell most heavily on low-income, predominantly African American residents, who were displaced from aging central city neighborhoods and only occasionally provided with suitable replacement housing' (2016: 17). In Chicago, no individual played a greater role in that concurrent transformation than Richard J. Daley, who served as Chicago's mayor from 1955 until his death in 1976. As mayor, Daley oversaw the expansion of the Cabrini projects and the opening of the William Green Homes, but those developments were tailored to maintain and even intensify racial inequities and exacerbate economic inequality. The Daley administration repeatedly refused to direct city agencies towards desegregation efforts, even after the CHA was found liable for racial discriminatory practices in *Gautreaux et al vs. Chicago Housing Authority* in 1969. While the Loop and Gold Coast began to expand and Chicago's finance sector blossomed, urban renewal projects largely exacerbated housing segregation, facilitated white flight to the suburbs and invested in corporate-friendly projects in affluent neighbourhoods. These were the kind of real estate development deals that would eventually lead to the destruction of the Cabrini-Green Homes. The result of these simultaneous and mutually reinforcing developments was that Chicago became a *deindustrialized* city for a disproportionate amount of its Black and brown residents, and a *postindustrial* city for its affluent, mostly white, residents and tourists.

Nostalgia is perhaps a natural response to living in a place like the Rust Belt. Nostalgia is, after all, characterized by the simultaneous mixture of pleasurable reminiscence of times gone by and painful recognition that those times will never return. Similarly, to inhabit a place of deindustrialization, is to constantly be reminded that some degree of prosperity and achievement has given way to divestment and despair. *Cooley High* clearly works to prompt nostalgic feeling for 'the good old days' of Cabrini-Green in the 1960s. At the same time, the film illustrates both the cracks in the foundation of the city's industrial economy and the federal, state and local government's active roles in enforcing the racialization of urban space. Close attention to *Cooley High* showcases that the public housing committees that served the working-class Black and brown residents began to corrode long before the city showed its rust.

Notes

1   Throughout this chapter, I use the capitalized adjective 'Black' rather than 'African-American'. My intention in doing so is to refer to the particular culture, traditions and experience of a racialized group that exceeds any particular ethnic heritage, national location or continental ancestry. This experience is related to, but distinct from, other racialized populations (including but not limited to indigenous, Latin American, or Middle Eastern peoples) that live alongside and within Black communities in the United States. To respect the particularities of the Black experience in America while acknowledging the parallel dynamics that impact other racialized populations, I occasionally use the phrase 'Black and brown'. I do not capitalize 'brown' to emphasize that it is a category imposed from the outside, rather than a specific cultural identity.

2   It bears mentioning that these very same drawbridges were lifted in Chicago during the protests following the murder of George Floyd in 2020, ostensibly to protect Chicago's downtown from its neighbouring residents. See: Mick Dumke, 'In Lori Lightfoot's Chicago, Bridges Have Become Barricades', ProPublica, 14 August 2020, https://www.propublica.org/article/draft-bridges.

3   For an interactive map of locations in the film, see http://bit.ly/cooleyhighmap.

References

Bensman, David and Mark R. Wilson (2005), 'Iron and Steel', in *Encyclopedia of Chicago*, Chicago: Chicago History Museum and the Newberry Library. Available online: https://encyclopedia.chicagohistory.org/pages/653.html (accessed 12 July 2018).

Delmont, Matthew F. (2012), *The Nicest Kids in Town: American Bandstand, Rock 'n' Roll, and the Struggle for Civil Rights in 1950s Philadelphia*, Berkeley: University of California Press.

Dowd, A. A. (2017), 'The Riotous Cooley High Is a Chicago Movie for People Who Really Live Here', *The AV Club*, 31 March. Available online: https://film.avclub.com/the-riotous-cooley-high-is-a-chicago-movie-for-people-w-1798259824 (accessed 29 May 2019).

Dumke, Mick (2020), 'In Lori Lightfoot's Chicago, Bridges Have Become Barricades', *ProPublica*, 14 August. Available online: https://www.propublica.org/article/draft-bridges (accessed 6 September 2021).

Dwyer, Michael D. (2015), *Back to the Fifties: Nostalgia, Hollywood Film, and Popular Music of the Seventies and Eighties*, Oxford: Oxford University Press.

Dwyer, Michael D. (forthcoming), 'That Nostalgic Feeling', in *Pop Nostalgia? The Uses of the Past in Contemporary Popular Culture*, Tobias Becker and Dion Georgiou (eds), London: Palgrave.

Hemphill, Jim (2015), '"We Didn't Even Have Time for a Table Read": Cooley High Director Michael Schultz', *Filmmaker Magazine*, 21 April. Available online: https://filmmakermagazine.com/93892-we-didnt-even-have-time-for-a-table-read-cooley-high-director-michael-schultz/ (accessed 29 May 2019).

Hirsch, Arnold R. (1998), *Making the Second Ghetto: Race and Housing in Chicago 1940–1960*, Chicago: University of Chicago Press.

Hunt, D. Bradford (2009), *Blueprint for Disaster: The Unraveling of Chicago Public Housing*, Chicago: University of Chicago Press.

John, Derek (2015), '40 Years Later, The Cast of "Cooley High" Looks Back', *NPR*, 26 June. Available online: https://www.npr.org/sections/codeswitch/2015/06/26/417185907/40-years-later-the-cast-of-cooley-high-looks-back (accessed 9 August 2021).

Lipsitz, George (2011), *How Racism Takes Place*, Philadelphia: Temple University Press.

Mitchell, John L. (2006), 'Plotting His Next Big Break', *Los Angeles Times*, April 14. Available online: https://www.latimes.com/archives/la-xpm-2006-apr-14-me-monte14-story.html (accessed 1 July 2020).

Murphy, Arthur D. and *Variety* Staff (1975), 'Cooley High', *Variety*, 1 January. Available online: https://variety.com/1974/film/reviews/cooley-high-1200423493/ (accessed 1 July 2020).

Neumann, Tracy (2016), *Remaking the Rust Belt: The Postindustrial Transformation of North America*, Philadelphia: University of Pennsylvania Press.

Rosenbaum, Jonathan (1985), 'Cooley High', *Chicago Reader*, 26 October. Available online: https://www.chicagoreader.com/chicago/cooley-high/Film?oid=1065849 (accessed 1 July 2020).

Rothstein, Richard (2017), *The Color of Law: A Forgotten History of How Our Government Segregated America*, New York: Liveright Publishing Corporation.

Salzmann, Joshua (2018), 'How Chicago Transformed from a Midwestern Outpost Town to a Towering City', *Smithsonian Magazine*, 12 October. Available online: https://www.smithsonianmag.com/history/how-chicago-transformed-from-midwestern-outpost-town-to-towering-city-180970526/ (accessed 5 June 2020).

Siskel, Gene (1975), 'Anger, Comedy, Love in "Cooley High"', *Chicago Tribune*, 27 June, sec. 3: 3.

Slater, Jack (1975), '"Cooley High" – More Than Just a Black "Graffiti"', *The New York Times*, 10 August. Available online: https://www.nytimes.com/1975/08/10/archives/cooley-high-more-than-just-a-black-graffiti.html (accessed 1 July 2020).

Taylor, Keeanga-Yamahtta (2019), *Race for Profit: How Banks and the Real Estate Industry Undermined Black Homeownership*, Chapel Hill: University of North Carolina Press.

Thomas, Kevin (1975), 'Cooley High's Universal Appeal', *The Los Angeles Times*, 13 July, sec Calendar: 36.

Trescott, Jacqueline (1975), '"Cooley": Growing Up Black in the '60s', *The Washington Post*, 16 July, sec. D: 1–2.

Walley, Christine (2013), *Exit Zero: Family and Class in Postindustrial Chicago*, Chicago: University of Chicago Press.

8

Franklin Wong's *Below the Lion Rock* television series: Community dialogue in 1970s Hong Kong public housing

Chung-kin Tsang

Introduction

After the Second World War and the Korean War, economic development was often commemorated by connecting national symbols with a sense of pride, like the Miracle on the Rhine in West Germany and the Miracle on the Han River in Korea. Likewise, Hong Kong's postwar development has been celebrated with the name *The Spirit of Below the Lion Rock*. Like the above two counterparts, this narrative of the spirit of Hong Kong connects with a landmark, the iconic Lion Rock Hill, which rises prominently above the densely populated urban areas of Kowloon and the New Territories. However, this narrative is also different from the above for originating from and articulating with a television series, *Below the Lion Rock* (*BLR*).

BLR is a renowned and popular television drama series since 1972 that was produced by Radio Television Hong Kong (RTHK), the sole public broadcaster under the colonial government in Hong Kong before 1997. The early episodes of *BLR*, which were produced around the years 1972–6, are set in public housing (the Resettlement Estates) about a family of two generations, the Tak family, in the form of a drama with comedy elements (genre categories in the Chinese language use '劇' to signify drama, and this series is categorized as 處境喜'劇', or 'situation comedy drama'). These early episodes of *BLR* narrate several intersecting thematic contexts: spatially, it was set in public housing with extremely limited personal privacy where a clear distinction between public and private space was almost impossible to maintain; temporally, it was produced in the 1970s during the city's transition from a traditional to a modern society; socially, it depicted the way of life of the local grassroots (working-class and poor residents) through the negotiations between the refugee generation and the local-born generation; and politically, it was a public broadcaster's programme with a tension between promoting the colonial government and the social critique made by director-producer, Franklin Wong Wah-kay.

As I will argue in this chapter, within these thematic contexts, Wong's episodes reflect and become a part of a social and cultural turning point in the city's history, around 1974. *BLR* accomplishes this through its depiction of community dialogue about individual and social problems within the blurred public and private spaces of the Wang Tau Hom (橫頭磡) Resettlement Estates, where the director-producer stages the series. In the spatial design of the show, the door of the small public housing unit where the Tak family resides is always open. They welcome neighbours, friends and relatives to come by for a chat at their table, and even unsolicited visitors are welcome.

This depiction of spatial and social blurriness between public/private enables the characters in the early episodes to openly discuss and connect their private issues beyond their immediate surroundings with a more public perspective. In other words, through community dialogue the characters discover the social roots (and potential cures) of their individual problems. These onscreen discussions about Hong Kong society become a unique enactment of the struggles of life in the colonial city. Shared dialogue provides both the refugee generation who came to Hong Kong from Mainland China as well as the local-born generation who grew up in Hong Kong in the 1950s–60s a collective experience of the city's identity as it was modernizing in the 1970s.

In addition, the popular drama series serves as the representational and discursive foundation of Hong Kong as an imagined community, where Tak's family and their friends help each other unconditionally. Although this depiction fantasizes the community by neglecting the real, daily conflicts caused by cramped living conditions, these onscreen representations of communal effort and cooperation continued to become part of the narrative of *The Spirit of Below the Lion Rock*. In the following, I will outline the history of Wong's *BLR*, followed by a discussion of the thematic contexts within the series, which are visible onscreen in the development of public housing and the economic, social and political transition from traditional to modern Hong Kong. I will also examine the relationship between tenants and the colonial government as articulated by the show's characters through their community dialogue located in the blurred public/private spaces of Hong Kong public housing. I will conclude with the long-lasting influence of *BLR* and its connection to the collective identity of the city below the Lion Rock.

Below the Lion Rock: Production history, propaganda and popularity

Below the Lion Rock (*BLR*) is a long-running television drama series with more than 200 episodes. These episodes were produced from 1972 to 1980, and occasionally every few years throughout the 1990s to 2010s until 2022. I agree with Hio Leong Che's proposal to divide *BLR* into two eras by the year 1976 (2021: 245). Those episodes produced before 1976 are the old style, which I call the early episodes, and will be the focus of this chapter. The main reason is that the episodes after 1976 are in a more 'experimental style' (Chin 2009: 81), gradually shifting away from the studio-produced public housing setting and the format of family-centred drama/comedy to become a darker, location-shot anthology series by the end of the 1970s. Therefore, since I will be discussing the onscreen representation of public housing in 1970s Hong Kong, the early episodes (between 1972 and 1975) by director-producer Franklin Wong Wah-kay[1] are the foundation of my analysis. Among these episodes, forty were re-run by RTHK in 2014 (*Revisiting the Classics of Below the Lion Rock* 2014); several of these will be discussed in this chapter. These episodes were set in a public housing estate, Wang Tau Hom (橫頭磡), below the Lion Rock Hill (see Figure 8.1), the most prominent mountain that separates Kowloon and

Figure 8.1 Wang Tau Hom Estate, the public housing estate shown in the opening of *Under the Lion Rock* © RTHK (Radio Television Hong Kong) 1973–1977. All rights reserved.

the New Territories. Besides its geographical significance and visibility, at the time when the early episodes were produced in the mid-1970s, Kowloon was crowded with public housing estates and squatter areas situated below the Lion Rock landmark.

Franklin Wong's episodes reveal the tension between highlighting a community's social concerns and the series' propaganda value to the colonial government. On the one hand, naming the series *Below the Lion Rock* was intended to represent the way of life among the city's grassroots neighbourhood of the working class and the marginals, as recounted by Franklin Wong (*Revisiting the Classics of Below the Lion Rock* 2014, Ep. 1), and many of these episodes are concerned with social problems. The production crew would do a site visit, witness first-hand the living condition of the lower class and then depict their problems in *BLR* (Chin 2009: 82). Having trained at the BBC, Wong deployed 'the spirit of public broadcasting' (Chin 2009: 82) to reflect social reality with a neutral stance, while still critiquing (and praising) the government. For example, one early episode criticized local police corruption and, although it received many complains from civil servant organizations, Wong stood by his television production and refused to apologize (Chin 2009: 82).

On the other hand, Che (2021) proposes that Wong's episodes also functioned as a form of cultural support for the colonial government after a 1967 uprising seriously challenged its legitimacy. This riot has often been regarded as the watershed in the history of the city's colonial governance. Lasting for seven months, it was based in the labour movement and led by sympathizers of the Chinese Communist Party (CCP) in Hong Kong. Before the riot, the colonial state took a hands-off approach to the well-being of the population. Afterwards, social reforms, including free education, labour protection and health care, were implemented in the 1970s. The establishment of a Public Affairs Television Unit under RTHK in the early 1970s was part of these social reforms 'to develop and sustain strong links between the Government and the people' and provide information and messages with 'credibility and impartiality' (*RTHK Annual Report, 1970/1971*, cited by Che 2021: 244). In this way, RTHK and their *Below the Lion Rock* television series reflected the wider government policy to close the information gap between the elite and the masses, the rulers and the ruled.

This propaganda in support of the colonial government was strengthened in two major types of Wong's episodes in *Below the Lion Rock*: the first type promotes the spirit of 'assiduousness, endurance and communal support' to improve social stability, while the second type improves 'the government's image' (Che 2021: 249). Examples of the former include an episode with the civic-minded message of helping neighbours survive a city water shortage, and trying to convince public housing tenants to support a rent raise that will help provide more public housing and resettle people stuck in terrible housing conditions. The series also bolsters the image of the government by challenging public perceptions of the police as corrupt and civil servants as lazy (Che 2021: 249).

To Che, *BLR* was 'a situation comedy with coloniality' (2021: 253), as its attention to the colonial government also gave the series elements of a 'living-room drama' (2021: 255). This genre context facilitates the show's conservative bent, emphasizing the importance of family and maintaining the status quo and social stability. The narrative of the series values smooth family dynamics in which each member properly performs their own designated role. This tradition means the father has to work and earn a salary, the mother is a housewife and takes care of the family and the children must study hard in school. As befits the narrative's television format, the conflicts in *BLR* are often about misunderstandings that can be resolved at the end of the episode. In this same run of the series (and under pressure from the colonial government), a favourable image of the police was required to be promoted in *BLR*, so a policeman with positive characteristics was added after 1974 (Che 2021: 259).

With this format and these characters, the early episodes were very popular in the 1970s. The viewership of *Below the Lion Rock* was 780,000 in 1973 and increased to 2,700,000 by the end of 1974. It became the most popular television programme of the year (Wu 2020: 122; Che 2021: 247). Given the population of Hong Kong at four million people and the competition from the other two commercial television stations at the same time, this viewership could be described as extremely high. A report from 1974 showed that 'only 1 per cent of the local population had never watched the show' (Wu 2020: 123), while another reported that the series was well-received, with over 85 per cent of the interviewees rating the series as 'excellent' and 'good' (Wu 2020: 123). In 1976, after Wong left the production team of *BLR*, a government report recognizes that *BLR* was well-received by the population living in public housing, an audience who saw their daily lives being articulated onscreen in a relatable setting (as cited by Che 2021: 261). In contrast, the more experimental episodes after Wong's period were less popular for not providing this kind of 'balanced view' and for having endings described as 'disillusioned and unhappy' (Che 2021: 261). Therefore, it is to the Wong episodes we turn now.

In the following, I will argue that, between the social concerns of the community and the propaganda message of colonial governance, it is the spatial setting of the Tak family's public housing units depicted in *BLR* that enhances our understanding of the cultural shift from a traditional to a modern city. By resonating with the Hong Kong people's common living experience in the 1970s, this on-screen representation imagines a collective way of living together through shared community dialogue within intersecting thematic contexts – spatial, temporal, social and political.

The Tak family home and the spatiality of public housing

The early episodes of *BLR* revolve around the lives of a local family: Tak's household, and its six family members in two adjacent 120 square-foot housing units of Wang Tau Hom (橫頭磡) Resettlement Estate. The family head, Uncle Tak (Leung Meng 良鳴), is a middle-aged man, educated with a traditional Chinese knowledge background and working as a letter writer for the illiterate on the public housing estate. He lives in one housing unit with his wife Auntie Tak (Fung Sui Chun 馮瑞珍) and younger daughter Yee (Kimmy Got Kim Ching 葛劍青). Auntie Tak is a housewife and Yee is a teenage student who went through secondary school to a polytechnic and works in factory by the end of Wong's era of the show. Their older son, Tin (Kenneth Tsang Kong 曾江), is a married young professional working as a journalist, living with his wife Sum (Chan Ka Yee 陳嘉儀) and their young son, Kau (Wu Kwan Mang 胡君孟), in the unit next to Uncle Tak's.

Wang Tau Hom (橫頭磡) Resettlement Estate, where Tak's family lives, is in the Mark II-style public housing provided by the government in the 1950s and 1960s. The estate's name came from the government's imperative to resettle homeless victims from several destructive fires that occurred throughout the 1950s in the city's squatter areas. These spaces were home to refugees from Mainland China after the Second World War, comprised of temporary huts constructed of highly flammable wood. For example, after the Shek Kip Mei blaze in 1953, the colonial government had to immediately resettle 50,000 homeless squatters (*Hong Kong Memory* 2012a). Hence, permanent six- to seven-storey buildings were erected as an early form of public housing for these tenants as well for victims of natural disasters (*Hong Kong Memory* 2012a); these constructions were typically sited in densely populated urban areas.

The Mark I (built from 1954 to 1960) and Mark II (built from 1961 to 1964) styles of resettlement estates became Hong Kong's first public housing. Both styles shared almost the same design, being seven-storeys tall with around sixty to seventy-two units per floor. The buildings were usually in an H-shape, with two parallel residential blocks as wings and connected in the middle with a block of shared staircases and public lavatories. In the middle of each wing near the staircases were shared facilities of water tap, public area for laundry and bathroom (Che 2017: 153; Ko 2021). Therefore, people living on the same floor in each wing (around thirty to thirty-six units) would usually share the same water source, public bathroom and public lavatories. Each unit was placed back-to-back to another unit at the centre of each wing, and all units were surrounded by a circular open corridor. The only windows and door of the housing unit are open on the same side to the corridor. As we can see in Figure 8.2, the space of the open corridor outside of each unit became an open

Figure 8.2 The corridor outside the public housing units is a shared communal space often used for cooking and laundry, shown in the opening of *Under the Lion Rock*
© RTHK (Radio Television Hong Kong) 1973–1977. All rights reserved.

kitchen as well as a laundry area, with wet clothes hung from the ceiling to dry. Spatially, this setting blurs the exterior public common areas with the private interior domestic space.

In terms of the interior design, the housing units in the Mark I and Mark II styles formed an empty rectangular space of 120 square feet with an open floor plan (Che 2017: 139), where 'the new tenant was faced with a room bare of services and finishes' (*Hong Kong Memory* 2012b). Because the housing unit is so small, it serves as the bedroom, living room and dining room for the whole family. In the onscreen representation executed through Wong's studio filming, the Tak family home features a foldable table under the window and beside the unit's open door, a central prop that blurs the threshold between interior and exterior spaces. This table becomes the site of community dialogue, by its location and by the discussions of residents seated around it in the episodes described below. Elsewhere, a double-deck bed is at the rear of the room where Uncle and Auntie Tak share the lower deck while their younger daughter Yee occupies the upper. The lower-deck bed also serves as a chair in scenes where Yee or Uncle Tak reclines on it during conversations with visitors. This spatial setting of Uncle Tak's housing unit was widely relatable to the audience's everyday experience of urban life in Hong Hong. In 1972, around 530,000 tenants out of a 4 million population (*Hong Kong Memory* 2012b) were living in these Mark I and Mark II resettlement estates. Including those living in the newer Mark III to Mark VI styles (built since the mid-1960s), approximately 1.5 million residents lived in public housing in the early 1970s (Che 2017: 139).

In this spatial setting, interior and exterior blurring makes any division between private property and lives inside tenants' homes and public spaces almost impossible to maintain. Cooking, bathing and toilet hygiene are all done in a shared space. The separation of the private small housing unit from the neighbourhood can only be achieved through closing the door and curtaining the window. Otherwise, daily life would be visible to any passer-by walking the open corridor. Unfortunately, fresh air and sunlight would also be blocked by closed doors and curtained windows. As Ng has recounted, resettlement estates like Wang Tau Hom sheltered those in need, but provided no private bathrooms and kitchens, and the long corridor outside each housing unit is a forced, reluctant public space (*Revisiting the Classics of Below the Lion Rock* 2014, Ep. 15).

This spatial blurring between public and private existed in the city's social reality as well. I will show that the early episodes of *BLR* translate this blurring to its onscreen narrative, enabling the formation of a collective community.

Producer-director Wong achieved this by connecting the characters' personal issues with the government's changing social policies as a way for them to make sense of, and become part of, the city's transition from traditional to modern in the mid-1970s. Yet, at the same time, this imagined community reinforced the myth of Hong Kong identity in which conflicts arising from the lack of privacy in public housing's confined living spaces are not included in Franklin Wong's narratives, which more positively convey the colonial government's propaganda around this form of communal living.

Generations and government

Local sociologists Ng Chun-hung (2012) and Lui Tai-lok (2007) both propose that 1974 is the watershed in the history of Hong Kong. Ng (2012) suggests that modern Hong Kong and its local popular culture were born in 1974. Prior to that year, the middle-aged post-Second World War refugee generation who came to Hong Kong in the 1950s and '60s was still not fully settled and had not yet treated this colonial city as their permanent home. These refugees tended to have an apolitical mentality (Tsang 2021: 54) and distanced themselves from the colonial state as they were kept busy struggling 'for daily economic survival' and 'keeping one's head down and staying out of the way of nationalist concerns as well as of the colonial regime' (Mathews, Lui and Ma 2008: 29). Through the pursuit of material success, together with their family members, these refugees adapted to the British colony with limited social welfare before the reforms of the 1970s (Lau 1978).

After 1974, political stability and economic prosperity helped define the young local-born baby boomers who gradually became the driving force that dominated the development of the city in the latter part of the decade. Yet, as Lui (2006) points out, the transition from the outbreak of social discontent in the 1967 riot to the birth of local culture in 1974 was not a smooth process. The seven years in between were marked by turbulence and chaos. Economically, the local stock market crash and the global oil crisis in 1973 caused economic recession, inflation and unemployment in Hong Kong society. Politically, the student and social movements continued to challenge the legitimacy of the colonial government in the context of corruption and, socially, labour rights and protections from the government were still very limited. However, these baby boomers were still in their teens or early twenties and were very different from the city's older residents; for instance, they were influenced by western popular culture, like Britain's The Beatles and the James Bond movie franchise. This younger generation was in the midst of making sense of a modern Hong Kong society when Franklin Wong's series hit their television screens.

The early episodes of *BLR* (1972–6) were part of this shift towards a modern Hong Kong. The stories *BLR* told not only spoke the dialogue of a new socially active community, one that was moving beyond the previous generation's refugee mentality, but also helped the colonial government achieve stability and legitimacy. When combined, these effects gave rise to the public belief that the modern state should provide social welfare and improve the well-being of the city's inhabitants. Wong achieved this by having his characters engage in shared community dialogue in the spatial setting of blurred public/private space. Almost every episode of *BLR* consists of at least one scene in which some or all members of the family, neighbours, relatives and/or friends discuss social problems when sitting together around the table in Uncle Tak's home, where the front door and the window's curtains are always open. As if it is an extension of the open corridor alongside the public housing unit, Tak's private home becomes a public space where community dialogue happens. Crucially, the role and responsibility of the colonial government are often openly discussed there.

This presence of the Hong Kong government in onscreen dialogue was remarkable in contrast to the media representation of it in the 1950s. For instance, one of the classic movies of that decade, *In the Face of Demolition* (Lee Tit 1953), is about a group of individuals who share the same tenement flat, living in cubicles and rented bedspaces as sub-tenants. These characters occupy the same living space and cooperate with one another as a community to fight against the greedy landlord and natural disasters like typhoons, which threaten the demolition of the whole building. Lui has noted that the role of the colonial government is totally absence from this film (2007: 58–9). Even when a typhoon does destroy the building, the focus remains on how the individuals resolve conflict with communal spirit. However, there is no social welfare available; individuals must survive hardships alone, by selling blood or being sex workers. Their isolation persists – for these tenants, Hong Kong is merely a temporary shelter after the Second World War, with no sense of the city as home (Lui 2007: 59).

In contrast, Wong's early episodes of *BLR* still emphasize communal effort but also encourage open discussions about the colonial government, even when the narrative concludes on a conservative note, without serious challenge to the status quo. In these episodes, the backdrop of Tak's home blurs the separation between the public and private to create a socially productive space where dialogue connects personal issues to their social roots and remedies. Hong Kong's public housing frames this connection through the episodes I sample below.

Around the table: Community dialogue and the personal/political connection

'Loan shark/貴利' (1974) is a story about communal effort and the elimination of social problems through state intervention. Uncle Choi (才叔) is a hawker in a street market who is being continuously exploited by a local loan shark. He is also a neighbour of Tak in Wang Tau Hom. Tak invites Uncle Choi and other neighbours (seven people in total) to join together in his home and discuss how to help Uncle Choi. Tak proposes to collect the money among them to pay the loan shark first and avoid the high rates of interest. All of the neighbours are generous and agree to lend money to Uncle Choi. Tak's son, Tin, comes back to their housing unit after the meeting and disagrees with the decision to pay the loan shark. To Tin, this is an act of community benevolence, but it cannot cure the social problem of criminal profiteering. Instead, he insists on calling the police to report the case as a more rational way to solve the problem. He says, 'Dad, you are kind-hearted. But how many people can you help? If we don't eliminate loan sharks, many people will still fall prey' (*Revisiting the Classics of Below the Lion Rock* 2014, Ep. 11: 00:08:27-00:08:40). This episode shows the significance of Tak's unit as a private gathering place of the public housing community to help people in need. To that, the show adds a positive political intervention by the state – the police force can be the root solution to the neighbourhood's social problem.

In another Wong episode, 'Temptation/誘惑' (1974), the characters discuss the issue of corruption and their expectation of a better society. A friend of Uncle Tak and Tin, Shing (成仔), is a young man who was recently promoted to be a government officer. He is in charge of Uncle Tak's Resettlement Estate and has the power to approve or reject housing applications. At the beginning of the episode, after rejecting a bribe from a subordinate for application approval, Shing is sitting in Tak's home at the table near the open door, describing his situation to the family. Uncle Tak praises him for making the right decision. Later, Shing visits his girlfriend's home and is reminded by her mother that he should be saving money to get married, so he begins to worry about his personal finances. His subordinate, though, continues to urge Shing to use corruption to get rich quick, so he returns to Tak's home for advice. He sits at the family table with Tin and Yee, while Uncle Tak reclines on the lower-deck bed and Auntie Tak washes dishes in the open corridor outside the unit. Shing confesses his frustrations about money and marriage with all of them. At this, Tin connects Shing's experience and the elimination of corruption to the ideal of long-term development in society and to the public good: 'People hope to live in a liberal, peaceful, stable place with no violence and no corruption' (*Revisiting the Classics of Below the Lion Rock* 2014, Ep. 7: 00:17:53-00:18:03). With the support provided through this community dialogue, Shing is inspired to reject the bribe again and, instead, reports it to the government's newly established office, the Independent Commission Against Corruption (ICAC). Wong's characters once again use Uncle Tak's home (and his family table by the open door and window) as the blurred public/private space where their interactive community brings a personal problem into dialogue with the pursuit of collective social and public good. Here, this 1970s television series situates Hong Kong public housing as a reflection of the colonial government's role in improving the well-being of its citizens.

Addressing another social problem in the transition to a modern Hong Kong, the episode entitled 'Never will there be Days of Peace/永無寧日' (1973) takes on noise pollution in the city. Tin's father-in-law visits Uncle Tak's home and sits at the table next to the open door to complain about the noise from the commercial aircraft flying overhead. Tin's father-in-law shares a newspaper clipping with Uncle Tak expressing the same health concerns. Later, Tin returns home and relays information about the recent government policy prohibiting night flights as well as the regulatory efforts of a new government committee to reduce noise pollution in the neighbourhood. Like an educational television programme, this episode aims to promote the colonial government's recent efforts to address the well-being of the city's inhabitants. The episode uses the private dialogue in these scenes to encourage the public expectation of a government that does more.

Finally, and to that end, 'The Long Stream/細水長流' (1975) tells the story of a water shortage that occurred at that time and helps the television audience visualize a version of Hong Kong identity based on the collective experience of endurance, communal effort and the government's improved policy initiatives. The episode depicts the hardships experienced by Uncle Tak's family and the whole neighbourhood during a difficult period of water restrictions. They have to queue at the water tap on their floor, use plastic buckets to collect the water and store these in their housing unit. Tak's family accidentally mistakes the neighbour's water bucket for their own, causing a brief conflict. Tin's wife, Sum, is kind-hearted and always helps the neighbour in collecting water. This benevolent behaviour resolves the conflict at the end of the episode, as Sum, Uncle Tak and the neighbour commiserate together in the open corridor their shared experience of life in modern Hong Kong. Sum summarizes: 'In the past, we have water restriction with water once every four days. We went through that. We are Hong Kong people, and we have lots of experience. These little things cannot stump us.' As in the other episodes discussed here, the positive role of the colonial government comes up when Uncle Tak adds: 'The government official from the Water Supplies Department said Hong Kong's water plan is world famous. I think if we save more water, we can have enough. We won't need to go back to the water supply four hours once every four days (as in the 1960s)' (*Revisiting the Classics of Below the Lion Rock* 2014, Ep. 20: 00:18:50-00:18:03). Around the Tak family table – at the public/private threshold in their housing estate – these repeated enactments of community dialogue connect the personal with the political.

Conclusion: The real world and an elephant in the room

These early episodes of *BLR* blur the spaces of the characters' lives while also closing the distance between the audience and the government. Their combined effect is to heighten the expectation of the population in regard to the state's role in improving and securing their well-being. However, the elephant in the room is that the unconditional communal efforts we see in Wong's televisual world remain an onscreen fantasy; the lack of privacy and the sharing of public resources can be the source of insecurity and severe competition among the tenants. Che (2017) concludes that the need for private space is not fulfilled in the early designs of public housing. For instance, she interviewed a female tenant who lived in the same kind of Mark II Resettlement Estate as seen in the TV series. The interviewee complained about the public facilities, pointing out that 'as a woman, using [a] public bathroom is not convenient and dangerous' (Che 2017: 140). James Lee (1999) interviewed a male tenant who lived in the Resettlement Estate as a child. This tenant recalled the vigilance required to survive the competitive living environment: 'When I was about ten, I was assigned by my mother as a "sentry" for the washing tap and the toilet. I developed a system of warning and communication with my family so that they knew exactly when to come forward to the communal place for washing. I mustn't let the fat lady next door get it first because if she did, we wouldn't be able to have the shower room before ten [o'clock]' (Lee 1999: 123). The community conflict suggested by these real-world public housing contexts is likewise visible as the television series moves on.

In the new style of *BLR* after Franklin Wong's era, 'The Move (喬遷)' (1976) is an episode by director Lo Chi-Keung and producer Cheung Man-Yi, with location shooting at the Wang Tau Hom estate. The episode follows Uncle Tak as he spends a single day in the Resettlement District. It begins with a conflict in the neighbourhood about using the water tap in the morning, when one resident is brushing his teeth, and another is cleaning the spittoon. It then follows with an argument about peeking into the female lavatory, then there is a girl who must hold up a curtain in the double-deck bed while she changes clothes, just to maintain her privacy. In the sunset, Uncle Tak breaks the fourth wall and talks to the television audience directly: 'In the morning, people fight for the toilet, then fight for water to cook. When people come home after work, they fight for the bathroom. We even fight for the road in the corridor when leaving the housing unit' (*Revisiting the Classics of Below the Lion Rock* 2014, Ep. 47: 00:32:32-00:32:57).

Against these conflicts shot in real-world Hong Kong's public housing spaces (and lacking the positive community dialogue around Uncle Tak's table), we can see that the strength of Wong's episodes rests at encouraging a more connected city dweller. The conversations between his characters brought together personal, social and government issues, balancing the concerns of the grassroots working class with narrative propaganda supporting government policies. Wong's design of a blurred public/private space at the family table next to the open door and the un-curtained window is where and how that balance was achieved, articulating to the citizens of the city, and to the viewers of the show, how to live in a transitioning Hong Kong. This Wong-era spirit was evoked in 2002 when the Financial Secretary Antony Leung Kam-chung recited the lyrics of the *BLR* theme song (by the same title) during his budget speech. With a deficit and harsh pay cuts looming, he appealed to frustrated Hong Kong residents to overcome the hardship of economic recession by returning to 'individual effort' and 'communal harmony' (Chan 2007; Lam 2020: 130), even referencing the days of water rationing as seen in the 1975 episode 'The Long Stream/細水長流'. Although Wong's *Below the Lion Rock* era of an unconditionally supportive, harmonious urban community remains a fiction, this chapter can contribute to further discussion about the roots of the *Spirit* and how 1970s Hong Kong public housing, framed spatially, socially and politically by producer-director Franklin Wong Wah-kay, opened a communal door to an iconic stone lion and its panoramic view of a modern city.

Note

1   Franklin Wong directed his last *BLR* episodes in 1975, when he became the Chief Promotion Officer at the Independent Commission Against Corruption (ICAC).

References

Chan, Eddy Ming Hong (2007), 'From "Below the Lion Rock" to Sam Hui's Songs to "Just Because You Are Here": The Relationship between "Hong Kong People's Song" and "Hong Kong People"', *Cultural Studies@Lingnan*, Issue 7: 1–22 (in Chinese). Available online: https://www.ln.edu.hk/mcsln/archive/7th_issue/pdf/feature_01.pdf (accessed 20 July 2022).

Che, Hio Leong (2017), 'Space and Biopolitics: Case study on Hong Kong Public Housing', in Siu Keung Cheung, Kai Chi Leung and Ka Ming Chan (eds), *Hong Kong, Society, Negotiation*, 137–62, Hong Kong: Infolink Publishing, Ltd. (in Chinese).

Che, Hio Leong (2021), 'Cultural Governance under Colonial Rule: The Early "Below the Lion Rock"', in Siu Keung Cheung, Gary Kin Yat Tang and Chung-kin Tsang (eds), *Hong Kong, Paradigm, Shift*, 241–63, Hong Kong: Infolink Publishing, Ltd. (in Chinese).

Chin, Horace Wan-kan (2009), *The Days of Public Broadcasting: RTHK 80 years*, Hong Kong: Ming Pao Publications Ltd (in Chinese).

Hong Kong Memory (2012a), *Resettlement Estates: Introduction.* Available online: https://www.hkmemory.hk/MHK/collections/public_housing/resettlement_estates/introduction/index.html (accessed 24 July 2022).

Hong Kong Memory (2012b), *Mark I & Mark II Blocks.* Available online: https://www.hkmemory.hk/MHK/collections/public_housing/resettlement_estates/mark_I_and_mark_II_blocks/index.html (accessed 24 July 2022).

Ko, Tim Keung (2021), *Memories of a Bygone Era: Resettlement in Hong Kong 1950–1972.* Available online: https://heritage.uchicago.hk/photos/Rotating-Exhibits/Resettlement/Resettlement_Leaflet.pdf (accessed 24 July 2022).

Lam, Sunny Sui-kwong (2020), 'The Two Logics of the "Lion Rock Spirit" Re-Represented by FortunePharmHK's Branding Television Commercial', in

Sunny Sui-kwong Lam (ed), *New Media Spectacles and Multimodal Creativity in a Globalised Asia: Art, Design and Activism in the Digital Humanities Landscape*, 123–39, Singapore: Springer.

Lau, Siu-kai (1978), *From Traditional Familism to Utilitarianistic Familism: The Metamorphosis of Familial Ethos among the Hong Kong Chinese*, Hong Kong: Social Research Centre, Chinese University of Hong Kong.

Lee, James (1999), *Housing, Home Ownership, and Social Change in Hong Kong*, London: Routledge.

Lui, Tai-lok (2006), '1974 – the Year of Insignificance', in Chun Hung Ng, Eric Kit-wai Ma and Tai-lok Lui (eds), *Hong Kong, Culture, Studies*, 21–44, Hong Kong: Hong Kong University Press (in Chinese).

Lui, Tai-lok (2007), *Please, Check the Bill – the Hong Kong Diary of a Sociologist*, Hong Kong: Oxford University Press (in Chinese).

Mathews, Gordon, Eric Ma and Tai-Lok Lui (2008), *Hong Kong, China: Learning to Belong to a Nation*, New York: Routledge.

Ng, Chun Hung (2009), 'Born in 1974: The past and present of Hong Kong popular culture', in Anthony Bing-leung Cheung (ed), *Hong Kong Experience: Cultural Heritage and Institutional Innovation*, 142–63, Hong Kong: Center of Asian Studies, Hong Kong University (in Chinese).

Ng, Chun Hung (2010), 'From "Shelter" to "Home" – How Do We Grow Up?', in *Get Lively with Homes Design: The Look of Hong Kong Homes & Households, 1960s–2000s: Visual Arts Thematic Exhibition*, 24–43, Hong Kong: Cultural Hulu.

Tsang, Chung-kin (2021), *Homeownership in Hong Kong: House Buying as Hope Mechanism*, London & New York: Routledge.

Wu, Helena (2020), *The Hangover after the Handover: Places, Things and Cultural Icons in Hong Kong*, Liverpool: Liverpool University Press.

Television drama series

Wong, Franklin Wah-kay, director (1973–1975), *Revisiting the Classics of Below the Lion Rock*. Hong Kong: RTHK, (Episodes 1–20). https://podcast.rthk.hk/podcast/item.php?pid=568 (accessed 20 July 2022).

Revisiting the Classics of Below the Lion Rock (2014), 'Episode 1 – Introduction', https://podcast.rthk.hk/podcast/item.php?pid=568&eid=37345&year=2014&display=all&list=1&display=all&lang=zh-CN (accessed 20 July 2022).

Revisiting the Classics of Below the Lion Rock (2014), 'Episode 7', https://podcast.rthk.hk/podcast/item.php?pid=568&eid=37339&year=2014&display=all&lang=zh-CN (accessed 20 July 2022).

Revisiting the Classics of Below the Lion Rock (2014), 'Episode 11', https://podcast.rthk.hk/podcast/item.php?pid=568&eid=37918&year=2014&lang=zh-CN (accessed 11 April 2023).

Revisiting the Classics of Below the Lion Rock (2014), 'Episode 15', https://podcast.rthk.
    hk/podcast/item.php?pid=568&eid=38086&year=2014&lang=zh-CN (accessed
    11 April 2023).

Revisiting the Classics of Below the Lion Rock (2014), 'Episode 20', https://podcast.rthk.
    hk/podcast/item.php?pid=568&eid=38090&year=2014&lang=zh-CN (accessed
    11 April 2023).

Revisiting the Classics of Below the Lion Rock (2014), 'Episode 47', https://podcast.rthk.
    hk/podcast/item.php?pid=568&eid=39184&year=2014&lang=zh-CN (accessed
    11 April 2023).

9

Within the public housing flats: Interiorization of class drama in Singapore cinema

Meisen Wong and Chua Beng Huat

Introduction

Public housing estates in Europe have been popular sites of portrayal by documentary and fiction filmmakers. It is even formalized in French cinema as a distinct genre – *banlieue* or *beur* cinema. The geographically peripheral estates would serve as a diegetic backdrop to its inhabitants' social and economic marginalization and estrangement from the city centre and all the possibilities it has to offer (Nwonka 2017: 70). The onscreen portrayal of public housing estates and its residents is a consequence of state disinvestment since the 1970s. Existing social housing stock was sold to sitting tenants at a very substantial discount, turning working-class tenants into homeowners. The residual social housing stock was left for racially, economically and otherwise socially disadvantaged people. The steadily declining residual estates came to be widely (mis)perceived, amplified by media reports, as urban 'ghettos': structurally unsound racial enclaves steeped in gang criminality and violence, unemployment and social unrest (Taunton 2009; Boughton 2018). Such perceptions have strengthened governmental calls for demolition and urban redevelopment (Adesina, Brennan and Greenwood 2018).

In reel life, the estrangement of public housing estates and their residents would drive drama and plot development, affixing an underlying social critique of class rage and institutional violence. Higbee (2001) argues that despite certain filmmakers' best intentions to critique and highlight social and economic marginalization, the cinematic space of public housing estates and its inhabitants ironically reinforces its own Other-ing. There are exceptions. Joe Cornish's *Attack the Block* (2011) and Fanny Liatard and Jérémy Trouilh's

Gagarine (2020) are examples that disrupt the angry young Black male trope. The main characters of both films, Moses and Youri, respectively, are recast as creative and resilient defenders of the estate as community and home. Their valiant efforts are ultimately celebrated as heroic.

In contrast to the class drama and resistance that have been externalized and spatialized in the cinematic portrayal of European housing estates and their inhabitants, this chapter argues that the screen imaging of the Singapore public housing system serves as an inversion of class-related conflict. The experience of institutional violence or structural injustice is never externalized. Instead, it is inverted as individualized anguish, alienated and mostly confined within the 'interior' of the flat. Before our film analysis to explicate this interiorization of class drama in Singapore cinema, a brief history of the public housing system and its role in homogenizing lifestyles is necessary.

Public housing in Singapore: Post-war to the present

In Singapore, the provision of public housing has been continuous and unabated since its inception in 1960. The British colonial government had woefully fallen short in resolving the problems of urban overcrowding and the proliferation of informal settlements in the urban fringes. In 1959, the very first fully enfranchised, popularly elected parliament of the People's Action Party (PAP) immediately set out to fulfil its election promise to improve the living conditions of the new citizens. It established a national public housing authority – the Housing Development Board (HDB) – to oversee resettlement of the informal housing and construction, distribution, allocation and management of subsidized public housing units and estates. The publicly subsidized high-rise flats were sold to citizens on a ninety-nine-year lease; the leaseholders are endowed with the full rights of homeownership. The mortgage payment was facilitated by monthly withdrawal from a state-enforced social security savings scheme – the Central Provident Fund. A percentage of one's monthly wage plus an additional contribution from the employer are withheld and credited into one's CPF account. The monthly mortgage is withdrawn and paid directly to the HDB without the involvement of any commercial financial institutions. Public housing ownership is thus highly dependent on uninterrupted employment, disciplining a compliant labour force for national economic development. Within a decade, alongside rapid industrialization, the overcrowding and informal settlements were cleared, and the population housed in the high-rise, high-density, comprehensively planned public housing new towns.

Since its establishment in 1960, the HDB has received a total of S\$36.22 billion to provide housing for up to 85 per cent of the population (Ng 2020); more than 80 per cent hold a ninety-nine-year lease on their flats, and the remaining 5–6 per cent are housed in very low-cost rental flats.[1] Given full ownership rights, the ninety-nine-year lease can be freely traded in the open market among eligible citizens. Thus, like all other housing assets, public housing in Singapore has been commodified and transformed into an investment vehicle for private capital accumulation (Chua and Wong 2018: 108). Except for two or three short periods of price decline during brief national economic recessions, the value of public housing has increased without interruption since its inception. Unsurprisingly, the commitment to near-universal provision of affordable public housing, the HDB's housing stock currently accounts for 1.1 million housing units ('Households' 2021) and has been a vital source of the ruling PAP's political legitimacy (Chua 1997).

The public housing new towns are comprehensively planned for self-sufficiency in terms of providing daily necessities to the residential population: primary schools, medical clinics, markets and food courts, public transport services. This means the daily needs of an overwhelming majority of Singaporeans are equally served and their life within the housing estates relatively homogenized, with minimal visual evidence of social class differences. Singapore's tropical weather also reduces visual distinction by fashion, as informal casual dressing is the norm within neighbourhoods. Given near-universal homeownership of public housing and a social visual environment of homogenous lifestyles, dramas of gender, racial, and especially, class differences are thus interiorized and individualized in Singapore cinema.

Under an uninterrupted sixty years of a hegemonic PAP regime, Singapore's class struggles have never been spatially externalized. Between 1959 and 1960, the PAP had captured the labour union movement of the 1950s through union-busting policies, arrests and the establishment of the National Trade Union Congress (NTUC) that would unify labour organization. However, the NTUC has since then been symbiotically tied to the PAP government, with interchangeable leadership. Without avenues for collective action, any class-related conflict experienced by an individual has nowhere to go but to turn inwards and manifest itself as a problem of the Self and the family. This is further reinforced through institutionalized meritocracy that has socialized an individualizing of success/failure as a consequence of effort (or the lack thereof). As such, class-related drama manifests only as individual alienation and family violence enacted within the interior domestic spaces of the public housing flat; the dynamics of what may be said to constitute part of the Singaporean Self will be examined through the Singaporean films analysed in this chapter. They include Eric Khoo's *12 Storeys* (1997), Kevin Tong and Jasmine Ng's *Eating Air* (1999), Boo Junfeng's *Apprentice* (2016) and K Rajagopal's *A Yellow Bird* (2016). It is perhaps noteworthy that *12 Storeys*, *Apprentice* and *A Yellow Bird* have received critical acclaim and have appeared in the international film festival circuit, most notably at the Cannes Film Festival. A few other Singaporean films, including two short films, will also be referenced because they feature public housing flat interiors as dramatic sites.

The *Kopitiam* as a class community?

Before delving into the public housing flat interior, it is necessary to briefly discuss how cinema might feature and symbolically utilize exterior/outdoor spaces. In films, two such exterior spaces may be found. First is the colloquially named 'void deck'; this is the ground floor of each housing block which is left as an open but sheltered space. In addition to facilitating pedestrians passing through the blocks, void decks are also where some public amenities such as letterboxes or public furniture can be located (National Heritage Board 2013: 5). Socially, the open space enables neighbours to meet and bond or hold community events such as funerals and weddings (NHB 2013: 13). The other exterior space featured is the commercial shops on the ground floor of selective blocks of flats. The most prominent one is the *kopitiam* – a vernacular term for coffee shop, that hosts affordable drinks and food stalls of various ethnic cuisines.

In films such as *12 Storeys* (1997) and *Money No Enough* (Tay 1998), the *kopitiam* is where characters hang out, forming a community who meet in a ritualistic fashion, usually before or after working hours. This community is both gendered and class-biased: they are male and represent the so-called 'heartlander'.[2] The men sit around a table and engage in what is known in the vernacular as 'talking cock' over food and drinks. The conversations involve cheeky commentary about government policies, current events, political gossip and making sexualized quips about female passers-by. Yao (2006) argues that 'talking cock' is a pleasurable and cathartic exercise where male individuals vent about the pressures of life in a public space and is potentially subversive.

Nonetheless, any potentiality of class consciousness or subversion evolving from talking cock at the *kopitiam* is ultimately diminished in the aforementioned films, displaced by an individualized fantasy of winning the national lottery. The three main characters in *Money No Enough* discuss financial woes over breakfast, and Ong and Hui conclude that winning the lottery will solve all of life's problems. In *12 Storeys*, a young man jumps to his death from a high-rise housing block in one of the earliest scenes. His mangled body is on public display on the ground. There are a few onlookers. A man runs over to check on the body, asking if anyone has called for help. None responds. The man rushes off, exclaiming at the uncaring crowd. Since this is before the ubiquity of the personal mobile phone, we can assume he has gone to call the police. The victim's tragic death could have led to a community of concern, no matter how ephemeral. However, the witnesses speculate about the victim with little sympathy, connoting that the young man remains socially isolated even in death. Instead, the date and time of his death are turned into potential winning numbers for the local weekly lottery, hopefully turning one's misfortune into another's good fortune. If the exterior does not produce an emergent community, how does Singapore cinema portray the dramas of the socially marginalized within the interior?

Minimalism and *Démodé* vintage of the marginalized in cinematic space

The interior is a product of modernity. Urbanization and new forms of governance have increased public visibility and forced intimacy. Individuals have responded with reduced sociability and increased introspection, investing more in the interior (Sennett 1977; Rice 2007). This emergence of the interior is accordingly spatialized as home or shelter, 'a world in itself' that establishes the Bachelardian dialectic of inside/outside and its meanings (Shepheard 2017: 4). The investment in the home and what is contained within (e.g., home decor) is thus perceived as an expression of the Self, an individuality differentiated from its public variations. Daniel Miller, in *Home Possessions*, argues that the materiality of what lies within reflect the dwellers' 'agency and sometimes their impotence' (2001: 1). We thus begin with the diegetic portrayal of the *interior* that frames the lived experiences of the socially marginalized in Singapore.

Material austerity is the oft-representation of choice for the poor in Singapore cinema. The starkest illustration of this forced minimalism is the interior of the flat of Siva's ex-wife in *A Yellow Bird*. Siva, a recently released ex-convict, seeks out his ex-wife, who had divorced him during his incarceration and has since refused contact, denying him access to their daughter. He finds the two-room flat she lives in with her new husband and children. The audience, like Siva, is denied entry or a full view of the interior. He manages to glimpse the interior by lifting the metallic window louvres; following the camera, he first sees two toddlers sleeping on a towel laid out on the floor. As the camera pans across the living room, we see a small table, a picture frame on the wall, a medium-sized cabinet and an electric fan placed in front of the sleeping children. There is no adult present. The emptiness is even more severe in the bedroom, containing merely a mattress and an oxygen tank connected to his paralyzed daughter, who needs assistance in breathing. The walls are stained with age and dirt.

As public housing ownership is the norm for Singaporean households, the lowest-income and abject poor are afforded the lowest-cost public housing rental flats of single or two rooms. The lack of basic amenities such as sofas or doorbells projects poverty and the temporary character of rental tenancy. The interior of the onscreen flat in *A Yellow Bird* clearly communicates temporary shelter, not permanence. The furnishings show little semblance of coherence or aesthetics besides their utility; there is 'no sense of the person as the other, who defines one's own boundary and extent' (Miller 2008: 8). It is common for the poor to inherit furniture left behind by previous tenants or glean items discarded by those living in excess. It is therefore almost impossible to curate an interior that speaks of the inhabitant's individual or household identity. If the toddlers do not even sleep on a simple mattress and have been left unattended (presumably for work), its inhabitants are not even living a functional life but merely eking out a bare subsistence. This is illustrative of filmmakers' diegetic use of the interior decor to symbolize class positions.

By contrast, the interior of working-class households is less austerely presented on screen. Although the films are set in contemporary times, the furnishings and decor found in the onscreen flats often have an outdated or vintage look; this results from the furnishing being discarded and found objects than of a purposefully elevated fashionable 'vintage' aesthetic. In a flat interior featured in Royston Tan's *Bunga Sayang* (2015), as seen in Figure 9.1, the designs of the door grills and window louvres are typically found in public housing flats built in the 1960s–70s and discontinued since the 1980s. The cabinet centrepiece in the living room is reminiscent of ones popular in the 1950s. The low-seating teak sofa set, the electronic fan and the television express the same temporal disjointedness. Similar decors, especially the low-seating teak sofa set, can be

Figure 9.1 Outdated interior décor in *Bunga Sayang* directed by Royston Tan
© Chuan Pictures, 2015. All rights reserved.

found in flat interiors that feature in *12 Storeys*, Ah Girl's house in *Eating Air*, Royston Tan's other short feature *15* (2002), the main family home in *Singapore Dreaming* (2006) and in *Apprentice*. Metaphorically, the temporal disjointedness also symbolizes the estrangement of the economically marginalized from the here-and-now of a society where home-owning middle-class living standards have become normative.

A literal reading of this *démodé* vintage aesthetic could mean that its inhabitants reside in flats located in the earliest-built public housing estates and had little means to 'upgrade' to a better-designed flat in newer housing estates. Aspirational 'upgrading' is memorably portrayed by the character Keong in *Money No Enough*. Keong had experienced a windfall from his share market speculations and was also expecting a job promotion with higher wages. His material possessions had to cohere with the expected improvements in economic earnings. He accomplished this by purchasing a bigger flat with extensive renovations using the 'best' materials (e.g. Italian marble flooring), a new car (albeit a second-hand Mercedes he bought at a discounted price) and the latest models of household appliances. The biggest, newest and best were seen as 'necessities' to construct a comfortable middle-class lifestyle, a stark contrast between the spartan and outdated interiors symbolizing the poor and working-class lifestyles onscreen.

Density, privacy and escapism

If class positions define access to space and how much space, then the same applies to access to privacy. For Walter Benjamin, the conception of the interior (i.e. home) is an escape from the public realm, and where expressions of individuality can be freely expressed (Rosner 2005: 147). However, in the cinematic portrayals of the socially marginalized in Singapore films, the limited interior of a small rental public housing flat creates a lack of privacy and freedom of self-expression; overcrowding and friction between its inhabitants are unavoidable. The interior thus becomes a site of alienation, repression and violence. Often, escape is temporary and futile.

A bigger home that comes with wealth is obviously the ultimate escape. As mentioned earlier, winning the national lottery is a common wishful fantasy to escape class-related challenges in both real- and reel-life. This is the pretext of *Singapore Dreaming*, where the character Poh Huat, an avid buyer of lottery tickets, gets lucky and wins a S$2 million lottery. Unfortunately, he dies shortly after this stroke of good luck and does not get to enjoy the private apartment or country club membership he has long desired. Upward social mobility as fantasy is also exemplified in Meng's narrative in *12 Storeys*. Meng, a schoolteacher, has the means and ought to have achieved upward class mobility, but his role as the sole breadwinner for his siblings has trapped him to remain in their small two-bedroom public housing flat. He is the model Singaporean who speaks good English, sticking out like a sore thumb amongst his ethnic-vernacular language-speaking working-class neighbours. Like Poh Huat, he looks down on his residential estate and its residents. As there are only two bedrooms in the flat, Meng is reduced to sharing a room with his younger siblings Trixie and Di (the vernacular designation for a younger brother); the other bedroom is presumed to be reserved for the parents absent in the film. Financing his siblings' education, Meng hopes his sister will perform well academically in order to access a white-collar profession. Unfortunately, neither Trixie nor Di has any academic inclinations. Trixie is content to be a salesgirl working in fashion retail. He is indignant that all his 'sacrifices' have been futile and deems his siblings ungrateful. Meng meets Trixie's boyfriend, a car salesman with much lower educational qualifications than Meng but who can nevertheless afford the middle-class lifestyle that he is denied. The meeting devastates Meng as he realizes that upward social mobility seems to be more fantasy than an achievable reality. He is further exasperated by the active sexual relations between Trixie and her boyfriend, a theme that will be taken up later.

One of the most unforgettable portrayals of density within the interior is *Eating Air* (1999). Within the first few minutes of screen time, it is clear that the film's titular character, Boy, is from a working-class background. He lives in a crowded three-room public housing flat. His parents cook and package take-out food within the confines of their home. Each morning, Boy wakes up to the din of frenzied cooking. Absorbed with filling food orders, the parents move around each other in silence in the kitchen. To retrieve a tin of biscuits for breakfast requires a highly choreographed sequence of writhing and twisting to avoid touching or disrupting his parents cooking back-to-back in the narrow width of the kitchen. The necessity of the business, such as food materials, egg trays and Styrofoam takeaway boxes, is visibly overflowing in the living room. Boy has to rummage through all the stuff to find his motorcycle helmet buried beneath it. Contrary to Catherine Allerton's (2013: 54) suggestion that density in the home produces smell, noise and chatter, connoting intimacy, liveliness and homeliness between family members, Boy feels invisible and unnecessary in an interior of excess.

Boy's alienation and loneliness within the interior are resolved through escapism. First, he retreats further into his imaginary world. In Boy's imaginary existence, he is self-cast as a Chinese pugilistic hero constantly engaged in violent battle. These settings are differentiated onscreen by red lighting and flashing strobes to disorientating effect. In one scene, his parents are dressed in assassin costumes and attempt to kill him; he battles them and successfully kills them with his superior *kungfu* skills. In another, he emerges from his bedroom into his make-believe world where his parents are already dead, believed to be murdered. Certainly, his parents' imagined death symbolizes an underlying desire to be free from his unhappy family and home.

Second, the outside of the flat is also a space for escape where community and connection are to be found. Boy's primary community is a small group of delinquent friends in a motorcycle gang, constantly engaged in petty crimes and mischief. Later, he develops an intimate bond with Girl, a lonely teenage high-school student emotionally estranged from her single mother who is in constant search of male companions who are uncommitted to her. Boy and Girl bond over their disinterest in academics. Although school can be a site of formative relations for teenagers, the self-discipline needed for the highly competitive examination-based system can be alienating for youth from impoverished and distressed families. Boy nonchalantly quips, 'Books don't read me, so I don't read them' (*Eating Air* 1999: 00:49:28-00:49:30). Together, they plan to run away from their respective homes.

In one scene, Boy and Girl hang out on the rooftop of a public housing block. The rooftop is a site of escape for both. With a view beyond the insularity and density of the flat, the rooftop is a literal and symbolic extension of space and possibilities, where they can freely express their desires. They imagine a faraway destination as Girl points to the sea and repeatedly asks what lies beyond. Girl asks what comes after China, and Boy replies, his grandma's house. He asks Girl if she wants to be taken there. Given that his grandmother is absent onscreen, the 'there' is an ambiguous destination at best. The conversation is possibly an ominous sign that their planned escape will be an unfulfilled one. Ultimately, on the night of his getaway with Girl, Boy and his buddy are violently killed while escaping a motorcycle chase by their enemies. In the closing scene, Girl looks at Boy's body sprawled on the highway in a tunnel and walks away in grief and disappointment. Those who have promised her escape (both Boy and her mother) have failed her.

Another heart-breaking illustration of density within a constrained interior is the narrative of San San in Eric Khoo's *12 Storeys*. San San is a middle-aged, obese, unemployed single woman who is the primary caregiver of her elderly adoptive mother, a fact the latter never fails to bring up as her deserved entitlement to San San's gratitude. Her mother has another adopted daughter with academic, economic and marital success in life. For the mother, Rachel's success is the counterpoint of comparison to San San's failure, as she rains interminable verbal abuses on San San throughout the day. San San busies herself with housework, a feeble attempt to ignore these relentless castigations. Far from homeliness and intimacy, this is an interior dense with pain, alienation and revilement for San San. Unsurprisingly, she is severely depressed and desires to escape through suicide.

While attempting to jump to her death, she notices a neighbour staring at her. When the two depressed neighbours see each other, a connection that could offer companionship and comfort might have been made. However, the young man turns away in silence. Minutes after witnessing San San's attempt, the young man jumps to his own death. As previously discussed, this is the same man who jumped in the film's opening scene. He returns as a voyeur spirit, silently observing and empathizing with the pain of his neighbours, especially San San. When her mother passes away, San San feels no relief from the pain. The spirit hugs her in comfort, albeit a meaningless gesture to her. The scene perhaps exemplifies the director's insistence on atomizing the pain of the marginalized, refusing the potential of relations that could be formed in empathy and shared suffering.

The high-density interior is also a site of sexual repression. In *12 Storeys*, Trixie and Lili are women whose sexualities are curtailed by surveillance by men in their families. Trixie shares a room with her brothers, where the forced intimacy reveals Meng's incestuous desire for her. When a condom emerges from their younger brother's invasion of Trixie's private belongings, he feels betrayed that she might be sexually active. Without any space to maintain privacy, and alongside her elder brother's controlling behaviour and slut-shaming, Trixie is forced to seek refuge outside the flat. She stays out later each night, to escape the sexual repression found at home. The containment of Meng's sexual repression finally explodes in a drunken rage after Trixie returns from a late night out with her boyfriend, culminating in Meng's violence towards her.

For Lili, the Chinese migrant wife to the buck-toothed food-hawker Ah Gu, escape is in the form of romantic flings with wealthy men who might promise her upward social mobility. To her, the interior of the marital flat symbolizes class and sexual frustration. Although her husband is utterly devoted to her, she perceives the marriage as a scam. She accuses Ah Gu of inflating his material wealth when courting her in China. When Ah Gu claimed he was a homeowner, she had expected a private landed property, not a ubiquitous public housing flat. Alongside the material disappointment, Lili is repulsed by the looks of Ah Gu, thus impeding a sexually fulfilling marriage. Resentful and lonely, Lili seeks romantic companionship outside, cruelly taunting Ah Gu's inability to 'satisfy' her. Suspicious that Lili is cheating on him, Ah Gu rummages through her belongings. He finally finds a text message on her mobile phone that alludes to her sexual intimacy with another man. This invasion of privacy infuriates Lili, who threatens to leave her husband; however, in an anti-climax, Lili stays. After presumably unsatisfying makeup sex with Ah Gu, she masturbates to a picture of a former lover left behind in China. By staying, Lili seems to have thwarted possibilities of happiness and retreated further into an individualized, painful nostalgia of a past romance and happier days.

Within confined interior domestic space, sexual activity must also be camouflaged. Suhaila's character in *Apprentice* invites her boyfriend over when her brother is at work. She turns up the television volume to mask any sounds emitting from the bedroom. Unfortunately, her brother returns home and walks in on them during sex. In *A Yellow Bird*, Siva returns to his mother's three-room flat after his prison term, only to find out that his bedroom had been rented out to Chinese migrant workers. Unable to afford the services of a sex worker, Siva decides to relieve himself in his mother's flat. Without the privacy of an individual bedroom and closed doors, Siva masturbates in the kitchen corner after everyone is asleep, hidden in darkness. He is interrupted by a tenant who has awakened to use the toilet located in the kitchen. In another scene, his ex-sister-in-law sexually propositions him in the stairwell of a housing block flat. For those marginalized within the interior, stairwells can function as an extension of private space or an escape, used by residents and strangers to converse in privacy or engage in more illicit activities such as drug-taking or sexual activity (Wong 2021). While corridors serve the same function, stairwells enable greater privacy due to their reduced public visibility.

The notable exceptions in Singapore cinema where Benjamin's concept of the home as escape and a site to freely express the Self is found in Eric Khoo's *Mee Pok Man* (1995). Johnny, the main character, is a slow-witted hawker who sells noodles at a *kopitiam* in the red-light district of Singapore. His regular customers include sex workers and their customers. His shy personality further alienates him from everyone, and he is often the butt of ridicule and taunts from individuals with marginal social status, like the sex workers and pimps he serves. Unlike the other characters discussed previously, Johnny lives alone in his flat, an *escape* from the public where he can freely express himself. His flat is thus the setting of a warped romance he shares with Bunny, a sex worker he has long desired. One night, Bunny is hurt in a hit-and-run accident witnessed by Johnny, who takes her to his home instead of a hospital. Within his flat, he can freely express his romantic obsession with her; this culminates in necrophilia when Bunny succumbs to her injuries. While the interior of his flat allows Johnny's privacy and thus his freedom to engage in fetish, the film ends with Johnny being alone again. Ultimately, the interior space as escape is only a fleeting one.

Another filmic example of Benjamin's concept of home is in Royston Tan's *15*, where the self-contained flat is the teenage delinquents' escape shelter from school discipline, dysfunctional parents and street gang violence. Their class positions are represented through the *démodé* vintage aesthetic found within the two flat interiors featured. As discussed earlier, this temporal disjointedness symbolizes their estrangement from mainstream (read: middle class) lifestyles. The teens are members of a street gang fraught with internal conflict, which disrupts the sense of community they had sought through their membership. For a significant portion of the film's screen time, two different groups of teenage delinquents are holed up within the respective flats in the absence of parents or other family members. Within the flat, they take drugs, watch porn, rehearse gang chants and dances that are presented like a music video onscreen and find solace (at points, homoerotic romance) in each other. Yet, there is a shared understanding that hiding within the flat can only be a temporary escape. One of the characters, Armani, seeks a permanent escape through suicide, and his friends Shaun and Erick assist him by finding the perfect suicide spot.

Here, we have shown that Walter Benjamin's concept of home and the interior as a space of freedom for individual expression is contradicted by Singapore filmmakers in *12 Storeys* and *Eating Air*. Instead, the high-density interior is a space of alienation, surveillance, repression and violence – from which the characters are compelled to escape. Conversely, *Mee Pok Man* and *15* serve as counterpoints where the interior coheres with Benjamin's concept and functions as a site of escapism from class-related challenges, albeit a temporary and futile one. In the next section, we will explore how local directors utilize windows as a cinematographic tool to individualize and interiorize class drama.

Windows as interiorization of class drama

In nineteenth-century apartment living, the boundary between the interior and exterior was permeable (Marcus 1999: 3). Housing was never entirely enclosed. Instead, apartment living illustrated the continuity between the interior and exterior, the domestic and the urban. The same can be said of life in contemporary, high-rise public housing estates where individual flats are divided only by walls, doors and windows that insulate flat dwellers from the exterior. Instead of insulation, however, they function as Gaston Bachelard's concept of *thresholds* which he poetically conveys as 'an entire cosmos of the Half-Open', a vessel of possibilities for better or worse (1969: 222). Thresholds connect, open, protect, or close off those within from the possibilities that the exterior offers. Thresholds also allow a glimpse into the interiors of someone else's world. Windows are such thresholds. Using *Apprentice* and *A Yellow Bird*, the following will examine the use of windows and cinematography in the interiorization of class drama.

Looking out of windows is easily associated with voyeurism in movies, popularly exemplified by Alfred Hitchcock's *Rear Window* (1954). The advent of glass allowed one to be a passive observer of social activity in the exterior. Yet the act of looking out of the window is not simply voyeuristic if filmmakers can enable the possibility of the politics of what is seen or hidden to emerge. During the early days of the Covid-19 pandemic, social media documented heart-warming scenes of individual households standing by their windows (and balconies) singing songs of solidarity and strength in Italy and Wuhan. These scenes illustrate that, even if we live atomized lives within our respective flats, a community can emerge just by looking out the window and engaging with the exterior (Deshpande 2021). Instead, in *Apprentice* and *A Yellow Bird*, the cinematographic use of windows reiterates the alienation of those who are socially marginalized.

In Boo Junfeng's *Apprentice*, a pair of Malay siblings, Aiman and his sister Suhaila, live in a two-bedroom flat inherited from their grandmother. The siblings share traumatic family history, one imbued with much societal stigma as their late father had been a convicted drug smuggler sentenced to death by hanging. How the siblings relate to the past has created conflict between them. Suhaila is future-oriented and determined to leave the past behind, starting life anew in Australia with her boyfriend, John. On the other hand, Aiman is trapped in the past. Suhaila's decision to move forward is perceived as a betrayal and abandonment, even though he rejects her invitation to visit and move to Australia with her. Resolved to not be like his father, Aiman is ironically fixated with the prison executioner who hanged his father. He makes the baffling decision to hide his family history from the prison administrators in order to get acquainted with the executioner. The latter takes a liking to Aiman and intends to groom him as an apprentice. In a crucial scene, Suhaila discovers Aiman's inexplicable career decision. Confused and hurt, she asks him what he is trying to prove by working with the executioner. At this point, Aiman's back is towards Suhaila, facing the windows. Suhaila is still talking to Aiman, but she has been cut out from the shot (see Figure 9.2).

This window scene symbolizes Aiman's self-imposed alienation. The audience sees neither what is outside the window nor Suhaila, who is in the room. From this framing, Aiman is essentially disconnected. The cinematic focus on his face with sunlight from the exterior illuminating his profile indicates to the audience that Aiman's internal emotional turmoil takes centre stage. Aiman keeps his back facing Suhaila while she recounts the happy memories they shared with their

Figure 9.2 Windows as interiorization of class drama in *Apprentice* directed by Boo Junfeng © Clover Films, 2016. All rights reserved.

father. She sees her father as loving and filial (to their grandparents) and, more importantly, as a man who paid grievously for his mistakes. With his resolve not to look at his sister, Aiman rejects this version of their family history and father and thus remains estranged from any possible reconciliation with their painful past. Furthermore, to have Aiman look through the window and the (unseen) exterior can be read as his blindness to the structural conditions that impinge on their family,[3] thereby individualizing the film's class-related drama.

A similar framing is evident in *A Yellow Bird*. Siva, a repeated convict, faces immense challenges with social reintegration outside the prison walls. Upon release, he has been ordered to stay with his mother during his rehabilitation process. His room has been rented out. He is displaced to the living room, not entitled to even moments of privacy. His family members enforce this estrangement. His mother treats him with indifference and silence, and his ex-wife has refused contact. In one scene, Siva stares out of the kitchen window. As in the framing of Aiman in the previous example, the exterior that Siva sees is hidden from the audience. There is a light source from the streetlamps outside, leaving most of his profile shrouded in darkness and shadow, with his face only dimly lit by the orange-tinged exterior light source. Again, the audience is meant to see Siva's internalized frustrations from this enforced estrangement and marginalization in his own home. However, if the camera is a window that shows us a view of ex-convicts and the challenges they face due to stigma, it also reinforces the audience's estrangement from the character. We can never see the same as he sees. The audience watches as voyeurs, observing *difference*. In this scene, the protagonist remains alone in his despair; he is alienated onscreen and from those watching through the screen.

Shekhar Deshpande argues that windows are merely boundaries that delimit the world inside; 'the existential condition of the inner spaces determines how the exterior world is seen' (2021). In both *Apprentice* and *A Yellow Bird*, the exterior is hidden from the audience. The cinematography and lighting draw attention to the profile of the respective protagonists, and through the emotions portrayed on the face, it is only the interior that is revealed. In both scenes, the windows function to invert class-related drama internally, individualizing the characters' existential angst.

Conclusion

Conceptually and empirically, public housing in Singapore is radically different from those in continental Europe. In the latter, public housing is residual housing for people left behind by a capitalist market economy. Since the 1970s, European housing policies had transformed public housing estates to 'residual' housing to accommodate those racially, socially, economically and politically marginalized. Spatially segregated within these housing projects, residents could not meet even their daily needs, let alone maintain their rental flats and the general estate environment. The spatial concentration of the marginalized creates the potential for collective action against their marginalization. This potential for collective rage against social injustice is often featured in films formalized as 'ghetto' or 'hood' films such as the *banlieue* cinema popularized by Mathieu Kassovitz's *La Haine* (1995; see McNeill, this volume). Whether in despair, desperation or heroic resistance against institutional violence, characters act not merely as individuals but with social positionalities affixed.

In contrast, Singapore public housing is state-subsidized flats sold to citizens at affordable prices for up to 90 per cent of the working population. Ownership of public housing is the norm. The size of one's flat depends entirely on one's ability to consume and reflects individualized economic success or failure in a highly competitive meritocratic society. Under such normative conditions, the socially disadvantaged are stigmatized by others and by themselves as 'failures'. Self-isolated in their material deprivation and psychological sufferings, marginalized individuals are atomized. They can only turn inwards, both psychologically and physically, within the limited, high-density domestic space of their small (rented or owned) public housing flats. There is no undertaking of collective action to resist or challenge the structural injustices of the society responsible for their conditions. Instead, they can only act out their inner personalized anguish violently against the Self, ultimately, in suicide or as violence towards family members, in both real and imagined scenarios. All of this interiorized class drama takes place within the confines of the flat. As we have demonstrated, the social reality of the marginalized has been abundantly captured, symbolically or through realism, by Singaporean filmmakers, particularly in critical arthouse production like *12 Storeys*, *Apprentice* and *A Yellow Bird*.

Notes

1   The remaining 10 per cent live in privately developed houses or condominiums.
2   Heartlander is in binary opposition to the cosmopolitan, categories popularized by PAP ministers in the 1990s. Whereas the cosmopolitan is a high-flying jetsetter who is fluent in English and whose occupational skills (e.g. banking) are globally relevant, the heartlander speaks mostly vernacular Singlish, has lower-

waged occupations relevant to the local community and spends more time in the 'heartlands' (i.e. public housing estates).

3   In Singapore, racial minorities – especially those from lower-income strata, witness an over-representation in incarceration and recidivism rates (Ganapathy and Lian 2016: 2). The government has singled out the Malay community for disproportionate drug use (Amin 2019), although a more critical analysis will identify class as a crucial factor of drug usage and what kind of drugs are consumed. The Singapore state is staunchly anti-drugs and maintains capital punishment for drug traffickers found in possession of drugs. Given Singapore's drug policies, the intersections of class and race in relation to drug usage and trafficking do make low-income Malay households more vulnerable to losing family members to incarceration. This risk likely reproduces class impoverishment.

References

15 (2003), [FILM] Dir. Royston Tan, Singapore: 27 Productions.
12 Storeys (1997), [FILM] Dir. Eric Khoo, Singapore: Brink Creative.
Adesina, Zack, Claire Brennan, and George Greenwood (2018), 'Dozens of London Council Estates Earmarked for Demolition', *BBC News*, 3 September. Available online: https://www.bbc.com/news/uk-england-london-45196994 (accessed 20 September 2021).
Allerton, Catherine (2013), *Potent Landscapes: Place and Mobility in Eastern Indonesia*, Honolulu: University of Hawai'i Press.
Amin, Amrin (2019), 'Review 2019 – "United Against Drug: Community Progress and the Way Forward" – Speech by Mr Amrin Amin, Senior Parliamentary Secretary, Ministry of Home Affairs and Ministry of Health', *Ministry of Home Affairs*, 16 March. Available online: https://www.mha.gov.sg/mediaroom/speeches/association-of-muslim-professionals-community-in-review-2019 – united-against-drug-community-progress-and-the-way-forward – speech-by-mr-amrin-amin-senior-parliamentary-secretary-ministry-of-home-affairs-and-ministry-of-health/ (accessed 27 September 2021).
Apprentice (2016), [FILM] Dir. Junfeng Boo, Singapore: Akanga Film Productions.
Attack the Block (2011), [FILM] Dir. Joe Cornish, UK: Screen Gems.
Bachelard, Gaston (1969), *The Poetics of Space*, translated by The Onion Press, Boston, MA: Beacon Press.
Boughton, John (2018), *Municipal Dreams: The Rise and Fall of Council Housing*, London: Verso.
Bunga Sayang, From Anthology, *7 Letters* (2015), [FILM] Dir. Royston Tan, Singapore: Chuan Pictures.
Chua, Beng Huat (1997), *Political Legitimacy and Housing: Stakeholding in Singapore*, London: Routledge.

Chua, Beng Huat and Meisen Wong (2018), 'No One Left Homeless: Universal Provision of Housing in Singapore', in Rebecca L.H. Chiu and Seong-Kyu Ha (eds), *Housing Policy, Wellbeing and Social Development in Asia*, 106–22, UK: Routledge.

Deshpande, Shekhar (2021), 'The Ontology of Windows and Cinema in the Pandemic: E-Flux and International Short Film Festival Oberhausen's Film Series 2020', *Senses of Cinema*, 98 (May). Available online: http://www.sensesofcinema.com/2021/ feature-articles/the-ontology-of-windows-and-cinema-in-the-pandemic-e- flux-and-international-short-film-festival-oberhausens-film-series-2020/?utm_ content=bufferb9efa&utm_medium=social&utm_source=facebook.com&utm_ca mpaign=buffer&fbclid=IwAR1nMaUsHmHCab1x02rEZUUy77MFM8Jf9NTzJ cfgoBpvX0gk9mRR4pAZvc (accessed 10 May 2021).

Eating Air (1999), [FILM] Dir. Kelvin Tong and Kin Kia Jasmine Ng, Singapore: YTC Pictures.

Ganapathy, Narayanan and Kwen Fee Lian (2016), 'Race, Reintegration, and Social Capital in Singapore', *International Journal of Comparative and Applied Criminal Justice* 40 (1): 1–23.

Higbee, William (2001), 'Screening the "other" Paris: Cinematic Representations of the French Urban Periphery in La Haine and Ma 6-T Va Crack-Er', *Modern and Contemporary France*, 9 (2): 197–208.

'Households' (2021), Department of Statistics, Singapore, *SingStat*. Available online: https://www.singstat.gov.sg/find-data/search-by-theme/households/households/ latest-data (accessed 20 September 2021).

Marcus, Sharon (1999), *Apartment Stories: City and Home in Nineteenth Century Paris and London*, Berkeley, Los Angeles: University of California Press.

Mee Pok Man (1995), [FILM] Dir. Eric Khoo, Singapore: 27 Productions.

Miller, Daniel (2001), 'Behind Closed Doors', in Daniel Miller (ed), *Home Possessions*: *Material Culture behind Closed Doors*, 1–22, Oxford, UK: Berg Publishers.

Miller, Daniel (2008), *The Comfort of Things*, Cambridge, UK: Polity Press.

Money No Enough (1998), [FILM] Dir. T. L. Tay, Singapore: JSP Group of Companies.

NHB (National Heritage Board) (2013), 'Community Heritage Series III: Void Decks', *Singapore: National Heritage Board*. Available online: https://www.nhb.gov.sg/~/ media/nhb/files/resources/publications/ebooks/nhb_ebook_void_decks.pdf (accessed 22 September 2021).

Ng, Michelle (2020), 'Housing Programmes See HDB's Deficit Grow to $2.66b, the Highest so Far', *The Straits Times*, 23 October. Available online: https://www. straitstimes.com/singapore/housing/housing-programmes-see-hdbs-deficit-grow- to-266b-the-highest-so-far (accessed 20 September 2021).

Nwonka, Clive James (2017), 'Estate of the Nation: Social Housing as Cultural Verisimilitude in British Social Realism', in David Forrest, Graeme Harper and Jonathan Rayner (eds), *Filmurbia: Screening the Suburbs*, 65–78, UK: Palgrave Macmillan.

Rice, Charles (2007), *The Emergence of the Interior: Architecture, Modernity, Domesticity*, UK: Routledge.

Rosner, Victoria (2005), *Modernism and the Architecture of Private Life*, New York: Columbia University Press.

Sennett, Richard (1977), *The Fall of the Public Man*, New York: Alfred A. Knopf.

Shepheard, Paul (2017), 'Foreword', *Interiors* 8 (1–2): 4–7.

Singapore Dreaming (2006), [FILM] Dir. Colin Goh and Yen Yen Woo, Singapore: 5C Films.

Taunton, Matthew (2009), *Fictions of the City: Class, Culture and Mass Housing in London and Paris*, UK: Palgrave Macmillan.

Wong, Kayla (2021), 'Residents at Pasir Ris Blk 101 Complain of Couples Engaging in Sexy Time at Staircases', *Mothership*, 21 March. Available online: https://mothership.sg/2021/03/pasir-ris-sexy-time-stairs-complain/ (accessed 23 September 2021).

Yao, Suchao (2007), '"Talking Cock": Food and the Art of Lying', in *Singapore: The State and the Culture of Excess*, 121–39, UK: Routledge.

A Yellow Bird (2016), [FILM] Dir. K. Rajagopal, Singapore: Akanga Film Productions.

Part Three

Home screens: Public housing in serialized television drama of *The Wire, Treme* and *Show Me a Hero*

10

Ignoring women and communities of care:
Public housing in *The Wire*

Kalima Young

Any concrete, spatial location where one can rest, find nourishment and establish a sense of security can become one's home. That is because home is both a location and a place of meaning making. Incidents and situations that occur within a place become fundamental memories. Whether good or bad, these place-based memories provide the narrative bones for the way we shape our lives. They provide a foundation for growth. As a physical location and a place of meaning making, home can take the shape of even the most under-resourced locales – even public housing developments in cities like Baltimore.

Government-subsidized housing came to Baltimore City on 4 October 1934, when ground was broken at 'Area H', a site on the corner of Poppleton and Saratoga Street in West Baltimore. Upon its opening in 1940, this housing project would formally go on to be called the 'Poe Homes'. The Poe Homes was a part of a larger project to replace the series of make-shift homes that housed a vast population of Black residents in the city, many of whom moved into the city from rural Maryland and/or migrated from states below the Mason-Dixon line in the nineteenth century, only to experience continuous displacement throughout the twentieth century. Eventually, the Poe Homes would go on to house 298 families who would finally have access to indoor plumbing and other amenities to improve their quality of life. Poe would later be joined by the Latrobe, McCulloh and Douglass Homes. By 1956, Baltimore had built its first high rises with Lafayette Courts and Flag House. Shortly thereafter, these high-rise housing projects were joined by Murphy Homes and Lexington Terrace Towers.

Despite protest by Black leaders, Baltimore's housing projects were racially segregated from their inception, with 'white sites' located in more desirable areas of the city than 'black sites' (Jacobson 2007: 2). Real estate agents were less concerned about uplifting people from poverty than they were with clearing 'slums' from areas deemed profitable for development, a trend that continues to this day. Baltimore has the dubious history of being the first municipality to embrace racial zoning laws. This partnership between local and federal government and real estate agencies created Residential Security Maps which 'redlined and underdeveloped Black neighborhoods in more than 200 cities' (Brown 2021: 2). Redlining, public housing and a long history of segregated public education systems in Baltimore ensured white neighbourhoods could remain white and Black neighbourhoods could remain Black. The highways and byways of urban renewal programmes from the 1950s through the 1980s in Baltimore also helped to keep the rich from having to see the poor. Throughout the 1990s, Baltimore City began demolishing the high rises through the Home Ownership and Opportunity for People Everywhere (HOPE VI)[1] (see Morgan Parmett and Macek, this volume), with Lafayette Courts falling in 1995, Lexington Terrace Towers falling in 1996, Flag House Courts and the Murphy Homes in 1999 and Perkins Homes in 2019. The mixed-income housing that has replaced many of these communities has unevenly implemented the community engagement plans designed to allow former residents the right to return to their communities. Baltimore's crisis of vacant housing, homelessness and resident displacement exists because of segregation, inequality in public and private development contracts, suburban sprawl, white flight and divestments in Black and brown communities after the 1968 uprisings in response to the assassination of Dr. Martin Luther King Jr. Discussing Baltimore's vacant housing, Eli Pousson rightly surmises that 'the conversation about how to solve the vacant building problems often starts and ends with demolition. Tearing buildings down is easier than integrating the city's segregated neighborhoods, reforming the tax sales process, or reversing decades of automobile-oriented development. Imagining alternatives – more comprehensive and lasting solutions – requires a broader perspective' (2019: 54). Television is one of the most powerful tools for harnessing broader perspectives and imagining alternative solutions to social ills, such as Baltimore's ongoing crisis of public housing and displacement.

Seeing public housing

Running from 2 June 2002 to 9 March 2008, HBO's *The Wire* captured the imaginations of the audiences, journalists, media scholars and policymakers interested in watching a fictional police procedural with a tinge of ethnographic reportage. Former *Baltimore Sun* columnist turned author and television director, David Simon, created the series with former Baltimore City Police officer and public-school educator, Ed Burns. Drawing on their experiences in their respective fields, *The Wire* presented a wide range of storylines about policing, drug cartels, informal economies, political corruption, public education and the role of journalism in Baltimore City. *The Wire* is often hailed as one of the best television series of all time. In *The Wire* 'individual stories opened out into an analysis of an overarching, and at times irresistible, system shaping each aspect of society. The series demonstrated the potential of television narrative to dramatize the nature of the social order, a potential that TV drama has long neglected or inadequately pursued' (Sheehan and Sweeney 2009). Despite its critical reception and innovation, *The Wire* suffered from a series of blind spots in its depiction of public housing and its Black female inhabitants. This is mainly due to the hypervisibility of its medium, subject matter and subjects.

From the 1950s to the 1990s, television was a symbol of modernity and a post-Second World War emphasis on private pursuits over public leisure. Watched at home and interwoven with domestic routines, the small screen was not perceived as a space of high cultural prestige. Black people have appeared on television as long as the medium has been around, but Black actors were relegated to playing servants or providing comic relief. More rounded portrayals of Black Americans and their experiences did not infiltrate the television landscape until the late 1960s. Until then, the majority of Black representation on television was through television news. Televisual depictions of Black life often labour under a documentary or ethnographic impulse (Torres 2003: 13) that is largely concerned with capturing the authenticity of Black life. When not being fashioned to fit narratives of white supremacy through stereotyping, this authenticity relied on stories of Black poverty and struggle. In the 1960s television news coverage of the civil rights movement allowed Black bodies to symbolize America's tense but forward moving racial progress. By the 1980s, televisual depictions constructed the Black body as a site for criminality, irresponsibility and addiction. Hypervisibility is the state of being always in view – but never fully *seen*. Because of its overreliance on Black bodies as sites of information gathering and symbolic progress/decline, the medium of television has historically hyper-visibilized Black bodies and majority Black spaces.

Unlike New York City, Miami or Los Angeles, Baltimore was not a site for televised fiction. From the 1950s through the 1990s, Baltimore's national television identity was gleaned primarily through footage from the civil rights movement, specifically the riots that followed in the wake of Martin Luther King Jr's assassination in 1968. Charlotte Brunsdon suggests prior to NBC's *Homicide: Life on the Street*, Baltimore was a 'televisual city' (2018: 199) whose perception of itself was largely shaped by local television and local concerns. From 31 January 1993 to 12 May 1999, *Homicide* was seen as a smart and cutting-edge take on the police procedural. It provided a new visual backdrop for the genre, not just in its hyper-locality but in its use of Black actors and Black cultural sites in Baltimore. In the early twenty-first-century cable television programming began to adopt more cinematic conventions, ushering in the era of masculinist quality television shows such as HBO's *The Sopranos* (1999–2007). As quality television became more cinematic, television cities became more complex. By establishing Baltimore as a place grounded in 'realness', *Homicide* opened the door for *The Wire* to claim itself as an authentic portrayal of an American city for a more cinematic television landscape. But when claims of authenticity are made about majority Black spaces and subjects, erasure through hypervisibility is sure to follow.

The authors of *Public Housing Myths: Perception, Reality and Social Policy* posit that the public's understanding of public housing is troubled by myths. They suggest that reporters in the United States 'have developed a series of persistently demeaning and dehumanizing public housing memes and tropes. Mostly middle-class reporters find public housing as a convenient shorthand for all urban poverty, government malfeasance, rampant criminality, and dependence' (Bloom, Umbach and Vale 2015: 11). These stories have ignited the imaginations of middle- and upper-class readers for decades. These same themes have infiltrated mediated representations of public housing. In the cultural imagination, public housing is often believed to be high-rises in dangerously under-resourced city neighbourhoods. In reality, a number of public housing projects are in rural and suburban areas. Some are mixed-income housing with potential residents often on years-long waiting lists to gain entry. Public housing is not just for the poor. It was designed essentially for families and the elderly. For many, it has long been a bridge between low-income and the middle class. There is a perception that public housing in the United States is a crumbling den of unsanitary living; however, most current public housing 'meets or exceeds federal quality standards' (Bloom, Umbach and Vale 2015: 13). Researchers have long identified discrimination and lack of access to opportunities, not housing structures, as drivers of criminal activities. Public housing in neighbourhoods with access to employment, commerce, good schools and other community institutions have crime rates comparable to other neighbourhoods. Additionally, the assumption that public housing is primarily inhabited by only Black and brown residents overlooks that fact that, for example, between 2000 and 2013 '53 per cent of households living in public housing identify as white' (Bloom, Umbach and Vale 2015: 21).

These myths persist because public housing in the United States has long been complicated by hypervisibility. Joseph Heathcott notes that even the casual language of 'housing project' or 'the projects' illustrates the distinct isolation which society sees as characteristic of public housing (2015: 31). Public housing is a place that is *a-part* of the community, one that is bounded by firm metaphorical and architectural borders. There are specific rules and regulations about who gets to live in them, while the overabundance of densely packed concrete towers contributes to the notion that those who live in them are separate from the rest of the community. Architectural separation combined with seemingly uniform inhabitants makes public housing projects hypervisible. Regardless of its initial origins as a movement to create sanitary urban utopias for a multi-racial working class, public housing projects operate like the abject figures in horror cinema. These structures create a concrete border between 'normal' and 'abnormal' citizenry. Hypervisibility and its abject effect are quintessential components of a society invested in the surveillance of Black bodies. If surveillance means to observe or to watch over, then it becomes necessary to see *Black* surveillance as not only about collection of data for social control, but also about the hypervisibility that comes with being Black and being perceived as different. For Black people in the United States, this difference is often interpreted as deviance, making the actions of Black inhabitants of public housing hypervisible to those who are not Black.

State concerns about the unruly and violent poor contribute to an over-surveillance of poor Black communities, such as those who inhabit housing projects in Baltimore. From child-welfare systems to monitoring programmes for domestic-abuse offenders, large swaths of data are routinely gathered by the state. Often, data from excessive monitoring of impoverished Black Americans are fed back into police systems that support a cycle of surveillance and punishment (Waddell 2016). When the hypervisibility of television and public housing is combined with Black surveillance, it becomes almost impossible to legibly *see* public housing as a place where 'normal' citizens create a life for themselves.

Communities of care: Women in public housing

Female-headed households make up three-quarters of those living in public housing. Gender-inequality plays an important material and ideological role in these numbers. Women, regardless of educational status, consistently make lower wages than their male counterparts. Ideologies about family structures persistently equate work outside the household as worthy of wages while other socially reproductive activities (cleaning, cooking, child-rearing, kinship caretaking, activism) are not deemed labour at all. Spearheaded by female-led households, communities of care in public housing can be thought of as small voluntary networks that form around those who are experiencing difficulties. Difficulties can range from loss of a loved one to those who manage care for the elderly and disabled. Communities of care can also be ascribed to support groups, 'where individuals discuss mental health issues openly and without stigma' (Stebleton 2019: 1). Communities of care are also social networks where people look out for one another to help manage fiscal instability, food insecurities and other social ills, especially when these are exasperated by spatial isolation. Combating the notion that public housing residents foment a culture of poverty, Pittman and Oakley found that 'most public housing residents regard themselves as living in communities with problems rather than "problem communities"' (2018: 22). They also found that studies highlighting the positive aspects or benefits of living in public housing do not ignore the challenges its residents experience; they instead show that 'residents report depending on the communities they build to mitigate the negative aspects of living in public housing' (Pittman and Oakley 2018: 22). In the early years of public housing (1940s–50s), Black female-headed households invested in making public housing feel like 'home' by creating communities of care and, in the years of divestment, Black female-headed households have continued to hold policymakers accountable to that vision. The devaluation of public housing communities overshadows residents' real experience of community ties and supports (Leventhal, Brooks-Gunn, Kamerman 1997: 182–206).

Baltimore's Lexington Terrace Towers was one of the most activist-oriented public housing projects in the city, up to its demolition in 1996. After several letters and petitions for better living conditions and safety were ignored by the Baltimore Housing Authority in 1993, tenants of the Lexington Terrace organized a rent strike and invited politicians to a sleep over to experience the living conditions of the mothers and children living there. Only one politician, Mary Pat Clarke, took the mothers up on their invitation. The mothers' activism began to be noticed by the *Baltimore Sun* and allegations of corruption and mismanagement began to shake up the Baltimore Housing Authority. The *Baltimore Sun* ran an article entitled, 'LIVING HELL Lexington Terrace families must struggle daily to endure' (Simmons 1993). The article describes the families as having 'a bunker mentality. They are survivors in the cruel game of life in Baltimore's public housing projects' (Simmons 1993). President Bill Clinton's

US Department of Housing and Urban Development (HUD) Secretary, Jack Kemp, visited the towers in 1993 and claimed to have witnessed an open-air drug exchange while there. The continued pressure and activism of the mothers living in the Lexington Terrace Towers eventually led to the HOPE VI grant and the demolition of the Lexington Terrace Towers three years later. After its demolition, these same mothers found themselves fighting a leasing provision in their new mixed-income homes that made it legal to evict an entire family for one family member's drug offense. And with 4,000 residents displaced and not enough mixed-income housing for them to live in, the criminal activities that became synonymous with public housing simply shifted location.

Communities of care are support systems of which activism is but one facet. The activism of these mothers speaks to a larger cultural community able to exist in an extremely challenging environment. Black women's unpaid community activism is work and it makes community 'a primary site of nonmarket production by Black women and other racialized women' (Banks 2020: 344–62). Black women's activism in public housing exemplifies a culture of *living*, regardless of the environment. Are these mothers and grandmothers 'survivors' as the reporters frame them? Or are they 'warriors' who improve the lives of their families? The framing of the narrative matters. As Jacqueline Leavitt notes, 'any attention to public housing is a de facto recognition of a largely woman's world' (1993: 109). Public housing and the communities of care within them are the spatial realm of the female. Women's worlds are often sites of socially reproductive labour, the unpaid activities that create and nurture future workers. Domestic tasks maintain and reproduce life on a daily basis. It often goes unrecognized and is commonly linked to essentialist rhetoric about what it means to be female. Compounded by the hypervisibility of public housing as a place that is seen but not seen, communities of care are easily ignored. This is evidenced throughout HBO's *The Wire*, from the writing room to the set.

Public housing and the women of *The Wire*

The spectre of *The Wire* haunts Baltimore natives and its transplants. David Simon's Baltimore captured the public's imagination, presenting a gritty and corrupt version of the city potent enough that, over a decade later, Baltimore politicians are still attempting to distance the city from it[2]. Much of this rested on Simons's ability to convince viewers that what they were seeing was authentic, informed by the observations of a resident who was also a journalist. In the introduction to Rafael Alvarez's *The Wire: Truth Be Told*, David Simon goes out of his way to position *The Wire* as an authentic depiction from Baltimore storytellers. He provides his and Ed Burns *bona fides* as reporter and cop. He describes first season writer George Pelecanos as a former shoe salesman and barkeep who understands Black life, and Rafael Alvarez as qualified to represent Baltimore because of his father's time on the Baltimore shipyards. He goes on to set his creative team as outside of the Hollywood television machine. Simon claims that 'we are none of us from Hollywood; soundstages and backlots and studio commissaries are not our natural habitat' (2009: 12). Simon's use of 'natural' and his desire to distance himself from the Hollywood machine make a compelling argument for the truthfulness of the narratives being woven over various seasons. The familiar streets, accents and nods to specific aspects of Baltimore culture all contributed to a viewing experience more akin to watching a documentary than a serial narrative (Kelleter 2015: 46). Even fictitious spaces were patterned after real landmarks. Modelled after both the former Lexington Terrace and George B. Murphy Homes Projects, the Franklin Terrace Towers was a computer-generated rendering of a mixed-use high-rise public housing complex of six buildings located on Fremont Avenue. Acting as the background of the show in its first two seasons, before its demise in the beginning of season three, the Franklin Terrace Towers set created a bustling landscape of drug selling and using, all seen through the panoptic gaze of the police officers trying to intervene. But for a show dedicated to authenticity, *The Wire*'s Franklin Terrace Towers was curiously absent of the women who would inhabit this space and who would be dedicated to creating a community of care there, even in the most desperate circumstances.

As a police procedural, *The Wire* follows in the footsteps of the vast majority of television by creating a largely masculinist world. Such worlds generally relegate women to a few secondary roles – lady cops, lady prosecutors, ex-wives, mistresses, strippers, mothers, daughters and always – corpses. In many ways, *The Wire* offers a bit more variety to the police procedural landscape with the inclusion of multi-faceted women. The show includes characters such as Shakeema Greggs (Sonja Sohn), an openly lesbian single mother who is also a cop, Assistant State's Attorney Rhonda Pearlman (Diedra Lovejoy), who has an on again/off again relationship with the show's lead detective, Jimmy McNulty, the squad's Lieutenant Daniels's politically savvy wife, Marla (Maria Broom), stripper turned nursing student, Shardeen (Wendy Grantham), season two's transportation cop, Beatrice Russell (Amy Ryan), as well as Avon Barksdale's sister and co-leader of the Barksdale Gang, Brianna (Michael Hyatt). Discussing the women of *The Wire*, Laura Lippman notes only one woman worked in the writers' room in the first two seasons of the show and in season three, only three episodes were directed by women.[3] She goes on to observe that, although there were women behind the scenes, few of them were in the writing room. She credits men with giving these secondary female characters complicated lives, noting that 'many of the women in *The Wire* appear in secondary roles, but that is a simple truth about the world it portrays – and the point of view through which it is filtered' (Lippman 2009: 60). Her observation that women are secondary because of the male writers' points of view is spot on, but a show that prides itself on authenticity and realism fails, time and again, to develop realistic characters to inhabit its most visible landmark of authenticity, the Franklin Terrace Towers.

Exploring the women of the Barksdale gang, Courtney D. Marshall says that '*The Wire* allows for women's participation in crimes other than prostitution, and it invites us to see "fallen" women as complicated characters' (2009: 149). She goes on to trace how these complicated female characters provide a glimpse into 'black women's economic and organizational live' (Marshall 2009: 149). Marshall describes Brianna Barksdale as the deadly matriarch of the gang. We are introduced to her in her capacity as a mother when she brings D'Angelo (Lawrence Gilliard Jr.) a hearty lunch as he oversees drug dealing in the Pit – a large courtyard amidst the Franklin Terrace Tower's mid-rise housing. We then see her as the protective mother when she demands her brother look out for D'Angelo after he is arrested with a car full of drugs. The interactions between Brianna and Avon Barksdale (Wood Harris) hinge on her clear understanding of the duality of her position – she is a mother anxious about the health and safety of her son, as well as one of the primary reasons her son is living the life of a drug dealer. She is one of the leaders of the Barksdale gang and uses her position to keep her son in line, making sure his desire to escape the life of crime does not result in their family living, 'down in the fucking Terrace on scraps' (Marshall 2009: 154). Brianna's life depends on the Barksdale gang's enterprises to avoid having to live in that imagined panoptic space. Missing from the portrayal of Brianna and other female members of the gang's lives is any consideration that there may be communities of care in the towers capable enough to provide them with alternatives to a life of crime.

Who is Shante? Dialogue as erasure

The HOPE VI initiative comes to HBO's *The Wire* when the Franklin Terrace Towers is demolished. This segment enacts the historical demolition of public housing projects in Baltimore and other US cities in the mid-1990s. On 27 July

1996, spectators assembled in West Baltimore to watch the Lexington Terrace housing projects implode. There was a parade, balloons and speeches from government officials eager to destroy the complex. Baltimore Mayor Kurt L. Schmoke told the crowd, 'What we have done is torn down what essentially have become warehouses of poverty, and what we're creating is town houses of choice' (McCraven 1996). *The Wire* faithfully recreates this spectacle in the cold open at the beginning of season three. Surrounded by developers in suits and hard hats, Mayor Royce (Glen Turman) rallies the crowd, hyping the demolition as the first step in the creation of a 'new Baltimore' while framing the Franklin Terrace Towers as a structure that 'sadly came to represent some of the city's most entrenched problems' (*The Wire* 2004: 00:39:00). As Royce orates in front of a cartoonishly huge red 'detonation' button, mid-level drug dealers Preston 'Bodie' Broadus and Malik 'Poot' Carr (J. D. Williams and Tray Chaney) slice through the crowds, offering their differing views about the meaning of the housing project. Poot recalls fond memories of his time spent living and working there: 'I been seen some shit happen up in them towers, it still make me smile, yo.' In Poot's view, the towers were home, shaping his life and his view of himself. 'I'm talkin' about people,' he says, 'Memories an' shit'. Meanwhile, Bodie views the towers as merely functional, unattached to those who inhabit the space. 'Y'all talkin' about steel and concrete, man'. He replies to Poot, 'Steel and fucking concrete'. He later elaborates, 'They gonna tear this building down, they gonna build some new shit. But people? They don't give a fuck about people' (*The Wire* 2004: 00:39:00-00:51:00). Poot fondly recalls having his first sexual experience in tower 221 with a neighbourhood girl named Shante. As this exchange is taking place, Mayor Royce describes the demolition as an example of his administration's 'philosophy', which seems to hinge on the idea that tearing down buildings and displacing residents is a new kind of 'reform'. Bodie's concern about the tower's demise is related solely to the loss of prime real-estate for drug dealing. To Bodie, if you live in the projects, 'you ain't worth shit, but you selling product there, you got the game by the ass' (*The Wire* 2004: 01:06:00-02:39:00). When Royce finally pushes the button and the towers fall, smoke, debris and dust blow back onto the crowds of onlookers, choking them and briefly causing chaos.

However, one of the most interesting aspects of this dialogue as it relates to the Franklin Terrace Towers is the *kind* of memories Poot associates with the towers. Since the towers are not real, we never see these interactions take place in the character's life. We see Poot on the corner, in the Pit or at the Barksdale gang's funeral home office. We know the towers through his reminiscence –

unattached to actual scenes. If Poot associates the towers with fond memories of his multiple sexual conquests, what does it say about the women and girls who lived in the towers? Who is Shante? How does everyone know that Shante has had multiple partners? Do they know for sure or is this just the kind of rumour that sometimes follows young women in the 'hood'? In the same scene, Bodie mentions the way Poot must adjust his stride when walking to the 'clinic' for treatment of his STIs. Which clinic are they referring to? The Franklin Terrace Towers is modelled after the Lexington Terrace Towers near the University of Maryland School of Medicine. Since 1994 there has been an active paediatric and young adult clinic close to that location that provides HIV and STI counselling for young people. These services were offered in public housing projects at the behest of Black women activists who crafted a community of care around adolescent reproductive health when the city would not. Yet, the scene provides zero mention of these culturally important markers that could flesh out the towers as a space where people *lived*. These omissions further highlight *The Wire*'s tendency to follow in the footsteps of masculinist police procedurals that render communities of care and the women who manage them invisible. It is not problematic for a television show to craft a scene to prove a thesis; however, this cold open illustrates the way public housing in *The Wire* is merely shorthand for an assemblage of problems plaguing Baltimore. In the framing of the towers as such, *The Wire* allows the audience to fill in the blanks with their own cultural myths about public housing and the people who live in it. Poot and Bodie's dialogue erases Shante and the supportive networks she may have utilized to stay safe and healthy in the Franklin Terrace Towers.

In this scene, Poot says, 'I feel like I don't have a home'. As Bodie responds by positioning the loss of the towers in terms of economics, he counters with, 'Housing just moved your mama up to Poplar Grove, didn't it? You ain't homeless nigga, you got a home. Shit, you just damn near outta work' (*The Wire* 2004: 02:10:00-02:21:00). This dialogue is significant for several reasons. First, it counters the impression made of Poot's living situation that was explored in season one, episode six, 'All the Pieces Matter' (*The Wire* 2002). In this scene, Wallace (Michael B. Jordan), a now-deceased corner boy, and Poot discover the body of Omar Little's (Michael K. Williams) partner, Brandon (Michael Kevin Darnell). We see Poot and Wallace living with a group of younger children in an abandoned home, powered by an orange extension cord that siphons power from another resident's house to their condemned domicile. According to this scene, Poot *is* homeless, regardless of where his mother lives. For Poot, home has nothing to do with his mother and whatever she may provide in terms of domesticity. For Poot and Bodie, home does not include mothers or women with things to do other than stay absent or help spread STIs. The show, therefore, misses the opportunity to acknowledge the positive female community presence that would ground *The Wire* in both reality and authentic writing.

Whose couch was this? Residents as props

As told in *The Wire: Truth Be Told*, art director Vince Peranio was scouting locations for the pilot episode when he found the iconic orange crushed velvet couch propped up against a dumpster (Abrams 2018). The couch became the centrepiece of the Pit, the headquarters of D'Angelo Barksdale's drug dealing territory throughout the first season of *The Wire*. Since the Franklin Terrace Towers set was an assemblage of various locales throughout Baltimore, as well as computer-generated images, the Pit was physically located in the courtyard of the Murphy Homes project's low rises. The couch belonged to someone who lived there, someone who has never been identified and became a prop which figured in nearly every scene of the Pit, more of a character than the actual background players in the scenes.

We are introduced to the Pit (see Figure 10.1) and Franklin Terrace Towers (see Figure 10.2) in season one, when D'Angelo Barksdale is stripped of his leadership in tower 221 and sent to oversee the Pit in the low rises. An older Black woman waits at a bus stop. Behind her, a Black man sits on the bus

Figure 10.1 The Pit, *The Wire* © HBO 2002–2008. All rights reserved.

Figure 10.2 The front of Franklin Terrace Towers, *The Wire* © HBO 2002–2008. All rights reserved.

bench in conversation with another older Black woman. When the bus arrives, the first woman steps onto the bus as D'Angelo Barksdale steps off, a look of homecoming on his face. Rubbing his hands in anticipation of proving himself a worthy, capable drug dealer, he comes face to face with Stringer Bell (Idris Elba), the lieutenant of the Barksdale gang. As Stringer breaks the news to D'Angelo, it is clear from their exchange that tower 221 was prime real estate, while the Pit was for the low-level workers still learning the tricks of the trade. By the superb acting in this scene, you can also glean that Stringer Bell views the younger D'Angelo as soft. As Elizabeth Bonjean surmises, 'though a Barksdale by blood, D'Angelo does not have the edge that his relatives and other members of the Barksdale crew possess; his uncle Avon reprimands him for his "emotional" responses to situations, while Avon's business partner, Russell "Stringer" Bell lectures D'Angelo about the importance of never "show[ing] weakness" to others' (2009: 165). Tensions within the Barksdale gang are made starkly clear in these scenes. What is unclear in this exchange is exactly how those not involved in the informal economy feel about this characterization of the spaces they inhabit. Who has it better – those in the towers or those in the Pit?

By the way the set is dressed, the 221 towers are inhabited by more than the Barksdale gang. From the residents waiting on the bus, to the occasional mothers and children seen entering and leaving the space, there is evidence that the Franklin Terrace Towers are a home. Yet, the background players – the mothers, grandmothers, children, fathers and elders are never more than static figures, wandering through the milieu of the ethnographic gaze of David Simon and Ed Burns. Over in the Pit, the background players are also devoid of any reaction to the violent world around them. We enter the Pit from a bird's eye view of the orange couch. As D'Angelo walks towards the couch, followed by corner boys, Wallace and Poot, we are introduced to the residents of the Pit. From a window, a young boy looks down on the yard while listening to music. Two women and a young man sit in front of an apartment door. A young woman of middle school age attempts to come out that door and one of the women violently closes it on her. A mother hugs her daughter close as D'Angelo walks towards the orange couch. A faceless Black woman walks confidently across the Pit carrying a briefcase. There are clothes drying on the lines in front of various apartments and little children run past the couch, enamoured in their play.

These vignettes are designed to make the Franklin Terrace Towers appear *real* but, for a place to be lived in, it must be a place where people *reside*, not occupy. Occupation is commonly defined as taking ownership of a space. To occupy infers an entrenchment, a lack of permanence, a contested or embattled inhabiting of a space. Space is often perceived as a container (spatial or metaphorical) that is undifferentiated or general. Place refers to a container that can be located and is ascribed with meaning by those who live there. When someone resides in a *place,* they are there for a long period of time. They set down roots. Cities are sometimes unstable due to migratory flows that allow people to settle for brief periods in a space where they can live in relative anonymity. This contrasts with rural areas where people often root in proximity to one another for generations. Since cities are constantly being changed because of policy, economics and environmental factors, it takes a particular level of mental nimbleness to put down roots in them. Mindy Fullilove takes up urbanist Jane Jacobs's concept that we can view neighbourhoods as theatrical stages where every person knows their part. Navigating a place in a neighbourhood is likened to a street ballet:

> a way of describing our ability to master and run the maze of life, the mazeway, the near environment within which we find food, shelter, safety, and companionship. We love the mazeway in which we are rooted, for it is not simply the buildings that make us safe and secure but more complexly, our knowledge of the scene that makes it so.
>
> (Fullilove 2016: 19)

A space may provide us soil with which to root and demarcate with memory but knowing one's role and how to perform the street ballet is what makes it a home. Later in this episode, the character Johnny (Leo Fitzpatrick), a regular drug customer on the series, cheats Wallace by folding fake money in with a ten-dollar bill. When Bodie realizes what has happened, he commands Poot to 'grab that muthafuka, the white boy', then he and Poot give chase through the Pit (*The Wire* 2002: 46:24:00). As the chase ensues, children are seen hanging on fences, curious, while an elder looks on from his front door. Johnny side-steps a woman with a leashed pit bull and continues to run. In this sequence we see a little bit more of the Pit, including a playground, as Johnny rounds a corner and one of the unknown Barksdale crew trips him. He falls to the ground and Bodie confronts him, punching Johnny in the face. As D'Angelo and Wallace join them, Bodie waits for D'Angelo to give the signal that they are allowed to throw Johnny off the Franklin Expressway. When D'Angelo declines to harm Johnny any more than he already has been, Wallace, Poot and Bodie beat Johnny to a pulp. Again, I call the attention to the background players of the towers. Johnny's beatdown occurs just outside of a playground, where we catch glimpses of children in play. There are mothers on the periphery keeping watch. As this violent encounter occurs, we never see the mothers shielding the children from the violence or taking them away from the scene. They are mute spectators, merely occupying space. In a study of young people's perceptions of public housing, participants reported that they felt like 'the people in the community were connected; that there was a sense of being known' (Cole, Ramirez, et al. 2019: 65). Being known in a close-knit community has its upsides and its downsides as people are frequently aware of their neighbours' private information. The study also revealed that, when they were small children, there were resources and programmes that helped them feel safe and cared for in public housing. These young people's perception of connection with one another and support from adults runs counter to the portrayal of Johnny's beatdown on *The Wire*. In a close-knit community that is under-resourced, parents, friends and neighbours keep watch and try to shield young children from violence.

Home is elastic, stretching beyond physical locale and creating affective connections between people even when they are not in the place where they jointly reside. Baltimore is a city that calls itself a town. *The Wire* captures what Polly Stewart calls 'a region's consciousness of itself defin[ing] the region' (2015: 74). It is a state of mind that makes a region into a place. By using Baltimore colloquialisms, cultural foodways and recreating historical events in urban policy making, *The Wire*'s male creators demonstrate their understanding of Baltimore's regional consciousness. Missing in *The Wire*'s landscape are the women residents of Baltimore's housing projects who build the communities of care that enable people to set down roots and turn a space into a place called home. The residents of the Franklin Terrace Towers are written to be background players who do not react to their physical environment. At no point do women seem to have an opinion about the violent informal economy marring the place where they reside. At no point do we see relationships between the occupiers (the Barksdale gang) and the women residents. They have no parts to play other than to serve as props.

The Franklin Terrace Towers in *The Wire* is crafted like a space that is occupied by an invading force – the users and the dealers. It is a contested space created and maintained through a combination of entrenched inequities and ethnographic myths. As a masculinist police procedural created by male writers, *The Wire* privileges the fate of the characters over their agency. It is a show committed to highlighting the cyclical nature of Baltimore hardships. But in choosing to use the Franklin Terrace Towers as a hypervisible backdrop for its overall thesis, *The Wire* fails in its claim of authenticity by ignoring the Black women who, through a combination of community care, kinship and street ballet, maintain a loving and contentious relationship with the place they call home. That too is a story of Baltimore.

Notes

1   Created by Congress in 1993 to fund and revitalize the nation's distressed public housing, the HOPE VI programme addressed three areas: physical improvements, management improvements and social and community services to address resident needs.
2   In 2014, then Baltimore City Mayor Stephanie Rawlings Blake and former Police Commissioner Anthony Batts were quick to dismiss the impact of *The Wire* on Baltimore, proudly proclaiming they never watched the show as the city celebrated the five-year anniversary of the show's final season.
3   Female writers and directors on *The Wire* include Joy Lusco Kecken (writer), Gloria Muzio (director), Leslie Libman (director), Agnieszka Holland (director) and Christine Moore (director).

References

Abrams, Jonathan (2018), *All the Pieces Matter: The Inside Story of The Wire*, New York: Penguin Random House.

Banks, Nina (2020), 'Black Women in the United States and Unpaid Collective Work: Theorizing the Community as a Site of Production', *The Review of Black Political Economy*, 47 (4): 343–62, https://doi.org/10.1177/0034644620962811.

Bloom, Nicholas Dagen, Fritz Umbach, and Lawrence J. Vale (2015), 'Introduction', in Nicholas Dagen Bloom, Fritz Umback, and Lawrence J. Vale (eds), *Public Housing Myths: Perception, Reality, and Social Policy*, 1–30, Ithaca: Cornell University Press.

Bonjean, Elizabeth (2009), 'After the Towers Fell: Bodie Broadus and the Space of Memory', in Tiffany Potter and C. W. Marshall (eds), *The Wire: Urban Decay and American Television*, 162–74, New York: Bloomsbury Academic.

Brown, Lawrence T. (2021), *The Black Butterfly: The Harmful Politics of Race and Space in America*, Baltimore: Johns Hopkins University Press.

Brunsdon, Charlotte (2018), *Television Cities: Paris, London, Baltimore*, Durham: Duke University Press.

Cole, Andrea, Luis Alfredo Ramirez, Melissa R. Villodas, Shelly Ben-David, and Michelle L. Munson (2019), '"I want to rise above it all": Perceptions of the Neighborhood Among Young Adults Living in Public Housing', *Children and Youth Services Review*, 103: 63–9, https://doi.org/10.1016/j.childyouth.2019.05.031.

Fullilove, Mindy Thompson (2016), *Root Shock: How Tearing Up City Neighborhoods Hurts America, and What We Can Do About It*, New York: New Village Press.

Heathcott, Joseph (2015), 'Public Housing Stands Alone', in Nicholas Dagen Bloom, Fritz Umback, and Lawrence J. Vale (eds), *Public Housing Myths: Perception, Reality, and Social Policy*, 31–46, Ithaca: Cornell University Press.

Jacobson, Joan (2007), 'The dismantling of Baltimore's public housing: Housing Authority cutting 2,400 homes for the poor from its depleted inventory – A 15-year trend shows a decrease of 42 percent in occupied units', *The Abell Report*, 20 (2): 2–20.

Kelleter, Frank (2015), 'The Wire and Its Readers', in Liam Kennedy and Stephen Shapiro (eds), *The Wire: Race, Class and Genre*, 33–70, Ann Arbor: The University of Michigan Press.

Leavitt, Jacqueline (1993), 'Women under Fire: Public Housing Activism in Los Angeles', *Frontier: A Journal of Women Studies*, 13 (2): 109–30, https://www.jstor.org/stable/3346732.

Leventhal, Tama, Jeanne Brooks-Gunn, and Sheila B. Kamerman (1997), 'Communities as Place, Face, and Space: Provision of Services to Poor, Urban Children and Their Families', in Greg J. Duncan, Jeanne Brooks-Gunn and J. Lawrence Aber (eds), *Neighborhood Poverty, Volume 2: Policy Implications in Studying Neighborhoods*, 182–206, New York: Russell Sage Foundation.

Lippman, Laura (2009), 'The Women of the Wire (No, Seriously)', in Rafael Alvarez (ed), *The Wire: Truth Be Told*, 55–60, New York: Simon and Shuster.

Marshall, Courtney D. (2009), 'Barksdale Women: Crime, Empire, and the Production of Gender', in Tiffany Potter and C.W. Marshall (eds), *The Wire: Urban Decay and American Television*, 149–61, New York: Continuum.

McCraven, Marilyn (1996), 'Lexington Terrace Will Fall Today Controlled Explosions Will Destroy City's High-Rise Project', *The Baltimore Sun*, 27 July. Available online: https://www.baltimoresun.com/news/bs-xpm-1996-07-27-1996209055-story.html (accessed 27 November 2021).

Pittman, LaShawnDa, and Deirdre Oakley (2018), '"It Was Love in All the Buildings They Tore Down": How Caregiving Grandmothers Create and Experience a Sense of Community in Chicago Public Housing', *City and Community*, 17 (2): 461–84, https://doi:10.1111/cico.12280.

Pousson, Eli (2019), 'Vacant Houses and Inequality in Baltimore from the Nineteenth Century to Today', in P. Nicole King, Kate Drabinski and Joshua Clark Davis (eds), *Baltimore Revisited: Stories of Inequality and Resistance in a U.S. City*, 52–66, New Brunswick: Rutgers University Press.

Sheehan, Helena and Sheamus Sweeney (2009), '*The Wire and the World: Narrative and Metanarrative*', *Jump Cut* 51 (Spring). Available online: https://www.ejumpcut.org/archive/jc51.2009/index.html (accessed 24 January 2021).

Simon, David (2009), 'Introduction', in Rafael Alvarez (ed), *The Wire: Truth Be Told*, 2–34, New York: Simon and Shuster.

Simmons, Melody (1993), 'LIVING HELL – Lexington Terrace Families Must Struggle Daily to endure', *The Baltimore Sun*, 20 January. Available online: https://www.baltimoresun.com/news/bs-xpm-1993-01-20-1993020108-story.html (accessed 27 November 2021).

Stebleton, Michael J. (2019), 'Building a Community of Care: Mental Health Is Everyone's Business', *JCC Connexions*, 5 (4). Available online: https://www.naspa.org/blog/jcc-connexions-vol-5-no-4 (accessed 28 June 2021).

Stewart, Polly (2015), 'Regional Consciousness as a Shaper of Local History: Examples from the Eastern Shore', in Barbara Allen and Thomas J. Schelereth (eds), *Sense of Place: American Regional Cultures*, 74–87, Lexington: University of Kentucky Press.

Torres, Sasha (2003), *Black, White and In Color: Television and Black Civil Rights*, New Jersey: Princeton University Press.

Waddell, Kaveh (2016), 'How Big Data Harms Poor Communities', *The Atlantic*, 8 April. Available online: https://www.theatlantic.com/technology/archive/2016/04/how-big-data-harms-poor-communities/477423/ (accessed 12 November 2021).

The Wire (2002), [TV programme] HBO, 2 June.

The Wire (2002), [TV programme] HBO, 7 July.

The Wire (2002), [TV programme] HBO, 21 July.

The Wire (2004), [TV programme] HBO. 19 September.

11

'People need to come home': *Treme*, abandoned housing and post-Katrina New Orleans

Helen Morgan Parmett

Introduction

'We finally cleaned up public housing in New Orleans. We couldn't do it. But God did'.

> – Republican Representative from Baton Rouge, Richard H. Baker, following Hurricane Katrina (Babington 2005)

Baker's statement – made shortly after the levee failures ravaged the city in August 2005 killing thousands of mostly Black, poor and elderly citizens and displacing thousands more – is now an infamous testament to the racialized and classed implications of Katrina's human-made disaster. Baker expresses, in overt and no uncertain terms, the dominant viewpoint that has long characterized public housing in the United States – that it is a (moral) abomination. Baker's statement is offensive, but it is also misleading. Hurricane Katrina did not 'clean up' public housing in the way it seems Baker is suggesting; that is, neither the hurricane nor the broken levees destroyed public housing to make way for its 'cleaning up' via demolition. Public housing infrastructures were relatively unscathed in the aftermath of Katrina. What the failure of the levees did do was displace thousands of residents, including those in the city's public housing. And it is that displacement that Baker is crediting as a successful cleaning up, as the decision by government officials to not reopen public housing to allow residents to return to the city and their homes resulted in permanent displacement for many and what some argue is a whitewashing of the city (Dyson 2006). Thus, for Baker, as well as other elites who share his view, cleaning up public housing meant, and continues to mean, ridding the city of 'undesirable' populations – namely, the Black and poor populations that make up the majority of the city's public housing residents. The HBO series *Treme* (2010–13) focuses on the struggles of individuals and neighbourhoods to return and rebuild New Orleans after Katrina. Taking up debates over opening the city's public housing largely in its first season, this chapter situates *Treme*'s representation of public housing in New Orleans in the context of the politics of the city's post-Katrina housing struggles. I suggest *Treme* humanizes public housing by representing it as well-built, functional and, especially, as a home. In so doing, the series exposes what Giroux (2016) refers to as a biopolitics of disposability, wherein Katrina revealed how the intertwining racialized and classed logics of neoliberalism rendered whole segments of the population disposable and abandoned by the institutions whose duty it was to care for them. The series thus counters dominant representations of public housing in US media, which often portray public housing and residents as destructive, pathological and criminal. Instead, the abandoned public housing of New Orleans stands in for how government abdicated its responsibility to care for its citizens, thus positioning governmental abandonment as what is indeed criminal. Contesting the dispossession of Black and poor residents of New Orleans via the state's abandonment and eventual demolition of the city's public housing, *Treme* makes a strong call for public housing as a right through connecting it to the discourse of the right to return. A central means through which the series harnesses this discourse is by portraying the struggles over public housing in New Orleans through the character of Albert Lambreaux (Clarke Peters), Chief of the Mardi Gras Indians tribe Guardians of the Flame. This portrayal politicizes the struggle over public housing by connecting it to histories of Black cultural practice as forms of resistance and political struggle in New Orleans. Although *Treme* counters dominant representations of public housing, I conclude by reflecting on the political limits of the show's representational interventions in struggles over the city's housing.

Public housing pre- and post-Katrina

Although it was after Hurricane Katrina that federal, state and city government officials seized the opportunity to raze the city's public housing to build mixed-income developments, officials had long problematized public housing in New Orleans. Housing and Urban Development's (HUD) HOPE VI programme, initiated in the 1990s, promoted a discourse that the nation's public housing projects were 'severely distressed' and pushed demolition and redevelopment initiatives throughout the country. The programme greatly reduced affordable housing in the United States by as much as 20 per cent, as most initiatives were demolition only (Vale and Freemark 2019). Redevelopment took place largely through public/private partnerships, and private developers were granted government contracts and land along with tax breaks and incentives to include a percentage of affordable housing within mixed-income units. The shift from public housing projects to mixed-income/affordable housing was largely predicated on the theory of concentrated poverty, which assumes the concentration of impoverished households within housing areas and neighbourhoods perpetuates poverty because residents are unable to gain social capital through networking with wealthier neighbours. Deconcentrating poverty was believed to break the 'cycle of poverty' and decrease crime and violence within impoverished communities. Although research overwhelmingly disproves the concentrated poverty thesis, as poverty is caused by joblessness, discrimination and other factors rather than spatial location (which is more often the effect of poverty rather than the cause), it remains a powerful discourse pervading the representation of public housing as an anti-social cesspool of poverty, drugs and violence from which residents cannot escape (Gans 2010). Mixed-income developments are theorized to encourage public housing residents to transform into self-responsible, neoliberal subjects who do not need to be dependent upon government.

Thus, by the time Katrina arrived in August 2005 and driven by the neoliberal impulses of HUD's HOPE VI programme, the city of New Orleans had already demolished half of its public housing stock.[1] Demolition was driven by discourses generated by media and elites that pathologized the projects as hotbeds of crime and violence (Arena 2011). Prior to Katrina, most of the city's public housing residents were Black – close to 99 per cent of approximately 49,000 residents (Bullard and Wright 2009; Finger 2011). This overrepresentation is a product of histories of colonialism, slavery, redlining, segregation and discrimination in the city that restricted where Black people could live (Woods 2009). After Katrina hit, residents were displaced and dispersed throughout the country. A major impediment to their return was lack of available housing.

Yet, most public housing in the city was relatively unscathed by Katrina, with little damage and only minor or no flooding since the majority were located on higher ground and brick and plaster built with sturdy materials.[2] However, the Housing Authority of New Orleans (HANO) – the authority that oversees the city's public housing, run by HUD – officials almost immediately

declared the public housing 'devastated' and refused to open it to enable people
to return home. HANO claimed they were concerned about mold but allowed
homeowners to return to homes that were often considerably more devastated
(Arena 2011). Housing officials would not even allow residents to return to
collect their belongings (Adams 2013). They soon declared they would not work
to repair the buildings but, instead, would proceed towards demolition. Within
three years of Katrina, all but one of the city's nine public housing units were torn
down, with the last (Iberville) finally demolished in 2013 after a protracted battle
waged by housing activists. In their place, the city contracted private developers
to build mixed income units, eliminating 4,500 units and only building 800
(Bullard and Wright 2009).

The demolition of New Orleans' public housing is an example of what Naomi
Klein (2007) refers to as the 'shock doctrine' of disaster capitalism, wherein
political elites use crisis and disorientation among the public to 'shock' the
system into implementing neoliberal privatization through aggressive austerity
programmes that shrink the social safety net and roll back social entitlements
while transferring public funds into the hands of private companies. Klein
argues disaster capitalism includes 'orchestrated raids on the public sphere in the
wake of catastrophic events, combined with the treatment of disasters as exciting
market opportunities' (Klein 2007: 6). Despite the housing projects being fully
recuperable, elites instead used the storm to implement the tenets of HOPE VI
to demolish the units and contract out new, profit generating opportunities to
private developers.

The racial implications of disaster capitalism in New Orleans are significant.
Many public housing residents along with thousands of other largely Black
and poor residents remained (and continue to remain) displaced well after
the storm, and the racial composition of the city shifted (Finger 2011). Even
today, the city contains less than 80 per cent of its pre-Katrina population, which
comprises at least a 7 per cent decline in Black residents (Casselman 2015).
For many, this was believed to be political elites' end goal – to rid the city of a
population they deemed dangerous, unproductive and, ultimately, disposable.
Disaster capitalism is thus also connected to what Giroux (2016), drawing on
Foucault, refers to as a biopolitics of disposability. Biopolitics is a form of power
that works to produce and maximize the conditions for life as they are tied to
the production of knowledge about biological populations (e.g. demographics,
health, behaviours) through which subjects get constituted as populations.
Foucault argues biopolitics reverses the sovereign right to 'make die' and 'let
live' to one in which power 'makes live' and 'lets die' (Foucault 2003: 241).

The biopolitics of disposability falls along race and class lines, as race becomes the dividing line of those who are 'made to live' (i.e. invested in and constituted by the productive power of governing institutions), and those who are 'left to die' (Foucault 2003). Giroux suggests Katrina revealed a whole segment of the population that had largely been abandoned, rendered disposable and left to die, by neoliberal privatization and the weakening of the social safety net. This includes the abdication of governmental responsibility for maintaining crucial infrastructure like the levees. New Orleans' levee system, built by the Army Corps of Engineers in the 1960s, was supposed to protect the city's low-lying areas from flooding in the event of storms like Katrina. Those areas are overwhelmingly occupied by the city's Black and poor populations. However, by the time Katrina hit, the levee system was in major disrepair, having been consistently underfunded by the federal government. Those populations were thus not made to live, but rather left to die.

Public housing residents too were rendered disposable, deemed failures and drains on the system that the city did not need to return, lacking the personal responsibility and agency needed to become homeowners in their own right. This is a form of neoliberal racism which 'imagines human agency as simply a matter of individualized choices, the only obstacle to effective citizenship and agency being the lack of principled self-help and moral responsibility' (Giroux 2004: 58). This logic fails to account for racial discrimination in both housing and employment that leaves many dependent on public housing. In the face of neoliberal racism and the biopolitics of disposability, residents and housing advocates joined together to protest the demolition of the city's public housing. Advocates utilized a discourse of a 'right to return', which counters the biopolitics of disposability and discourses of individualized responsibility by foregrounding a collective responsibility through the defence of housing as a social right and public good. It creates a very different vision of how New Orleans public housing has been figured in media by contesting the 'neoliberal "common sense", promoted by the local media and public officials, that public housing residents did not want to return to their "dysfunctional" communities' (Arena 2011: 160). Instead, it demonstrates how public housing is, indeed, home, and a home that a traumatized and displaced people sought to return to.

It is into this conjuncture that *Treme* enters and presents, in dramatized form, the struggle of displaced people to return home. Although the series addresses the fight over the city's public housing in just a few episodes in the first season, and only briefly returns to the protests around demolition again in Season 3, its representation of public housing diverges not only from media discourse around New Orleans public housing but also from most US film and TV depictions more generally, which often portray public housing and its residents as pathological and disordered, often standing in for urban pathology (Rogers, Darcy and Arthurson 2017). Those representations are racialized, attributing housing as part of the cause of what is represented as pathological Black culture (Mann 2011). Media representations of public housing thus contribute to 'territorial stigma' (Wacquant, Slater and Pereira 2014), or the stigma associated with racialized, post-industrial urban neighbourhoods that mark them as Other. Territorial stigma is produced by symbolic representations of place and 'is not a static condition, a neutral process, or an innocuous cultural game, but a consequential and injurious form of *action through collective representation fastened on place*' (Wacquant, Slater and Pereira 2014: 1278; emphasis in original). In other words, representations of places have material consequences for the people who live there and the places they live. The territorial stigma through which public housing in the United States is consistently portrayed has thus played a substantive role in legitimating their demolition and quelling resistance to the shortfall in affordable housing.

Because of the persistence in territorial stigma in representations of public housing, media that work to counter those representations are especially notable. There are few representations of public housing in television, especially fictional programming. Television developed in the post-war 1950s alongside and in conjunction with suburbanization and the idealization of the nuclear family in the single-family home, and therefore representations of housing, even those within the urban, have tended to replicate those ideals. David Simon's televisual oeuvre stands out for its depiction of urban life and, especially, its emphasis on life inside public housing. While Simon's depiction of public housing in *The Wire* and *Show Me a Hero* is more substantial and also subject to more debate and critique, as the other chapters in this collection note, little has been written about the portrayal of public housing in *Treme*. In what follows, I argue *Treme* offers three significant interventions and counter-representations to the portrayal of US public housing in media. First, the series challenges the representations of the buildings and residents as dilapidated and dysfunctional by humanizing the space and representing it as a home. Second, these representations construct public housing residents as agents with a collective right to return. Third, *Treme* counters the representation of public housing as a space of criminality and violence through representations of police brutality and systemic abandonment that demonstrate that dysfunction and pathology do not lie within public housing or its inhabitants, but with a system that abandons them.

Humanizing public housing as home

Perhaps the most significant intervention *Treme* makes in representing public housing is to humanize the space and demonstrate that it is a place in which people make a home. Whereas public housing is frequently represented as dilapidated and dysfunctional, *Treme* instead shows that the public housing of New Orleans was in fact in good shape, or at least in shape that was good enough for people to return to. *Treme* humanizes public housing not through the representation of residents but through the space itself, which is marked by humanity and the lived experience of a daily life that has been forced into abandonment. Notably, *Treme* presents public housing in opposition to the remainder of the city's housing, which is shown as largely destroyed. Throughout the season, many homes, especially those of Black and poor characters, are unlivable, strewn with debris, muddy, with tree branches going through them and, in one case, with a dead body. In contrast, viewers' first sights of the condition of the public housing units in the seventh episode of the first season – when the character Albert Lambreaux enters a unit with an intent to squat in protest for their reopening – show them in perfectly livable condition. Some of the first shots are a removal of boards over the outside of the windows, which reveals them in perfect, unbroken condition. The shot cuts to peer out the window, revealing the other buildings in the development, all with boarded up windows that would seemingly be similarly intact, with grass free of debris. There is no visible damage from the storm at all. Removing the boards over the windows lets light come into the apartment, and the shots in this scene reveal, little by little, pieces of daily life and home – curtains on the windows, bright yellow walls, a clock on the wall frozen in time, kitchen sink with cooking utensils at the ready, portraits hanging on a wall. As they move through to the back of the house to the living room, the camera pans to reveal children's toys on one side of the room. Everything is tidy except for one stuffed animal laying on the floor. It is pink and fluffy, suggesting no water damage (*Treme* 2010c).

The condition of the public housing unit shown in *Treme* stands in opposition to the news images of decimated New Orleans housing after Katrina. Those images are haunting and spectacular, showing a destroyed life as it is strewn across the landscape in the wake of destruction. In *Treme*, the scene of apparent abandonment – of homes left empty, dark and frozen in time – is similarly haunting, but in a completely different way. What we see is another kind of destruction, but it is destruction that largely appears invisible on the landscape. As opposed to the decimated houses of Katrina, public housing is shown in perfectly livable condition, and it is thus not the storm that is the site of destruction for these homes and of the people's lives that lay abandoned within, but the invisible hand of destruction lies in the form of the political machine intent on demolishing people's homes. This is exemplary of how neoliberal urbanism works by accumulation through dispossession (Harvey 2005) – these scenes reveal that what we are witnessing, what first appears as a site of abandonment, are in actuality sites of eviction and dispossession to make way for new forms of profit.

Further, the images in *Treme* of these fragments of home contest the typically pathologizing representations of public housing, which is often shown as dilapidated, run-down and disorderly in ways that suggest the people within it are not capable of maintaining an orderly home. Those images convey that public housing residents are not fit to be self-responsible and are to blame for their living conditions. The fragments of images in *Treme* instead unfold a dwelling place, representing public housing residents as humans with value and dignity. These signs of dwelling are further reinforced when Lambreaux finds that another squatter has taken up his protest, unfurling a sign from a second story window of the building across the green that reads, 'My home' (*Treme* 2010d: 00:19:37). These sensibilities of home reinforce the overarching narrative of *Treme* on the value of New Orleans and the need for it to be rebuilt in the face of critics suggesting it should have a smaller footprint after the storm, or even that it was not worth being rebuilt at all. Underlying those perspectives is a biopolitics of disposability, since it is the low-lying areas occupied by the city's Black and poor populations that were ever in danger of not being rebuilt. Emphasizing public housing as a vital part of New Orleans, as a place in which many of those populations made a home, serves to situate the series within the discourse of a right to return.

A right to return

Treme follows the pattern of a number of documentaries, such as *Land of Opportunity* (2010) and *St. Joe* (2009), that counter representations of public housing in New Orleans through the struggle over the right to return and represent public housing as a human right, emphasize the voices of those who lived there and stress their agency to advocate for change (Cook 2015). *Treme* evokes a similar discourse and situates the narrative of public housing activism through the perspective of the character Albert Lambreaux, the Chief of the Guardians of the Flame, a Mardi Gras Indians 'tribe'. The tradition of the Mardi Gras Indians is rooted in the history of New Orleans' Black neighbourhoods, where 'tribes' or 'gangs' of working-class Black men sew ornate costumes throughout the year and then wear them as they parade ('mask') in neighbourhood streets on Mardi Gras and St. Joseph's Day, 'battling' for who is the 'prettiest' when they meet other tribes. Though there are debates about the commercialization of Mardi Gras Indians, the tradition remains a powerful form of cultural resistance within poor, Black New Orleanian neighbourhoods in which those participating construct a sense of Black collective identity and power, especially in the performative ways in which the groups lay claim to neighbourhood space and the rights of Black bodies to occupy city streets (Lipsitz 1990). Thus, Lambreaux, even though not a resident of public housing, stands in for the moral voice of Black resistance and cultural power. The choice to situate him as the voice and body standing up for public housing connects housing activism to broader struggles of working-class and poor Black New Orleanians to make a claim to the right to the return and to the city more generally. As Lambreaux works to get his crew back together to sew and practice for Mardi Gras day, the story becomes hinged on his battle with the city to reopen the projects to provide a place for his crew to come home to. Thus, these two core narratives become intertwined, articulating the resistance embedded within Mardi Gras Indian tradition to the activism around public housing and its incipient discourse of a right to return.

Lambreaux returns to New Orleans after being displaced to Houston, despite his children's concerns about the safety of his return since his house in the Gentilly neighbourhood had been flooded and was uninhabitable. Gentilly, like many predominantly Black neighbourhoods in New Orleans, is located in the area locals refer to as 'back-a-town' – those neighbourhoods north of the so-called 'silver by the river', or the predominantly wealthy white neighbourhoods along the Mississippi River (Campanella 2006). The latter are on relatively higher ground and received minimal or no flooding during the storm, in sharp contrast to 'back-a-town' neighbourhoods like Gentilly that are protected by the levee system. Lambreaux is determined to return to maintain fidelity to the Mardi Gras Indian tradition. After finding his house uninhabitable, he returns to the neighbourhood bar where members of the Guardians of the Flame ordinarily gathered and decides he will clean up the bar and sleep there while he waits for his crew to return. By episode two, however, he learns few of them have returned since, like he found with his own home, housing in this neighbourhood was decimated. When he finds that one of his crew members had been squatting at the Calliope housing projects (located in Central City on the other side of the highway from the Superdome), he goes in search of them and talks with a security guard who had been hired to watch the buildings. The guard lets Lambreaux know that the squatters had been expelled from the building, to which Lambreaux responds, 'People want to come home, no place to live' (*Treme* 2010a: 00:27:59). From there, viewers are clued into the broader context of New Orleans public housing and government intention to tear them down long before Katrina.

Lambreaux's activism begins in the season's fifth episode when he decides to confront city councillor Ron Singleton (Kerrell Antonio) about opening up the housing projects, suggesting to a friend he meets at City Hall, who is trying to get a parade permit for a second-line, that he is there to demand the projects reopen, again repeating, 'People need to come home' (*Treme* 2010b: 00:13:58).³ This phrasing positions Lambreaux within the discourse of housing advocates emphasizing a right to return, as his friend admonishes in return, 'It's like they don't even want New Orleans to be New Orleans no more' (*Treme* 2010b: 00:13:59). The friend is intimating the critique of how elites were using the storm to shift the city's population to permanently displace 'problem' populations. Lambreaux and his friend resist this discourse through an emphasis on Black cultural traditions – second-lining and Mardi Gras Indian parading – to demonstrate that New Orleans is only New Orleans because of these kinds of traditions. They resist the problematization and pathologization of this segment of the population and instead position them as cultural agents with a history, a tradition, that lend value to New Orleans as a place (Regis 1999).

Lambreaux finally confronts Singleton later in the episode, but Singleton abdicates responsibility, claiming 'you know that's not my call', because the projects are federal (*Treme* 2010b: 00:29:35). That is, because public housing is ultimately controlled by HUD and only administered by HANO, city officials did not have the ultimate call on whether they could reopen. But Lambreaux refuses to accept there is nothing the city can do, and this sets the stage for him to move from inquiry to activism in the next episode. Lambreaux states, 'it seems like they're trying to make it impossible for folks to come back. … Half my gang living like refugees in their own country. Somebody needs to make a stand, you know? Draw a line' (*Treme* 2010c: 00:45:06-00:45:42). Lambreaux's use of the term refugees here is significant, as in the immediate aftermath of Katrina, newscasters frequently referred to displaced Black New Orleanians as refugees. As critics pointed out, that language constructs them as non-citizens and draws on long-standing histories of dispossession and denial of citizenship rights to Black and poor peoples in the United States and in New Orleans in particular since slavery and colonialism (Dyson 2006). Lambreaux is thus connecting the right to return home to this broader struggle for Black citizenship rights. He refuses Singleton's attempt to placate him with an offer of a FEMA trailer and, instead, in the next episode, engages in direct action through squatting in the Calliope projects.

Treme represents Lambreaux as an active agent who resists the dominant narrative spun by city elites around the city's public housing. That resistance is articulated to Lambreaux's position as a guardian of Black cultural tradition. Lambreaux's refusal of the trailer further positions him in opposition to the autonomous individual idealized by neoliberalism and instead makes a broader, collective call for the right to return. It is clear Singleton views Lambreaux's status as a Mardi Gras Indian Chief as valuable, but Lambreaux refuses to acknowledge that value as being about his individual subject position and instead makes a claim for the value of all, especially those citizens deemed marginal and unworthy, to return. So too, he refuses to place a value on the individual home – rejecting the trailer – and instead offers up a powerful defence of public housing not as a space for transforming citizens into self-governing, individualized units, but as constituting a fundamental right.

Crime, police brutality and systemic abandonment

Treme's representation of public housing residents as active agents of resistance demanding a right to return refuses to make a division between the deserving and undeserving. In so doing, the series exposes governmental abandonment and abdication of responsibility of care as what is ultimately pathological and criminal, reversing the typical media representation of public housing residents in these terms. For example, in the season's fifth episode we learn that a comeback second-line parade ended in a shooting. This could have been an example of *Treme* reifying stereotypes of poor, Black criminality – a trope frequently circulated within New Orleans and used as justification to deny parade permits to clubs. Second-lines, like the projects, are viewed as hotbeds of potential crime and violence. The shooting was, unfortunately, reflective of actual events. The decision to include this in the show reveals that crime and violence are a reality of New Orleans, but in the parade shooting scene, the camera shifts focus from Black perpetrators to Black victims. This shift demonstrates the trauma of the largely Black paradegoers and their experiences of violence. A later scene in the episode shows a bar with a news show playing in the background, and we hear the reporter state the shooting was a reminder of a 'New Orleans that many hoped had been washed away' (*Treme* 2010b: 00:48:36). Watching the reporter recount this on TV through their own screen, viewers are enjoined to situate the reporter's comments within the context of the narrative of the Chief demanding a right of return. As viewers, we are forced to live with both realities – crime and violence *are* factors of living in New Orleans, but, unequivocally, people need to come home. *Treme* does not allow the viewer to divide the deserving and undeserving, those who should be allowed to return and those who should be 'washed away'. Crime and violence in *Treme* are not the result of pathological individuals who are thus undeserving, but, rather, pathological institutions and systems.

Refusing to create a division between those who do and do not deserve to return home, *Treme* complicates the biopolitics of disposability made manifest during Katrina. In many ways, public housing is a result of a biopolitics of disposability, particularly as it has been privatized and defunded, leaving many of these structures in disrepair and using the housing as a space for collecting, and abandoning, largely Black and poor populations. In the wake of Katrina, those populations were literally left to die. But *Treme* offers a different reading of public housing, while also not foreclosing the reading of them as products of a biopolitics of disposability. In placing emphasis on the habitability and the relative safety of the housing in comparison to the rest of the city's private housing, *Treme* demonstrates that it is neither the housing nor the residents that are the 'problem' to be solved. Rather, it is the systems that abandoned both the people and the housing that are to be blamed – HANO, HUD and HOPE VI are the subjects positioned as forces of destruction and violence. In emphasizing these structural causes of housing dysfunction, *Treme* counters the biopolitics of disposability by utilizing the state of abandoned housing as a haunting spectre of the state's abandonment of New Orleans's most vulnerable.

Treme further reverses the typical threat relation portrayed in public housing. Typically, public housing and its inhabitants are represented as a threat to police and state, but *Treme* reverses this and constructs the state and police as the real violent threat. In the season's seventh episode, Lambreaux is brutally beaten by police after he refuses to vacate the projects (*Treme* 2010d). The scene of the beating serves to reinforce the symbolic connections between the Chief as standing in for the voice, power and agency of public housing residents in ways that contest the biopolitics of disposability and neoliberal racism. It shows that the real threat is not the pathologized public housing residents as they are typically represented, but the police who target them and other Black citizens. The representation of police in this scene is part of a broader narrative thread in

Treme that problematizes police corruption and anti-Blackness. The images of police violence in the scene are significant especially in the context of the larger narrative arc in this season where the character Ladonna (Khandi Alexander) is searching for her brother who has been missing since Katrina. In this same episode, she learns the police have had him all along and that he died in their custody – abandoned, the ultimate subject of a biopolitics of disposability. When the police come to arrest Lambreaux, the officers burst into the unit and demand he gets down on his knees with his hands on his head, to which he responds, 'No hum-bow' (*Treme* 2010d: 00:39:57), a phrase chanted by Mardi Gras Indians, roughly translating to 'we won't bow down' and signifying 'the individual's spirit and not surrendering in the face of adversity' (Hinton 2020). As the cops move in on Lambreaux, the handheld camera work shows the beating from the Chief's perspective, taking place largely in darkness, and we see only the officers' arms, holding, grabbing, hitting as Lambreaux flails and tries to keep them off him. The scene is brutal and startling. As the white officer punches him, repeatedly, we hear another officer yelling, 'Stop resisting! Stop resisting!' (*Treme* 2010d: 00:40:09). This takes on a larger meaning in terms of demanding Lambreaux and the people he represents stop resisting, that they 'bow down'. But Lambreaux's 'no hum-bow' instead supports the possibility and necessity of resistance. It connects the resistance around public housing activism to the resistance of Black culture bearers such as the Mardi Gras Indians, whom the series shows are also frequently targets of police harassment and brutality, demonstrating that both are centrally about the right for Black bodies to live lives of dignity and lay claim to New Orleans. Representations of police brutality and resistance in *Treme* thus work to support the larger protest for public housing as it articulates it to a call for a right to return and the broader claim for Black citizenship rights.

Conclusions: On the limits of *Treme*'s politics

Though *Treme* poses a strong argument for the potential for resistance by the city's most dispossessed residents and a call for their right to return, like the calls of the real-life activists in New Orleans, Lambreaux fails to have the projects reopened. After he is arrested, Lambreaux returns to the Calliope housing projects in the season's eighth episode to find the National Guard, just having returned from Iraq, reconstructing the fence around the projects. The images here are palpable in how they show the investment of government in sources of profit, moving from exploitation of the oil fields in Iraq to securing public housing projects to guarantee private profits (Cook 2015). As Lambreaux is watching them rebuild the fence, a Black youth looking on observes the protest had changed nothing, but Lambreaux responds, 'Lost a battle is all', and he affirms to the kid that this is the reason he wants to 'mask', or parade as a Mardi Gras Indian (*Treme* 2010f: 00:50:29). The exchange here is significant in that it acknowledges the lost battle over public housing which did indeed play out in New Orleans, but it connects that battle to the longer history of struggle of Black New Orleanians fighting for their rights in New Orleans. It hinges that longer battle on Black cultural traditions like Mardi Gras Indians and second-lining, as practices of resistance that are engaged in political struggle over the city's future and who it is for. The Chief ultimately returns to his home in Gentilly and starts the long process of rebuilding. The next season shows him navigating the failures of the Road Home project, as his struggle to represent the right to return continues to expose how government failed and abandoned New Orleans's most vulnerable citizens.

Like Lambreaux's failed occupation of the Calliope projects, *Treme*'s defence of public housing in New Orleans did not stop the final projects from being demolished and transformed into the HOPE VI vision of mixed-income housing. Perhaps the series creators would like viewers to see this not as a failure, but just as one failed battle, as part of a longer struggle to contest the changes being wrought by disaster capitalism and neoliberal urbanism. Simon's turn to public housing as a major focus for *Show Me a Hero* (see Macek, this volume) demonstrates his commitment to positioning his storytelling as part of that longer struggle. *Treme*'s representations of public housing are a significant part of that in how they diverge from what we largely see in mainstream media, especially journalistic and televisual representations. It provides a powerful defence of the right to housing via a right to return and shifts the narrative of pathology and destruction from housing and citizens to the systems that create housing precarity.

Although these are welcome and important contestations that intervene into the wider debate about public housing, they are also limited. While Lambreaux stands in for a broader collective movement, especially since he serves as Chief of Guardians of the Flame which marks him as both a moral voice of the show as well as a symbol of community, collectivity and relationality, the failure to show the movement against the razing of New Orleans public housing as a collective, rather than individual effort, is disappointing. The series gestures towards others following him in squatting in the projects and briefly in a season three protest that shows opposition to public housing demolition (*Treme* 2013), but there is no attention given to the substantial collective organizing effort that went into that resistance. In that sense, *Treme* follows most televisual representations of resistance and social movement – that it is the result of singular, great individuals who stand up for justice. Although that serves the interests of televisual narrative and drama, that is rarely, if ever, how social justice works. Indeed, the organizing around New Orleans public housing was rooted in difficult, multiracial coalition work that required multiple groups to negotiate, at times conflicting, interests to further the goals of preserving the city's public housing and the rights of residents to return (Arena 2011). Of note as well is that the movement was largely organized and spearheaded by Black women, who disproportionately occupy public housing in New Orleans and the nation more broadly and whose images are most often used in the problematizing discourses and representation of public housing that represent them as pathological (e.g. the image of the 'welfare queen'). But *Treme* traffics in the well-worn erasure of Black women's collective, political resistance, instead reimposing the idea of the need for strong, Black masculinity to return to (the family) and retrieve the failing projects. The erasure of Black women's agential resistance and valorization of Black masculinity is indicative of Simon's work more broadly (see Young, this volume; Ault 2013). Championing the singular efforts and moral voice of Chief Lambreaux, as a great man and patriarch of the community, *Treme* risks reifying a neoliberal, entrepreneurialization of cultural identity untethered from collective social action in the form of social justice movements and protest (see Morgan Parmett 2019).

Furthermore, the series lays blame largely in the hands of the government for its abdication of responsibility for caring for its citizens, abandoning them during Katrina and in its aftermath. But the picture of government failure is more complicated, as those failures are largely the result of longer histories of privatization and market-based governance that had largely gutted government programmes by contracting to private entities (Adams 2013). The continual reminder to viewers that the city's public housing is under federal control seems to pit city and state authorities against a failed federal system, but it lends little visibility to the market forces that have long driven HUD's approach to public housing (Vale and Freemark 2019). In so doing, the series risks furthering the justification for rolling back government because of its failures and thus making *more* room for privatization, rather than contesting the privatizing, neoliberal forces that contributed to government failure.

Although *Treme*'s politics are limited, this is also too narrow a view of the specific political work *Treme* is engaged in with regards to public housing representations. It remains significant that the series portrays public housing in good condition, well-built and functional. As Lambreaux continues to demand government live up to its responsibilities by enabling people to come home and to reinvest in public housing, the series does open to a call for government responsibility rather than a further waning of that responsibility. And it does so through what is a rare representation on TV of a defence of public housing as a right. Thus, even if imperfect, *Treme* is a valuable contribution to representations of public housing in US television.

Notes

1   In 1998, for example, the St. Thomas Development was demolished after a series of highly publicized shootings there. St. Thomas was frequently represented by city government as a site of concentrated poverty and referred to in the news as 'one of the most violent and dangerous public housing projects'. Although violence and crime were factors of St. Thomas, their demolition was driven by the value of the real estate, as they were located in the Lower Garden District adjacent to the city's wealthiest neighbourhood. The demolition eliminated 1,500 housing units replaced by mixed income development with 200 'affordable' units (see Arena 2011).
2   The city's public housing was 'lauded as "some of the best public housing in the United States"' (Finger 2011).
3   'Second-line' refers to a parade in which a social aid and pleasure dances to a brass band and is followed by parade watchers in a 'second line' of the parade. On the tradition of second-lines and their relationship to Black cultural resistance, see Regis 1999.

References

Adams, Vincanne (2013), *Markets of Sorrow, Labors of Faith: New Orleans in the Wake of Katrina*, Durham and London: Duke University Press.

Arena, John (2011), 'Black and White, Unite and Fight? Identity Politics and New Orleans's Post-Katrina Public Housing Movement', in C. Johnson (ed), *The Neoliberal Deluge: Hurricane Katrina, Late Capitalism, and the Remaking of New Orleans*, 152–83, Minneapolis: University of Minnesota Press.

Ault, Elizabeth (2013), '"You Can Help Yourself/but Don't Take Too Much": African American Motherhood on The Wire', *Television & New Media*, 14 (5): 386–401.

Babington, Charles (2005), 'Some GOP Legislators Hit Jarring Notes in Addressing Katrina', *Washington Post*, 10 September. Available online: http://www.

washingtonpost.com/wp-dyn/content/article/2005/09/09/AR2005090901930.html (accessed 1 December 2021).

Bullard, Robert D. and Beverly Wright (2009), 'Race, Place, and the Environment in Post-Katrina New Orleans', in Robert D. Bullard and Beverly Wright (eds), *Race, Place, and Environmental Justice after Hurricane Katrina: Struggles to Reclaim, Rebuild, and Revitalize New Orleans and the Gulf Coast*, 19–47, Boulder, Colo.: Westview Press.

Campanella, Richard (2006), *Geographies of New Orleans: Urban Fabrics before the Storm*, Lafayette, LA: Center for Louisiana Studies.

Casselman, Ben (2015), 'Katrina Washed Away New Orleans's Black Middle Class', *FiveThirtyEight*, 24 August. Available online: https://fivethirtyeight.com/features/katrina-washed-away-new-orleanss-black-middle-class/ (accessed 1 December 2021).

Cook, Bernie (2015), *Flood of Images: Media, Memory, and Hurricane Katrina*, Austin: University of Texas Press.

Dyson, Michael E. (2006), *Come Hell or High Water: Hurricane Katrina and the Color of Disaster*, New York: Basic Civitas.

Finger, Davida (2011), 'Public Housing in New Orleans Post Katrina: The Struggle for Housing as a Human Right', *The Review of Black Political Economy*, 38 (4): 327–37.

Foucault, Michel (2003), *Society Must Be Defended: Lectures at the Collège de France 1975–76*, trans. D. Macey, New York: Picador.

Gans, Herbert J. (2010), 'Concentrated Poverty: A Critical Analysis', *Challenge*, 53 (3): 82–96.

Giroux, Henry A. (2004), *The Terror of Neoliberalism: Authoritarianism and the Eclipse of Democracy*, Boulder; Aurora, Ont.: Paradigm; Garamond Press.

Giroux, Henry A. ([2006], 2016), *Stormy Weather: Katrina and the Politics of Disposability*, London: Routledge.

Harvey, David (2005), *A Brief History of Neoliberalism*, Oxford: Oxford University Press.

Hinton, Matthew (2020), 'No Hum Bow: Wrongly Convicted, Mardi Gras Indians Chief Joe Jenkins Chose Love', *Very Local New Orleans*, 26 August 26. Available online: https://nola.verylocal.com/no-hum-bow-wrongly-convicted-and-never-wanting-revenge-mardi-gras-indians-chief-joe-jenkins-chose-love/159579/ (accessed 1 December 2021).

Klein, Naomi (2007), *The Shock Doctrine: The Rise of Disaster Capitalism*, New York: Metropolitan Books.

Lipsitz, George (1990), *Time Passages: Collective Memory and American Popular Culture*, Minneapolis: University of Minnesota Press.

Mann, Nicola (2011), 'Criminalizing "The Hood"', *Afterimage*, 38 (6): 21–5.

Morgan Parmett, Helen (2019), *Down in Treme: Race, Place, and New Orleans on Television*, Stuttgart: Franz Steiner Verlag.

Regis, Helen A. (1999), 'Second Lines, Minstrelsy, and the Contested Landscapes of New Orleans Afro-Creole Festivals', *Cultural Anthropology: Journal of the Society for Cultural Anthropology*, 14 (4): 472–504.

Rogers, Dallas, Michael Darcy, and Kathy Arthurson (2017), 'Researching Territorial
    Stigma with Social Housing Tenants: Tenant-Led Digital Media Production
    about People and Place', in Paul Kirkness and Andreas Tijé-Dra (eds), *Negative
    Neighbourhood Reputation and Place Attachment: The Production and Contestation of
    Territorial Stigma*, 178–93, London: Routledge.

Treme (2010a), [TV Programme] HBO, 18 April.

Treme (2010b), [TV Programme] HBO, 9 May.

Treme (2010c), [TV Programme] HBO, 16 May.

Treme (2010d), [TV Programme] HBO, 23 May.

Treme (2010e), [TV Programme] HBO, 6 June.

Treme (2010f), [TV Programme] HBO, 13 June.

Treme (2013), [TV Programme] HBO, 20 May.

Vale, Lawrence J. and Yonah Freemark (2019), 'The Privatization of American
    Public Housing', in Katrin B. Anacker, Mai T. Nguyen, and David P. Varady (eds),
    The Routledge Handbook of Housing Policy and Planning, 189–206, New York:
    Routledge.

Wacquant, Loïc, Tom Slater, and Virgilio B. Pereira (2014), 'Territorial Stigmatization in
    Action', *Environment and Planning A: Economy and Space*, 46 (6): 1270–80.

Woods, Clyde A. (2009), 'Les Misérables of New Orleans: Trap Economics and the
    Asset Stripping Blues, Part 1', *American Quarterly*, 61 (3): 769–96.

12

Public housing, social problems and defensible space in David Simon's *Show Me a Hero*

Steve Macek

Public housing is a central setting in many of David Simon's urban TV series. For instance, much of the action in the first two seasons of *The Wire* unfolded against the backdrop of the fictional West Baltimore Franklin Terrace Towers high-rises and the courtyards in between them. New Orleans' Calliope Projects were a main location in the first season of *Treme* (see Young and Morgan Parmett, this volume). At times, public housing in these and other Simon series functions as more than mere backdrop, and instead is thematized as both a key source and embodiment of broader social problems – racial segregation, poverty, crime, drug use, social disorder – and a focus of ideological and political struggles over how to ameliorate those problems (Clandfield 2009: 37–9).

Simon's treatment of modernist public housing towers as symbolic of the deep social divisions and profound injustices typical of the late-capitalist city is nowhere more evident than in his 2015 HBO miniseries *Show Me a Hero*, which dramatizes the real-life political battles that unfolded in Yonkers, New York during the late 1980s and early '90s over the building of court-ordered scattered-site public housing in all-white neighbourhoods. The series is notable, in part, because it includes as a main character architect and urban planner Oscar Newman, whose ideas about 'defensible space' and critique of high-rise public housing projects became popular with urban policy elites in the 1980s and '90s (and ultimately informed the US Department of Housing and Urban Development (HUD)'s HOPE VI programme, which caused the removal of so much of the nation's public housing stock in the 1990s). The series also stands out from much television fare in that it paints a richly detailed portrait of urban policy-making and local politics.

In this chapter, I argue that the consistent visual and narrative contrast drawn throughout *Show Me* between the living conditions in Yonkers' dilapidated, graffiti-covered William A. Schlobohm Houses and the new model scatter-site townhouses, into which a few fortunate Black and Latino former Schlobohm tenants move, appears to ratify Oscar Newman's claims about the essentially design-related failures of modernist public housing (which are presented to the audience, synoptically, by Newman as a character in a few key scenes in the series). This endorsement of Newman's views, I maintain, undercuts Simon's obvious intention to use this series and its nuanced stories about the daily lives of public housing residents to draw attention to and expose the way the reactionary, Not In My Back Yard (NIMBY) politics of predominantly white communities has contributed to the persistent segregation and systematic disadvantage of the Black and Latino poor and working class. It also quite uncritically reinforces what urban policy scholar Edward Goetz has called the discourse of public-housing-as-disaster, a demonization of state-provided housing that – at least in the United States – has been used to justify government abandonment of the poor to the ravages of private housing markets (2013: 40–2).

An allegory of political dysfunction tinged with hope

Based on a 1999 book about the Yonkers public housing battle by *New York Times* reporter Lisa Belkin, the six-part miniseries *Show Me a Hero* was written by David Simon and fellow *Wire* writer William F. Zorzi, directed by Paul Haggis and features a cast that includes recognizable stars. The series was shot entirely on location in Yonkers during the fall of 2014, with the William A. Schlobohm Houses and other high-rise Yonkers public housing projects serving as key locations throughout (Silberg 2015: 13). *Show Me* debuted in mid-August 2015 and aired, two episodes at a time, every Sunday night for three weeks. As a number of critics and reviewers have observed, the series marks a return to the sharp-edged, sociologically – and politically sophisticated critique of the dysfunctions and inequalities shaping contemporary American cities that many viewers valued about *The Wire* (Rotella 2015; Hale 2015). Indeed, Simon has said that he viewed the story of the Yonkers public housing fracas as 'an almost perfectly allegorical argument about how our political processes are no longer equipped to recognize or solve problems' (Mulholland 2014). In many ways, though, *Show Me* is more hopeful about the possibilities of progress than Simon's other TV shows, as it presents the eventual construction of new scattered-site housing in Yonkers as at least a partial cure for the city's deep divisions.

The series uses the case of the Yonkers public housing fight to explore the toxic legacy of racial segregation in America and the flawed, divisive nature of local politics. A December 1980 lawsuit brought by the Justice Department and the National Association for the Advancement of Colored People (NAACP) against the city of Yonkers made the case that the city's schools were unequal because of the racial segregation of its housing, especially its public housing. Indeed, the suit alleged that nearly all of Yonkers' Black and Latino residents were concentrated into a single square-mile area west of Saw Mill River and most lived in the 7,000 units of public housing located there. Federal Judge Leonard B. Sand agreed, ruling in 1985 that the siting of public housing in Yonkers was 'the result of a pattern and practice of racial discrimination by city officials, pursued in response to constituent pressures to select or support only sites that would preserve existing patterns of racial segregation, and to reject or oppose sites that would threaten existing patterns of segregation' (Williams 1985). Refraining from mandating a specific plan for the desegregation of public housing in the city, Sand nevertheless ordered that 200 units of public housing – which HUD had agreed to build – be erected in the predominantly white eastern sectors of the city. In 1986, the City of Yonkers announced it would appeal Sand's court order and the city council spent the year dithering about adopting a plan for the new housing (Jovanovitch 1986). In response, Judge Sand appointed architect and urban planner Oscar Newman to identify potential sites for the new houses (Feron 1987). Sand's ruling in *United States v. Yonkers*, and his subsequent orders provoked a vociferous response from white homeowner groups on Yonkers' east side.

The central narrative thread of *Show Me a Hero* focuses on the rise and fall of ambitious, *wunderkind* local politician Nick Wasicsko (played by Oscar Isaacs), a former cop and first-term councilman, who becomes a central (and tragic) figure in the dramatic standoff between the city and the court over Sand's housing decree. In the opening episode, we meet Wasicsko on the eve of a contentious February 1987 city council meeting at which an ordinance designed to implement the court order will once again be discussed. Shortly before the meeting, the city's Democratic Party boss, Ralph Arred (Michael Kostroff), persuades Wasicsko to run for mayor against six-term Republican incumbent Angelo Martinelli (Jim Belushi). At the city council meeting, a group of angry white residents wave signs and shout at Martinelli and the other city councillors who vote in favour of the ordinance. Though Wasicsko's voting record on most issues, including the housing issue, is identical to Martinelli's, he ultimately turns the fact that he voted in favour of appealing Judge Sand's decision into his main selling point on the campaign trail.

The first episode also introduces viewers to other key players in the ensuing political drama: Republican city council member Henry 'Hank' Spallone (Alfred Molina), Vinni Restiano, Wasicsko's main ally on the council (Winona Ryder), NAACP lawyer Michael H. Sussman (Jon Bernthaal) and urban planner Oscar Newman (Peter Riegert).

In a key scene following the February 1987 city council vote, we see Newman – who has just been hired to help site the new housing – in a conference with Judge Sand (Bob Balaban). Newman declares that Sand's original plan for concentrating the 200 new units of public housing on two sites will not work and advocates for 'scattered site' housing instead. Shortly afterwards, Sand orders Yonkers to comply with his order or be held in contempt.

At a city council meeting called by the embattled Martinelli to ratify the housing plan, pandemonium breaks out, vividly illustrating the sort of fearful, reactionary sentiments driving opponents of the plan. One exasperated woman angrily suggests 'maybe this judge, if he likes the people who live in public housing so much, then he should have that kind of housing in his neighbourhood, where he lives. See how he likes it!' Another man objects that 'we're not prejudiced. Anyone is welcome to live in my neighbourhood if they have the money' (*Show Me*, Part 1 2015: 00:39:58–00:40:170). The council reluctantly approves the Martinelli plan. Despite having voted in favour of the plan, Wasicsko is elected mayor. Even before being sworn in, he learns that the city's appeal has failed.

At the start of the second episode, Sand instructs Wasicsko and the members of the city council to approve 'specific houses in specific locations' or he will impose escalating fines every day 'until the city of Yonkers is bankrupt' (*Show Me* Part 2 2015: 00:00:34–00:01:00). Wasicscko persuades a bare majority of the city council to comply with the court order, but pays a high price for this victory and is portrayed being spat at by protestors and threatened with bullets in the mail. In one notable scene, Wasicsko's car is swarmed by an angry mob of housing opponents who pound on the hood and shatter the windshield.

As the series shows, Hank Spallone was able to leverage racist anger over the scattered-site public housing to defeat Wasicsko in the 1988 mayoral election (Feron 1987). Spallone then disappoints his NIMBY base by complying with the court order after one last legal appeal fails. Construction on the low-rise, scattered-site housing begins amidst duelling protests from Black activists demanding desegregation, on the one hand, and white east side residents dead-set against it, on the other. In the final instalment of the series, we see public housing residents settling into their newly constructed homes. Wasicsko – back in city council but paranoid about being targeted by an impending corruption investigation – commits suicide. The tension between Wasicsko's personal tragedy and the triumph of the housing desegregation plan he championed adds a melancholy tone to what would have otherwise been a triumphant conclusion to the series.

The Schlobohm Houses

Although Nick Wasicsko's rise and fall as an elected official form the central story arc of *Show Me a Hero*, the real focus of the miniseries is the legal and political fight to create an alternative to Yonkers' racially segregated, crime-ridden high-rise projects. As in other Simon series, *Show Me* provides viewers with a panoramic view of Yonkers' social and political hierarchy, from the powerful to the impoverished. Indeed, as Matt Zoller Seitz has observed, the series' juxtaposition of stories about the city's policy making process with stories about the working-class and poor citizens affected by that process makes a powerful statement about how government 'can be disconnected from the people it wishes to serve' (2015).

Simon introduces us to several Black and Latino residents of the city's Schlobohm Houses, desperate for improvement in their living situations, as well as to several white politicians and ordinary residents of the white east side neighbourhoods resistant to the scattered-site housing. We meet Norma O'Neal (LaTanya Richardson Jackson), an older healthcare worker losing her vision due to diabetes, Carmen 'Alma' Febles (Ilfenesh Hadera), a Dominican-born single mom of three working a blue-collar job, Billie Rowan (Dominique Fishback), a teenage girl who gets pregnant after partnering up with a dashing young man who spends much of the series in jail and Doreen Henderson (Natalie Paul), a woman from the suburbs who ends up in the projects after becoming a single mother and develops a crack addiction. As Francesco Sticchi observes, these women exist in 'states of precarious motherhood' and all of them evidence 'the fragility and vulnerability of an existence deprived of networks of solidarity' (2021: 212). Each of these characters is depicted as having compelling reasons to leave Schlobohm. For instance, after Norma O'Neal is diagnosed with diabetes-related vision loss, her son arranges for a social worker to help her but the menacing gangs who loiter around the projects scare the social worker off. And Carmen Febles and her family routinely must push past boisterous young men playing dice in the hallways and are forced to take the stairs because the elevators have been taken over by drug dealers doing business.

The visual portrayal of the Schlobohm Houses throughout the series is especially noteworthy. When we first see the Houses, it is from the vantage point of a helicopter being used by Oscar Newman to survey the city for possible locations of the scattered-site homes. We see, from Newman's point of view, an aerial shot of eight cruciform red brick housing slabs about ten storeys high. Next, the camera cuts to a street-level shot of the entrance to one of the Schlobohm buildings (see Figure 12.1). The building is depicted as dilapidated and filthy. There is graffiti on most of the exterior walls, a conventional signifier of criminal activity in virtually all American TV shows and films. A battered couch sits on the sidewalk adjacent to the entrance and an overturned chair and several bulging black trash bags sit near the curb. Carmen Febles and her children are shown exiting a car and the camera follows them into the building. The interior communal spaces – the hallways and stairwells – are dimly lit and, like the outside of the building, trash-strewn and plastered with graffiti.

Interestingly, the interiors of many of the Schlobohm apartments that we see throughout the miniseries are tidy and well-preserved, indicating ever so subtly that the main problem with the projects is the neglect and abuse of their common spaces (hallways, entrances, sidewalks in front of the buildings). This is underscored by a scene in the fifth instalment in which a group of middle-aged white women visit Schlobohm families who have been selected to be the first tenants of the newly constructed townhouses. The visitors are visibly shocked

Figure 12.1 Entrance to the Schlobohm Houses, *Show Me a Hero* © HBO 2015. All rights reserved.

by the graffiti-covered walls and filthy hallways that greet them at the entrance of the first building they enter. They find that the building's main elevator is out of order and are warned by the guide accompanying them to avoid the 'bad stairs' where, presumably, illicit activities are taking place. Yet, when the visitors arrive at the homes of the families they are visiting, the apartments are cheaply furnished but warm and welcoming, with family pictures hung neatly on the walls, children playing games in their bedrooms and tea and cookies served up in the cosy living rooms. Still, the overall image of Schlobohm, and by extension other high-rise public housing projects like it, as derelict, dirty and chaotic established in the opening sequence of the first episode remains remarkably consistent throughout the series.

The residents of Schlobohm share animus against the projects with the white homeowners and local politicians, routinely expressing their criticisms of and misgivings about the place where they live. The son of Norma O'Neal, the aging home health worker, tells her at one point, 'This place ain't gonna get no better' (*Show Me* Part 1 2015: 00:08:52–00:08:56). Alma is shown more than once staring out her windows at loitering clusters of young men milling around outside, presumably drug dealers, with a perpetually worried look on her face. In one memorable scene, Doreen writes a letter to her infant son John. 'You are my son and I love you', we hear her say in the voice-over narration, 'but you've been born in a hard place. And you and your mama are alone now' (*Show Me* Part 3 2015: 00:50:35–00:50:48). Doreen's voice-over is accompanied by a shot of Alma and her own son, Phillipe, at the playground outside Schlobohm, a graffiti-covered wall in the background (see Figure 12.2). Phillipe bends down

Figure 12.2 Alma's son Phillipe picks up a used syringe at a Schlobohm playground, *Show Me a Hero* © HBO 2015. All rights reserved.

and picks up a used syringe as Alma reacts with horror and alarm. Though Phillipe disposes of the syringe in a trash can, the shot amply illustrates the sort of dangers that Doreen fears might be lurking in this 'hard place'.

Public-housing-as-disaster

Show Me a Hero's framing of high-rise public housing projects in late-1980s Yonkers as this kind of dangerous, uninhabitable environment overrun with crime and social pathology encodes and perpetuates the now-hegemonic conception of public-housing-as-disaster. As Edward Goetz has noted, during the New Deal era and through the immediate post-Second World War period, federally funded public housing was seen by policymakers and local politicians across the country both as an effective solution to urban slums and as a means of addressing a burgeoning postwar housing crisis. Typically solidly built, well-designed low-rise brick apartment complexes, the newly constructed projects helped to clear out tenements in central cities and were often viewed as a paradise by their working-class residents (Goetz 2013: 26). However, by the 1950s, federal government-funded slum clearance had actually exacerbated the shortage of affordable housing, particularly for low-income Black families displaced by the federal bulldozer. According to Gwendolyn Wright, federal slum clearance resulted in a net loss of some 300,000 units of low-income housing between 1949 and 1968 (1983: 234). In their classic study of urban poverty and the political functions of social welfare spending, *Regulating the Poor*, Frances Fox Piven and Richard A. Cloward point to evidence that the destruction of admittedly substandard, slum-quality low-rent housing available through the private market in the 1960s drove up dramatically the number of families who were forced to go onto welfare in order to make ends meet (1971: 287).

The rising demand for low-income units coupled with severe cost constraints led officials to erect more and more monotonous, unattractive, cement and cinder-block high-rises. Often, public housing authorities (PHAs) lacked the necessary funds to maintain, repair and replace these high-rise buildings as they aged and deteriorated. Several other trends conspired to undermine popular support for public housing and to marginalize and stigmatize the projects and their residents. Spurred by the welfare rights movement in the 1960s, PHAs 'began to emphasize families with severe need living on public assistance' (Goetz 2013: 37). As a consequence, single mothers and their children occupied a rising number of public housing units. By 1966, half of all public housing households were headed by a single parent and half had no employed adults. This trend continued through the 1970s. By 1980, the average income of the nation's public housing residents was one-fifth of the national average (Goetz 2013: 38). The disrepair and dilapidation that had become so common in the 1960s worsened. Because public housing authorities depended on rents to pay for repairs, as vacancy rates rose and the tenants of the average project became poorer, repairs to windows, heating and plumbing systems and elevators at a number of projects were postponed indefinitely. Moreover, the amount of money the federal government invested in new housing construction plummeted from US$28 billion in 1977 to just US$7 billion in 1988 (Clay 1992: 263).

By the time of the desegregation battle in Yonkers, the nation's aging public housing stock had come to be viewed by policy experts, government officials and the general public as housing of last resort and exclusively as a reserve for 'broken families', racist code for impoverished Black families. There was a consensus among commentators that the crime and violence associated with the most troubled high-rise projects were not caused merely by the racial segregation, discrimination, over-policing, poverty and unemployment endured by their residents but by the design of the buildings themselves.[1] Indeed, in the wake of the urban riots of the late 1960s, the National Commission on Urban Problems criticized high-rise public housing as 'not just inadequate but "anti-community"' and as the cause of at least some of the troubles of its majority Black tenants (Wright 1983: 237). As we will see, this is a view that was echoed and defended at length by urban planner Oscar Newman, a central character in the Yonkers drama, and is one that is at least tacitly endorsed by the makers of *Show Me a Hero*.

As Goetz among others has argued, the mainstream media contributed to an exaggerated discourse of public-housing-as-disaster by zeroing in on 'the most dysfunctional high-rise project, the fantastic failures of public housing, highlighting a largely [B]lack population living in dangerous and alienating communities' (2013: 40), such as Pruitt-Igoe in St. Louis and the Robert Taylor Homes in Chicago. Yet, as Goetz attests, the image of public housing communities as 'wildly out of control' and composed of violent criminals preying on cowering tenants never described the 'overwhelming majority' of the nation's public housing communities and, in fact, in 'most cities at most times' public housing provided low-income families with a desirable and affordable alternative to private-sector housing (2013: 42).

The discourse of public-housing-as-disaster that was popularized in policy debates and by sensational news stories in the 1970s, '80s and early '90s continues to inform visual representations like *Show Me's* depiction of the Schlobohm Houses and other narratives of public housing in film and television (Dreier 2005: 197; see also the individual TV news stories about housing projects discussed in Macek 2006). It has legitimated and continues to legitimate the federal government's abandonment of public housing as an antidote to the dismal failures of private real estate markets as a source of adequate shelter for poor people. It also implicitly demonized a particular housing type and architectural form, modernist high-rise towers, as inherently alienating and inhospitable. In the 1970s and '80s, the man who was arguably most responsible for popularizing the discourse of public-housing-as-disaster in policy circles and for blaming public housing's troubles on design was architect and urban planner Oscar Newman, a central character in both the real-life battle over public housing in Yonkers and in *Show Me a Hero's* retelling of it. His voice is centred, repeatedly, in the miniseries and the entire framing of the 'problem of public housing' in the series can be read plausibly as an endorsement of his ideas.

Oscar Newman, defensible space and the townhouses as Utopia

Oscar Newman's reputation and influence on urban policy stems largely from a single book, his 1972 opus *Defensible Space: Crime Prevention Through Urban Design*. The research for the book was financed 'by the New York City Housing Authority as well as the National Institute of Law Enforcement and Criminal Justice of the US Department of Justice' and 'was in fact a direct response to the urban crisis of the 1960s and the consequent reallocation of federal funds to studies of crime and urban violence' (Cupers 2017: 176). In it, he advanced the argument that crime and social disorder were flourishing in high-rise projects because of their scale as well as the modernist design of the buildings themselves. Underwriting this claim was his famous notion of 'defensible space', the architectural or design features most associated with single-family dwellings – front stoops, fenced in front yards, private entrances, private walkways – that make it easy for the inhabitants to recognize the zones over which they have influence and to control what takes place in them. Obviously, such features are absent from multistory towers like Schlobohm. As Newman explained:

> In a high-rise, double-loaded corridor apartment tower, the only defensible space is the interior of the apartment itself; everything else is 'no-man's-land,'

neither public nor private. The lobby, stairs, elevators and corridors are open and accessible to everyone. But unlike the well-peopled and continually surveyed public streets, these interior areas are sparsely used and impossible to survey; they become a nether world of fear and crime.

(1972: 27)

In order to demonstrate the purported connection between high-rise projects and the proliferation of crime, Newman conducted a study of the felony rate by building height in the projects run by the New York Housing Authority for the year 1969. Not altogether surprisingly, he found that buildings over six storeys tall in projects containing over 1,000 units had significantly higher crime rates than shorter buildings in projects with 1,000 units (Newman 1972: 28). He also found that the majority of serious crimes occurred in the interior public areas of the towers – especially, the elevator, the hallways and the stairs – rather than on the surrounding grounds or inside the apartments (Newman 1972: 32–22).

The centrepiece of Newman's argument is an extended contrast between two Brooklyn public housing complexes: the low-rise Brownsville Houses and the high-rise Van Dyke Houses. Though, according to Newman, the two projects had virtually identical tenant populations – both housed mostly poor Black and Puerto Rican families and a majority of residents were minors – he found that Van Dyke experienced nearly double the number of 'felonies, misdemeanors and offenses' (1972: 47). Moreover, Van Dyke required '39 per cent more maintenance work' than Brownsville, including experiencing more than twice the number of elevator breakdowns per month (Newman 1972: 48). Perhaps most significantly in Newman's eyes, police viewed Van Dyke as 'difficult to control' and questioned their own efficacy in fighting crime there while at Brownsville they were 'much more optimistic and, in subtle ways, respond[ed] to complaints with more vigor and concern' (Newman 1972: 49). All of this Newman attributed to the design features of the two projects. Everything about the Brownsville complex – the placement of the buildings on the site, the separate entries for each apartment, the open stairwells, the modest height (no house is taller than six storeys) – conspired to create a 'sense of propriety' among tenants who surveilled and took steps to control the eminently defensible spaces of the complex. By contrast, Newman argued that the 'no-man's lands' of the elevator, entry ways and corridors of the Van Dyke high-rises all but invited the disorder he discovered in his study.

In the end, Newman believed that building type did not matter very much for middle-class families with resources but thought that 'for poor and broken families, for immigrant, rural families new to urban life, the effect of living in a high-rise building is proving catastrophic' (1972: 188). Not surprisingly, his recommendation was that future housing projects for such families be closer in form to the Brownsville Houses. He advocated reducing densities to less than 100 units-per acre, erecting only low-rise housing and intentionally creating more 'defensible space' in all new construction by creating separate entrances, interior recreation areas, stairwells and corridors used by fewer apartments (Newman 1972: 187–208). He wanted 'privatized' public housing that gave individual tenants symbolic 'ownership' over the spaces they inhabited and eliminated as far as possible zones of communal control. Ultimately, the theory of defensible space essentially fetishized the detached, single-family home of the modern American suburb as the norm upon which the planning of residential areas should be based. *Show Me a Hero* explicitly validates Newman's diagnosis of the drawbacks of modernist, high-rise projects like Schlobohm and his notions about residential planning. Certainly, the visual representations of Schlobohm in the miniseries manifest every single problem or defect of high-rise public housing enumerated in *Defensible Space*. And, throughout *Show Me*, the character of Oscar Newman is given ample opportunity to articulate the philosophy laid out in that book. For instance, in the first episode of the series, when Newman elaborates on why he thinks the 200 units of housing ordered by Judge Sand should be scattered across several sites, his lines could have been taken word-for-word from *Defensible Space*. 'Too many units in any neighbourhood won't blend in with the community', he explains to Sand, 'it becomes isolated and divisive' (*Show Me* Part 1 2015: 00:22:25–00:22:31). Isolation, he adamantly insists, 'will allow a criminal element to flourish that the public housing residents alone can't control' (*Show Me* Part 3 2015: 00:41:26–00:42:19). While one of the NAACP lawyers attending the meeting at which Newman makes this statement counters that his perspective is fearmongering and potentially racist, the fact that Newman is given so much extended speaking time aligns the viewer and the series with his point of view. For example, Newman objects to the proposed design of the townhouses, which initially featured shared entrances and stairwells. 'Problems arise when projects have nebulous public areas that are a sort of no-man's-land', he declares, pointing out that such spaces are used for 'loitering' and 'drug dealing' (*Show Me* Part 3 2015: 00:46:03–00:46:18).

Even more significant than the platform that the Newman character is given to expound his ideas, *Show Me*'s rosy, soft-focus depiction of the townhouses as a desirable (if not frankly utopian) alternative to the hellish conditions in Schlobohm can be seen as a tacit validation of Newman's ideas. The townhouses, as pictured in the series, are designed exactly according to Newman's specifications. Each is no more than two storeys high, has a private entrance, a green front lawn and a fenced-in private backyard. Although they are attached houses and not free-standing single-family homes, their design mimics the domestic architecture of the surrounding middle-class neighbourhood with lawns, stoops, framed doors and windows and gabled roofs.

That the townhouses being built in the predominantly white neighbourhoods of East Yonkers represent a kind of Shangri-La, a veritable paradise, is never left in doubt. Consider, for instance, the raucous lottery at which a fortunate few families from Schlobohm are chosen to move into the new townhouses, a centrepiece of *Show Me's* fifth episode. Inside a gym packed with nervous Schlobohm tenants, the director of Yonker's PHA draws slips of paper from a raffle cage one-by-one and reads out the names. Each selection is greeted with loud applause, cheers and laughter and the people whose names are called jump up and down and hug each other. Of the characters we have followed throughout the series, only Carmen and her family leave the lottery empty-handed (and their dejection is palpable).

The completed townhouses are depicted as fully deserving of all the heartfelt longing. When the winners of the lottery arrive by bus to marvel at the new houses and later when they are shown moving in, the homes are shot with bright lighting, the warm colour palette of the scenes and the accompanying nostalgic Bruce Springsteen songs endowing the buildings with positive, upbeat emotional connotations (especially in contrast to the grim menace of the Schlobohm homes).

The finale of the series underscores for the viewers the stark contrast between the desirability of the townhouses and Schlobohm. Carmen Febles' niece, Rosa, who has happily settled into a townhouse, is carrying heavy shopping bags through a filthy, foreboding alleyway on her way into a Schlobohm building. Two men rush at her, steal her bags and gratuitously punch her in the face. Later, in her Aunt Carmen's apartment, Rosa makes a report to a police officer while holding a bag of ice to her bruised cheek. When the officer asks her where she lives, she proudly declares, 'I live in the townhouses now', while the camera lingers on her aunt's contemplative gaze (*Show Me* Part 6 2015: 00:16–33–00:16:36). Eventually, Carmen receives a letter from the Yonkers Housing Authority informing her that she and her children will be allowed to move into one of the new townhouses. She travels to the construction site with her kids and surveys the plot where her home will be erected while Rosa looks on approvingly. Soft piano and violin music play gently in the background, adding a slightly wistful tenor to the scene – Carmen clearly wants the life promised by these houses so badly it hurts. The better life symbolized by the townhouses is framed as the antithesis and antidote to the brutality of Schlobohm (the setting of the assault on Rosa) in a way that is impossible for viewers to ignore. Intertitles in the final scene describe what ultimately happened to the people the main characters are based on in real life. Carmen is shown entering her new home with her children excitedly running ahead of her. An intertitle tells us she became a grandmother of four and still lives in Yonkers – a success story.

In fact, the final minutes of *Show Me* suggest that the scattered-site public housing developments ordered by Sand were an unequivocal success. While the new Black and Latino residents of the townhouses initially endure the disapproval of the white neighbours and even shouted racial epithets, and while they must adjust to the eerie quiet of the middle-class neighbourhood, they are portrayed as very content with their new dwellings. Moreover, by the end of the miniseries, the Black and Latino residents of the townhouses have begun to integrate into the surrounding community and their white neighbours' hostility has begun to subside. Simon and company use the story of a white East Side resident, Mary Dorman (Catherine Keener), to illustrate this process. When we first meet her at the beginning of series, Dorman is a staunch opponent of the court-mandated housing. But after being recruited by the city's Housing Education Relocation Enterprise to assist tenants of the court-ordered housing acclimate to their new environment, she gradually becomes a defender of the townhouses and an ally of the tenants. She grows especially close with Doreen, who is elected as head of the townhouses' resident council. Significantly, at the end of the series, Mary and Doreen are shown sitting on chairs on Doreen's front stoop, chatting happily. Intertitles tell us that Mary remained active in the community until her death in 2011 and that Doreen still lives in her Yonkers townhouse. The closing image of interracial friendship and bonding set against the backdrop of the townhouses fittingly punctuates Simon's statement about the wisdom and success of Oscar Newman's solution to the problem of the projects.[2]

Widely accepted ideas?

In *Show Me a Hero*, many of the elements that made *The Wire* so distinctive and such an incisive indictment of the political status quo are once again present – precise sociological observation, a panoramic view of a city from the gutters to the halls of power, sympathetic treatment of the urban poor and a realistic, thoroughly unsentimental portrayal of the political process. Moreover, like

The Wire, Show Me skewers the bad faith and outright racism that distorts so many public policy debates, in *Show Me's* case about solutions to the affordable housing crisis besetting the urban poor. Critic Paul Owen went so far as to suggest that the miniseries was evidence that Simon had gotten 'his mojo back' after what he characterized as the occasionally 'unwatchably didactic' *Treme* (2015). Yet, unlike *The Wire, Show Me's* critical edge is blunted by its investment in Newman's demonization of high-rise public housing and the suspect ideological myths about public housing he perpetuated.

As I have argued, *Show Me* uncritically supports Oscar Newman's scapegoating of high-rise modernist architecture for many of the ills of public housing. An intertitle flashed over a shot of the Newman character at the end of the series declares 'the public housing theories of Oscar Newman are now widely accepted' (*Show Me* Part 6 2015: 01:03:14–01:03:19). However as urban policy journalist Jake Blumgart has pointed out, this is at best an overstatement and at worst simply untrue. While most housing theorists today agree that concentrating very poor people into a single location as happened in the 1960s was a recipe for disaster, Newman's explanations for notorious public housing failures like Pruitt-Igoe are oversimplistic and completely disregard the surrounding political-economic context. As Blumgart explains, 'Newman's theories completely ignored the vanishing industrial job base, the changing tenant demographics of public housing, and the neglectful management of some patronage-staffed housing authorities' (2015). Research by Fritz Umbach and Alexander Gerould demonstrates that the data Newman drew on in *Defensible Space* actually show that the ratio of adults to youth in the public housing projects he studied had a far more determinative impact on crime rates than the height of the buildings (2015: 69). D. Bradford Hunt, in an analysis of Chicago's Robert Taylor Homes, similarly has shown that the incredible concentration of young people in those projects, rather than the modernist architecture of the RTH's signature tower blocks, contributed to the social disorder that prevailed there (2015: 57). Moreover, Blumgart points out that a separate 1999 study using New York City Housing Authority data found that poverty rates in a given project, not the project's size or architecture, are the best predictor of their crime rates (2015). The scholarly consensus is clear: Newman's design determinism simply does not hold up under scrutiny. Unfortunately, Newman's single-minded focus on housing design obscured the importance of a host of socio-economic factors – class and income, the age mix of the tenant population, poverty and crime rates in the surrounding neighbourhoods, etc. – in shaping the fate of high-rise public housing projects for generations of policymakers.

Even worse, in my view, is the fact that in the process of televising Newman's ideas about 'defensible space' and adherence to the norms of middle-class propriety as the essential basis of any successful programme of state-provided shelter, Simon and the other creators of *Show Me* felt compelled to recycle stock images of high-rise public housing as a veritable hell on earth. This image has a grim history of being used to legitimate defunding of the social safety net. In the Clinton era, the demonization of high-rise housing was embraced by the federal Department of Housing and Urban Development and Housing Secretary Henry G. Cisneros which, in turn, led the government to tear down much of the nation's existing high-rise public housing stock. The demolished towers were replaced by low-rise, privatized, mixed-income townhouses modelled on middle-class condos and former tower residents were given vouchers to help pay for privately operated rental units. This approach, HUD's notorious HOPE VI programme, has been widely criticized for enriching developers while inadequately addressing the severe housing needs of the extremely needy (Hanlon 2010; Hanlon 2012; see also Bennett, Smith and Wright 2006). Because this programme for 'transforming' public housing did not mandate a one-for-one replacement rate for demolished units, it ultimately resulted in a net loss of housing for the nation's poorest families. According to HUD's own statistics, by 2017, some 43,274 units of public housing stock had been lost due to the HOPE VI programme (U.S. Department of Housing and Urban Development 2017). HOPE VI demolitions displaced thousands of long-time residents of high-rise projects from their homes without consulting them and a disturbing number of these residents subsequently found themselves completely cut off from housing assistance (National Housing Law Project 2002, iii). Moreover, while a majority of relocated public housing families using vouchers ended up living in better housing and in economically more stable neighbourhoods as a result of the programme, former residents with multiple, complex health and mental health issues ended up much worse off (Popkin 2006: 85). In some ways, HOPE VI was the perfect neo-liberal government programme. In the name of saving low-income, mostly Black and Latino families from confinement in racially segregated high-rise, modernist, government-run housing, it forced poor people to turn to the private housing market to find shelter, rendering the most vulnerable former residents even more economically vulnerable in the process. By uncritically reproducing the image of public-housing-as-disaster, *Show Me* reinforces the logic and rationale behind HOPE VI even as – left-liberal that he is – Simon himself doubtless would deplore the social casualties inevitably caused by that programme.

Show Me a Hero's detailed examination of the political struggle over the desegregation of public housing in Yonkers and the empathetic way that it explores the impact of that struggle on everyone from local political leaders like Wasicsko to Black public housing residents like Doreen Henderson is in many ways classic David Simon. It may, in fact, be the best single scripted TV treatment of the urban policy making process ever broadcast. Sadly, though, the miniseries' vision of high-rise public housing and its framing of the 'problem of the projects' owes far too much to the discredited (and crypto-reactionary) planning philosophy of Oscar Newman.

Notes

1   This, despite the fact that, as Nicholas Dagen Bloom has persuasively argued, New York City's public housing system – which is 'dominated by large, high-rise public housing developments' – at the time was remarkably successful at providing safe, well-run, affordable housing for low-income families in the midst of a very expensive city (2015: 91).

2   Francesco Sticchi attributes a very precise political meaning to this closing scene. In his view, 'the interaction and alliance between the two characters, if we look at the closing moments of the miniseries, is the element that, in fact, survives and is, in contrast, alternated to the intense images of Wasicsko's funeral, thus expressing a political force that proliferates beyond the limits of an institutionalized and crystallized (though utilizable) structure of power' (Sticchi 2021: 218–19). This interpretation of the scene reads a sort of anti-statist, anarchist ideology into the series that seems at odds with Simon's social democratic political sensibility. Given the series' heavy-handed endorsement of Newman's ideas, it is far more plausible that the closing image of the Doreen-Mary bond is offered as yet more evidence of the wisdom of Newman's residential planning scheme.

References

Belkin, Lisa. (1999), *Show Me a Hero: A Tale of Murder, Suicide, Race and Redemption*, New York: Back Bay Books.

Bennett, Larry, Janet L. Smith and Patricia A. Wright (eds). (2006), *Where Are Poor People to Live?: Transforming Public Housing Communities*, Armonk, New York and London: M. E. Sharpe.

Bloom, Nicholas Dagen. (2015), 'Myth #4: High-Rise Public Housing Is Unmanageable', in Nicholas Dagen Bloom, Fritz Umbach and Lawrence J. Vale (eds), *Public Housing*

Myths: Perception, Reality, and Social Policy, 91–120, Ithaca and London: Cornell University Press.

Blumgart, Jake. (2015), 'What HBO's *Show Me a Hero* Got Wrong about Public Housing', *Next City*, 3 September. Available online: https://nextcity.org/urbanist-news/hbo-show-me-a-hero-tv-show-public-housing (accessed 5 July 2022).

Clandfield, Peter. (2009), '"We Ain't Got No Yard": Crime, Development and the Urban Environment', in Tiffany Potter and C.W. Marshall (eds), *The Wire: Urban Decay and American Television*, 37–49, New York and London: Continuum.

Clay, Phillip L. (1992), 'The (Un)Housed City: Racial Patterns of Segregation, Housing Quality and Affordability', in George C. Galster and Edward W. Hill (eds), *The Metropolis in Black and White: Place, Power, and Polarization*, New Brunswick, NJ: The Center for Urban Policy Research.

Cupers, Kenny. (2017), 'Human Territoriality and the Downfall of Public Housing', *Public Culture*, 29 (1): 165–90.

Dreier, Peter. (2005), 'How the Media Compound Urban Problems', *The Journal of Urban Affairs*, 27 (2): 193–201.

Feron, James. (1987), 'Housing Aide Pursues Plan in Yonkers', *The New York Times*, 22 March. Available online: https://www.nytimes.com/1987/03/22/nyregion/housing-aide-pursues-plan-in-yonkers.html (accessed 19 May 2022).

Goetz, Edward G. (2013), *New Deal Ruins: Race, Economic Justice and Public Housing Policy*, Ithaca and London: Cornell University Press.

Hale, Mike. (2015), 'Review: "Show Me a Hero" Focuses on a Mayor in the Maelstrom of Desegregation', *The New York Times*, 13 August. Available online: https://www.nytimes.com/2015/08/14/arts/television/review-show-me-a-hero-focuses-on-a-mayor-in-the-maelstrom-of-desegregation.html (accessed 15 May 2022).

Hanlon, James. (2010), 'Success by Design: HOPE VI, New Urbanism, and the Neoliberal Transformation of Public Housing in the United States', *Environment and Planning A: Economy and Space*, 42 (1): 80–98.

Hanlon, James. (2012), 'Beyond HOPE VI: Demolition/Disposition and the Uncertain Future of Public Housing in the U.S.', *Journal of Housing and the Built Environment*, 27 (3): 373–88.

Hunt, D. Bradford. (2015), 'Myth #2: Modernist Architecture Failed Public Housing', in Nicholas Dagen Bloom, Fritz Umbach and Lawrence J. Vale (eds), *Public Housing Myths: Perception, Reality, and Social Policy*, 47–63, Ithaca and London: Cornell University Press.

Jovanovitch, Milena. (1986), 'Yonkers to Appeal in Bias Suit', *The New York Times*, 15 June. Available online: https://www.nytimes.com/1986/06/15/nyregion/yonkers-to-appeal-order-in-bias-suit.html (accessed 18 May 2022).

Macek, Steve. (2006), *Urban Nightmares: The Media, the Right and the Moral Panic over the City*, Minneapolis: University of Minnesota Press.

Mulholland, John. (2014), '*The Wire* Creator David Simon: Why American Politics No Longer Works', *The Guardian*, 28 September. Available online: https://www.

theguardian.com/media/2014/sep/28/wire-david-simon-interview-american-politics-show-me-a-hero (accessed 16 May 2022).

National Housing Law Project. (2002), 'False HOPE: A Critical Assessment of the HOPE VI Public Housing Redevelopment Program', Washington, DC: NHLP.

Newman, Oscar. (1972), *Defensible Space: Crime Prevention through Urban Design*, New York: Collier Books.

Owen, Paul. (2015), '*Show Me a Hero:* Is the HBO Mini-Series David Simon's Return to Form?', *The Guardian*, 11 August. Available online: https://www.theguardian.com/tv-and-radio/tvandradioblog/2015/aug/10/show-me-a-hero-david-simon-return-to-form (accessed 10 July 2022).

Piven, Frances Fox and Richard A. Cloward. (1971), *Regulating the Poor: The Functions of Public Welfare*, New York: Vintage.

Popkin, Susan J. (2006), 'The HOPE VI Program: What Has Happened to the Residents?', in Larry Bennett, Janet L. Smith and Patricia A. Wright (eds), *Where Are Poor People to Live?: Transforming Public Housing Communities*, 68–92, Armonk, New York and London: M. E. Sharpe.

Rotella, Carlo. (2015), '"No Dragons, No Zombies": David Simon of *The Wire* Returns to a New TV Landscape', *Chicago Tribune*, 9 August: 6, accessed 15 May 2022, ProQuest U.S. Major Dailies Database.

Seitz, Matt Zoller. (2015). 'The Radical Humanism of David Simon', *New York*, 13 August. Available online: https://www.vulture.com/2015/08/david-simons-radical-humanism.html (accessed 10 December 2022).

Silberg, Jon. (2015), '*Show Me a Hero:* Exploring the Social, Political and Economic Realities of 1980s New York', *Digital Video*, 23 (9): 12–14.

Sticchi, Francesco. (2021), *Mapping Precarity in Contemporary Cinema and Television*, London: Palgrave Macmillan.

Umbach, Fritz and Alexander Gerould. (2015), 'Myth #3: Public Housing Breeds Crime', in Nicholas Dagen Bloom, Fritz Umbach and Lawrence J. Vale (eds), *Public Housing Myths: Perception, Reality, and Social Policy*, 64–90, Ithaca and London: Cornell University Press.

U.S. Department of Housing and Urban Development. (2017), *Hope VI Data Compilation and Analysis*, 20 March. Available online: https://www.huduser.gov/portal/pdredge/pdr-edge-research-032017.html (accessed 19 May 2022).

Williams, Lena. (1985), 'Judge Finds Yonkers Has Segregation Policy', *The New York Times*, 21 November. Available online: https://www.nytimes.com/1985/11/21/nyregion/judge-finds-yonkers-has-segregation-policy.html (accessed 11 May 2022).

Wright, Gwendolyn. (1983), *Building the Dream: A Social History of Housing in America*, New York: Pantheon.

Further viewing

Future research on public housing in global film, television, and other media could include the additional shooting locations, production contexts, architecture, genres and national/regional/local screen narratives suggested below.

US films:

70 Acres in Chicago: Cabrini Green (Bezalel 2014), sequel to *Voices of Cabrini* (below)
Being Poor in New Orleans (documentary series, Kolker/Alvarez 1977–1979): *The Clarks* (St. Thomas housing project)
Clockers (Lee 1995)
Hardball (Robbins 2001)
Hatful of Rain (Zinnemann 1957)
Hoop Dreams (James 1994)
Judge Dredd (Travis 2012)
Judgment Night (Hopkins 1993, Robert Taylor Homes, Chicago)
Menace II Society (The Hughes Brothers 1993, Jordan Downs, L.A.)
The PJs (animated series, 1999–2001, Brewster-Douglass, Washington, D.C.)
Straight Out of Brooklyn (Rich 1991)
Training Day (Fuqua 2001, Imperial Courts, L.A.)
Voices of Cabrini: Remaking Chicago's Public Housing (Bezalel/Ferrara 1999)
What We Can Do for Joe (University of Southern California, 16-mm student film, Chester Kessler 1948)
World War Z (Forster 2013, Aylesbury estate, London)

US TV:

Boss (Lionsgate Television 2011–2012)
The Corner (HBO 2000)
Heard (Montgomery 2020)

US videogames:

Grand Theft Auto: San Andreas (Rockstar North 2004, depicts a recreation of the L.A. Jordan Downs projects as 'Willowfield Homes' in the fictional city of Los Santos, California)
Watch_ Dogs (Ubisoft Montreal 2014, reimagines Cabrini-Green as the 'Rossi-Fremont' housing project)

UK films:

Adulthood (Clarke 2008)
All or Nothing (Leigh 2002)
Brotherhood (Clarke 2016)
Children's Game, Heygate Estate (Lewis 2002)
Citadel (Foy 2012)
A Clockwork Orange (Kubrick 1974)
Dispossession: The Great Social Housing Swindle (Sng 2017)
Gregory's Girl (Forsyth 1981, set in Cumbernauld, outside Glasgow)
Harry Brown (Barber 2009)
Ill Manors (Plan B 2012)
Kes (Loach 1969)
KiDULTHOOD (Huda 2006)
Ladybird, Ladybird (Loach 1994)
Last Resort (Pawlikowski 2000)
The Legend of Barney Thomson (Carlyle 2015)
Made in Dagenham (Cole 2010)
Nil By Mouth (Oldman 1997)
Red Road (Arnold 2006)
The Selfish Giant (Bernard 2013)
Somers Town (Meadows 2008, Phoenix Court, Bristol)
Weekend (Haigh 2011)
Who Cares (Broomfield 1971)

UK TV:

The Bill (ITV 1984–2010)
Coronation Street (ITV 1960–present)
Luther (BBC1 2010, Aylesbury estate, London)

Misfits (Ch. 4 2009–2014)

Only Fools and Horses (BBC One 1981–2003, South Acton estate, now Acton Gardens, London)

Our Friends in the North (BBC2 1996)

Shameless (Ch. 4 2004–2013, set in Manchester, fictional Chatsworth estate)

as well as episodes of *Call the Midwife, Dr. Who, Law & Order: UK, Misfits, Top Gear,* and *Waterloo Road*

ARGENTINA:

Miserias (Albarracín 2009)

AUSTRALIA:

The Eviction (formerly known as *On the Rocks*) (Lucine 2018)

The Heights (ABC 2019–2020)

A Home of Their Own (Housing Commission of Victoria 1949)

Struggle Street (SBS One 2015/2017/2019)

Suburb 4 Sale (Delaney 2006, TV movie)

BRAZIL:

City of God (Meirelles/Lund 2002)

Favela Rising (Zimbalist/Mochary 2005)

FRANCE:

Banlieue 13 (Morel 2004) and *Banlieue 13: Ultimatum* (Alessandrin 2009)

Banlieues: sous le feu des médias (Del Debbio 2006)

Banlieusards (James/Sy 2019)

Le Chat (Granier-Deferre 1970)

Chronique d'une banlieue ordinaire (Cabrera 1992)

De l'autre côté du périph' (Bertrand and Nils Tavernier 1997) and *De l'autre côté du périph* (Charhon 2012)

Farenheit 451 (Truffaut 1966, Alton Estate, London)

Girlhood (Sciamma 2015)

Melodie en sous-sol (Verneuil 1963)
Les Misérables (Ly 2019)
Une poste à La Courneuve (Cabrera 1994)
Renoir des 4000 (Rastelli 2002)
Rue des Prairies (de La Patellière 1959)
Two or Three Things I Know About Her (Godard 1967)
La ville est à nous (Laroche 2000)

HONG KONG:

Rigor Mortis (Original title: *Geung si*) (Juno Mak 2014)
and see Tsang, this volume

MEXICO:

El Hombre de Papel (Rodríguez 1963)

RUSSIA:

The Fool (Bykov 2014)

SINGAPORE:

Heartlanders (MediaCorp TV, Channel 5, 2002–2005)
and see Wong/Chua, this volume

SOUTH KOREA:

The Tower (Ji-hoon Kim 2012)

SWEDEN:

Let the Right One In (Original title: *Låt den rätte komma in*) (Alfredson 2008)

Index

Note: Page numbers in *italics* indicate figures.

242; nostalgia 145–6; pathological representations 18, 226, 231; and police brutality 232–3; surveillance of 207; television representations of 8, 205–6; terminology 160 n.1; as victims of violence 231–2 (*see also* racial segregation)

Black women: and communities of care 210–11, 213–14, 216–18; and community activism 208–9, 213, 235; erasure of collective resistance 235; female-headed households 207–8; interracial friendships 252, 255 n.2; narrative framing 209; pathologizing representations of 235; in *The Wire* 205

Blake, Stephanie Rawlings 218 n.2

Blaxploitation films 146, 155

blockbusting 12, 19 n.6, 151

Bloom, Nicholas Dagen 255 n.1

Blumgart, Jake 253

Bolton, Lucy 129

Bonifazio, Paola 92

Bonjean, Elizabeth 215

Bortolotti, Lando 90

Bory, J. 69

Boundary Estate 6

Bristol, Katharine 32

Britain: Hong Kong colonial governance 163–4, 166–7, 171–2, 174–5; imperial exploitation 127; postwar reconstruction 127, 138; public housing in film and television 259–60; Singapore governance 182; socialized housing 6, 14, 127; social realism in films 129; tower block architecture 138; town planning principles 67, 78 n.4; working-class neighborhoods 6, 125, 127

British Mandate 67, 73

Broom, Maria 210

Brown, Sylvester, Jr. 36

Brownsville Houses 249–50

Brown v. Board of Education 43 n.3, 151

Brunsdon, Charlotte 205

Brutalism 9

built environment: Cabrini-Green 146; community displacement 4; confinement of Blacks in 146, 148–50; hostility to Black residents 153; impact

on inhabitants 16, 28–9; INA-Casa villages 85, 92–4, 98; and public housing residents 30; racialized space in 146

Bunga Sayang (2015) 186, *187*

Burns, Ed 205, 210, 216

Cabrini Extension 43 n.1

Cabrini-Green: confinement in 35, 146, 150, 154–5; in *Cooley High* 145–6, 152–3, *153*, 154–6, 158, 160; design 16, 43 n.1; destruction of 159; deterioration of buildings and services 35–6, 40; dominant narratives on 145–6; expressway boundaries of 29, 33; exterior/interior spaces 33–6, 38; gentrification 42; harsh realities of 8; in-between spaces 35–6; institutional repression 28–30; population increases 151; racialized space in 148, 150, 156, 159; uncanny architecture 27–9, 33–8, 40–3

"California Dreamin" (Womack) 139

Calliope Projects 229, 231, 233–4, 239

"Campi di Concentramento" (Pasolini) 89

Candyman (1992): aerial views of Chicago 28–9, 33; deterioration of buildings and services 35; exterior spaces 33–4, *35*; holes in units 40, 42; home in 28–9; in-between spaces 35–6; interior spaces 35–7, 40, 42; uncanny architecture 27–30, 33–8, 40–2; water and waste 34–5, 40–2

Candyman (2021) 42

Canteux, Camille 111

Capoferri, Federica 87

Carmon, Naomi 70

Carr Square Village 5

Cassie 137, 142 n.3

Cement (Gladkov) 56

Chaney, Tray 212

Chan Ka Yee 168

Che, Hio Leong 165–7, 175

Cheung Man-Yi 176

Chicago, Il.: Black migration to 147, 149; boundaries in 152–4, 156, 160 n.2; deindustrialization effects 17, 146–7, 157, 159–60; industrial development 146–9; Jane Addams Homes 18;

Index

www.ingramcontent.com/pod-product-compliance
Lightning Source LLC
Chambersburg PA
CBHW071843270326
41929CB00013B/2087